# EDUCATIVE
# DEMOCRACY

# UNIVERSITY OF HULL PUBLICATIONS

# Educative Democracy

*John Stuart Mill on Education in Society*

F. W. GARFORTH

*Published for the* UNIVERSITY OF HULL *by*
OXFORD UNIVERSITY PRESS
1980

Oxford University Press, Walton Street, Oxford OX2 6DP
OXFORD LONDON GLASGOW
NEW YORK TORONTO MELBOURNE WELLINGTON
KUALA LUMPUR SINGAPORE JAKARTA HONG KONG TOKYO
DELHI BOMBAY CALCUTTA MADRAS KARACHI
NAIROBI DAR ES SALAAM CAPE TOWN

*Published in the United States by*
*Oxford University Press, New York*

© *University of Hull 1980*

**British Library Cataloguing in Publication Data**

Garforth, Francis William
Educative democracy—(University of
Hull Publications).
1. Mill, John Stuart—Education
2. Education—Philosophy
I. Title   II. Series
370.19'3'0924    LB675.M/    79-40834

ISBN 0-19-713438-6

*Set, printed and bound in Great Britain by*
*Fakenham Press Limited, Fakenham, Norfolk*

*For*

*Helen and Laura,*
*Peter and Martin*

# Preface

MUCH has been written in recent years on those aspects of Mill's thought for which he is best known—social and political theory, ethics, and philosophy of science. There are, for instance, Robson's *The Improvement of Mankind*, van Holthoon's *The Road to Utopia*, Ryan's two books, *The Philosophy of John Stuart Mill* and *J. S. Mill*, and Duncan's *Marx and Mill*. His personal life too, including the peculiarities of his own remarkable education, has received considerable attention in such books as Himmelfarb's *On Liberty and Liberalism*, Mazlish's *James and John Stuart Mill*, and Kamm's *John Stuart Mill in Love*; and there is, of course, Packe's well known (but not so recent) biography. Yet none of these books, nor any previous that I know of, has attempted a detailed and systematic account of Mill's views on education and its role in society.

The reasons, I suppose, are not far to seek. Mill himself has left no extended work on education; the *Inaugural Address*, his only piece of specifically educational writing, was composed late in life for a university audience on the restricted theme of a liberal education; what else he has to say on education—and there is a great deal—is scattered throughout his writings and needs sifting out into a coherent picture. Moreover, Mill's achievements in other fields and the popular fame of his *Utilitarianism* and *On Liberty* have obscured the fact that education was an integral part of his social and political thinking. That this was so should cause no surprise: 'the improvement of mankind' (his own words) was his life's major purpose; the association psychology in which he was nurtured offered a view of human nature as amenable to such improvement in response to deliberate structuring of the environment; education, which for Mill included not only schooling but the totality of environmental influence, was therefore an indispensable means to social reform.

I have tried in the present book to elicit from the whole range of Mill's writings his view of the aims of education and its role in creating the improved society which he envisaged. Essential to that view is the concept of the educative or self-educative society, a concept whose significance will, I hope, emerge in the course of reading; and such a society, so Mill believed, can exist only within a democracy. Because education, for Mill, embraced the whole environment—'whatever helps to shape the human being, to make the individual what he is or hinder him from being what he is not'*—its role includes not only formal institutions of instruction, but all the multifarious activities of the community, including central and local government, and not least the influence of individual men and women (especially the gifted).

What is presented here is by no means the whole of Mill's educational thought. He has much to say on the theoretical bases of instruction (derived from his empirical account of human nature and its psychology) and on its methods and content. Indeed one can readily construct from his writings a coherent and persuasive theory of education which anticipates not a few of the now commonly accepted educational ideas and practices. This I have attempted in my *John Stuart Mill's Theory of Education* (Martin Robertson, 1979).

I have assumed in the reader a knowledge of the main facts of Mill's life—his education at the hands of his father, his 'nervous crisis', his career in the India Office, his relationship with Harriet Taylor (eventually his wife) and his brief period in Parliament. For amplification there are the *Autobiography*, Packe's *Life*, and the books mentioned above. I have also assumed some knowledge of the history of English education in the nineteenth century; those who wish to refresh their memories can find the details in, for instance, Lawson, J. and Silver, H., *A Social History of Education in England*.

*Westerdale,*
*August 1978.*

* *Inaugural*, p. 154.

# Acknowledgements

I AM greatly indebted for guidance, correction and encouragement to my colleague John Lawson, who read the typescript at an early stage in its composition and since then has patiently answered my many questions on historical details. To Professor V. A. McClelland I am indebted for advice on certain details of Irish education in the nineteenth century. My thanks are also due to the staff of the Brynmor Jones Library of the University of Hull for their help in procuring for me copies of some of Mill's less accessible writings; to the staff of the Institute of Education Library of Hull University for assistance in various ways; and to the University of Toronto Press and its editors, whose volumes of Mill's Collected Works have considerably eased my labours and whose *Mill News Letter* is an invaluable source of information on all aspects of Mill studies.

Francesca has again shared the burden of correcting the proofs and making the index.

# Contents

# I

# Aims and Values

It is abundantly clear that Mill believed in the fundamental importance of education as a powerful instrument of human purposes. This can be shown both from explicit statements and from his whole conception of the role of education in society. 'How unspeakable', he asserts in 'The Utility of Religion',

is the effect of bringing people up from infancy in a belief and in habits founded on it. . . . The power of education is almost boundless: there is not one natural inclination which it is not strong enough to coerce and if needful to destroy by disuse.[1]

Its efficacy is thus both positive in establishing habitual beliefs and attitudes and negative in controlling instinct and suppressing undesirable growth—man's duty is 'not to follow but to amend' nature, and education, especially early education, is his chief means for so doing.[2] He commends the view of those who think with Coleridge that 'national education . . . in any political society [is] at once the principal cause of its permanence as a society and the chief cause of its progressiveness' (anticipating a twentieth-century dictum that 'the educational purpose is to communicate the type and provide for growth beyond the type').[3] In a letter to Harriet Taylor he writes of 'the omnipotence of education' (an omnipotence, he adds, which must be subject to the authority of moral values); repeatedly he stresses the power, indeed the indispensability, of 'cultivated intelligence' for social improvement—it is 'the main determining cause' of social progress, for 'it is what men think', he states elsewhere, 'that determines how they act'.[4] In the life of the nation education contributes (among other important functions) to health, productivity, vocational training, population control, the extension of the franchise; conversely, 'the primary and perennial sources of all social evil are ignorance and want of culture'.[5]

In all this he is true to the utilitarian tradition inherited from his father and Jeremy Bentham. The latter, influenced by what he knew of education in France and Russia as well as Britain, was firmly convinced both of the importance of education and of the need for state intervention in providing it; he insists on the need for clearly defined educational purpose—'education is a series of conduct directed to an end; before any directions can properly be given for the education of any person, the end of education must be settled. The common end of every person's education is Happiness'[6]; and in his *Chrestomathia* he presents a detailed plan (little of which is strictly original) for the organization of schools based on the monitorial system of mutual pupil-by-pupil teaching. James Mill, who was a close friend, some would say a disciple, of Bentham, was no less an enthusiast for education, though his zeal was tempered by greater moral and cultural insight. Strongly influenced not only by Bentham but by Helvetius (as was Bentham himself) and other French writers, as well as by the supposedly unlimited practical efficacy of association psychology, he declared that 'all the difference which exists, or can ever be made to exist, between one *class* of men and another is wholly owing to education'[7]—an expansion of Helvetius' famous 'L'éducation peut *tout*'. This does not amount to a rejection of heredity or of innate differences, for Mill is referring to classes of men, not individuals; but it expresses a deep conviction of the tremendous power of education as a means of social improvement and reform, a power which it exercises by an almost equally decisive influence upon individuals. This enthusiasm for education was not confined to Bentham and James Mill but was a feature of the utilitarian movement as a whole; nor was it a merely theoretical commitment, for utilitarians were conspicuous in their efforts, both in Parliament and by other means, to extend education and improve its methods: Bentham and Mill supported the infant school movement initiated by Robert Owen in his experimental institution at New Lanark; Joseph Lancaster had utilitarian help in his scheme to provide cheap popular education by the monitorial method; and utilitarians were among those who secured the foundation in 1828 of the undenominational University College, London. In Parliament Joseph Hume and John Roebuck were prominent in the fight for a national system of education, and the latter's two speeches advocating this are a monument of educational good sense.[8]

In his article on education for the *Encyclopaedia Britannica*

James Mill had written: 'The end of Education is to render the individual as much as possible an instrument of happiness, first to himself, and next to other beings.'[9] To these two focuses of educational purpose, the individual and mankind, John Stuart was also committed; happiness too he accepted as the ultimate goal for both, though he qualified his father's statement by specifying more precisely the nature of the happiness he had in mind and by strongly suggesting that other values, such as love, freedom, truth, and individuality, are likewise intrinsically valuable and therefore worth pursuing in their own right. His dominant purpose was clearly 'the improvement of mankind',[10] and if Mill may be said to have had *an* educational aim inclusive of all others, this was it. In one phrasing or another the idea of human improvement, of human well-being in its widest possible extension, occurs repeatedly in his writings. 'The *ultimate* end . . . the alpha and omega' of his utilitarianism, he writes to Carlyle, is 'the good of the species'— though he adds here, what he affirms in *On Liberty* and elsewhere, that this can be achieved only by developing the best in every individual; in industrial relations the 'paramount principle' is 'the interest, immediate and ultimate, of the human race'; the education of women, he argues, would double the 'mental faculties available for the higher service of humanity', for 'where there is now one person qualified to benefit mankind and promote the general improvement', there would then be two; 'the general moral improvement of mankind through good government and education' is one of the aims (as it is also a condition) of the form of socialist society which he hoped to see established, and the same ideal is implicit in the 'religion of humanity' which he commends in 'The Utility of Religion' as a substitute for Christianity.[11] However, the improvement of mankind, of the human species as a whole, is a far distant goal, an ideal to kindle imagination and emotion rather than an immediate possibility; more proximate and attainable—and obviously an essential means to the further goal— is the improvement of particular societies. To this too Mill was no less firmly wedded; there can be few Englishmen who have given themselves so unreservedly as he, according to his talents, to the task of improving the intellectual, moral, political, economic, and cultural life of his own country, especially among the 'labouring classes'. Nor was his attention confined to Britain: he had, of course, a constant professional concern for India, which is reflected in his correspondence from India House; he was deeply distressed by poverty, depopulation and, in the winter of 1846–7, famine in Ireland, and he wrote article after article in *The Morning Chronicle* protesting and proposing remedies; he attacked slavery, defended the rights of American negroes, and showed sympathetic interest in the development of Australia—education, he wrote to his brother-in-law in Adelaide, is all the more important in a new country 'as the helps and instruments to self-cultivation are apt to be more scanty; and what is done or left undone now will determine in great measure what part the future Australian nation will take in the advancement of the world'.[12]

However, the meaning of 'improvement' is not immediately obvious, more especially when it refers in panoramic fashion to the whole of humanity rather than to this or that society. Clearly it implies movement towards a goal or goals whose attainment will result in a condition better (or deemed better) than that previously existing. But what goals? Until this is known, 'improvement' has no determinate meaning; it signifies little more than 'change' or 'alteration'. For Mill the ultimate goal is happiness, and this, he explains in *Utilitarianism*, means 'pleasure and the absence of pain'.[13] Lest he be misinterpreted he immediately enlarges this description by distinguishing qualities of pleasure, some kinds being 'more desirable and more valuable than others'; the criterion by which pleasures are ranked less or more valuable lies in the judgement of those whom experience and education have made competent to assess them; and such people, Mill asserts, 'give a most marked preference to the manner of existence which employs their higher faculties'. If the perfection of happiness is unattainable, at least:

It is better to be a human being dissatisfied than a pig satisfied; better to be Socrates dissatisfied than a fool satisfied. And if the fool, or the pig, is of a different opinion, it is because they only know their own side of the question. The other party to the comparison knows both sides.

Happiness in the sense of 'a continuity of highly pleasurable excitement' is clearly impossible:

A state of exalted pleasure lasts only moments, or in some cases, and with some intermissions, hours or days, and is the occasional brilliant flash of enjoyment, not its permanent and steady flame. Of this the philosophers who have taught that happiness is the end of life were as fully aware as those who taunt them. The happiness which they meant was not a life of rapture, but moments of such in an existence made up of few and transitory pains, many and various pleasures, with a decided predominance of the active over the passive, and having as the foundation of the whole, not to expect more from life than it is capable of bestowing. A life thus composed, to those who have been fortunate enough to obtain it, has always appeared worthy of the name of happiness.

It is only, he adds significantly, 'the present wretched education and wretched social arrangements' that prevent 'its being attainable by almost all'. Education is also vital, as he was well aware, in creating the informed and experienced judgement which is the final authority on the quality of pleasures.

Thus Mill seeks to ward off the charge of hedonism and to defend a quality of happiness which obviously reflects his own inclinations and which many nowadays would no doubt regard as 'élitist' and 'middle class'. Be this as it may, he certainly leaves many questions unanswered, and if this were a book on Mill's ethics it would be necessary to consider them. For instance, is happiness correctly identified with pleasure even of the most exalted kind? If the higher pleasures are unattainable to the fool, is his level of happiness any the less real or satisfying *for him*? Is Brahms necessarily better than Bingo? There is also the attempt at justification in chapter 4 of *Utilitarianism*—'the sole evidence it is possible to produce that anything is desirable, is that people do actually desire it'—which has been attacked for allegedly violating the logical distinction between 'is' and 'ought'.[14]

There is one problem, however, which is too important to be passed over, for it bears directly on Mill's educational aims and values. He makes it abundantly clear that when he speaks of happiness as the ultimate goal, he does not mean that of the individual 'but the greatest amount of happiness altogether'; indeed the individual may well be called upon to surrender his happiness for that of others, thus increasing the sum total of happiness while diminishing his own.[15] Such sacrifice requires a nobility of character, a single-minded altruism which Mill seems to regard, at least *for the individual*, as something valuable in its own right. For instance, in a passage at the end of *Logic* VI he asserts that although happiness 'is the justification, and ought to be the controller, of all ends', it 'is not itself the sole end'. He continues:

the cultivation of an ideal nobleness of will and conduct should be to individual human beings an end, to which the specific pursuit either of their own happiness or of that of others ... should, in any case of conflict, give way.

To the individual, elevation of character is itself 'a paramount end' (though, once again, it is happiness that constitutes the *ultimate* standard by which that elevation is to be judged).[16] Similar assertions occur in *Utilitarianism*:

Though it is only in a very imperfect state of the world's arrangements that anyone can best serve the happiness of others by the absolute sacrifice of his own, yet so long as the world is in that imperfect state, I fully acknowledge that the readiness to make such a sacrifice is the highest virtue which can be found in man.

(And when, one may well ask, will the world's state achieve perfection and so deprive this virtue of the status Mill here confers on it?) A little later, after reaffirming that the utilitarian standard is 'not the agent's own happiness but that of all concerned', he writes:

As between his own happiness and that of others utilitarianism requires him to be as strictly impartial as a disinterested and benevolent spectator. In the golden rule of Jesus of Nazareth we read the complete spirit of the ethics of utility. To do as one would be done by, and to love one's neighbour as oneself, constitute the ideal perfection of utilitarian morality.[17]

Consonant with this is his attack on Bentham for the spiritual poverty of his conception of man:

Man is never recognised by him as a being capable of pursuing spiritual perfection as an end; of desiring, for its own sake, the conformity of his own character to his standard of excellence, without hope of good or fear of evil from other source than his own inward consciousness.[18]

Finally, in *Comte and Positivism* he declares that beyond the minimum level of morality which is required of all, there is 'an unlimited range of moral worth, up to the most exalted heroism, which should be fostered by every possible encouragement'— though not, he adds, imposed as an obligation. He continues:

the direct cultivation of altruism, and the subordination of egoism to it, far beyond the point of absolute moral duty, should be one of the chief aims of education both individual and collective.[19]

There is no doubt of Mill's powerful attraction to nobility of character, ideal excellence, and disinterested virtue, all of them summed up in the *agape* of the New Testament; so much so that it rivals his claims for happiness as the supreme goal and creates a suspicion of ambivalence in his ethic—as if he were indeed undecided between his theoretical commitment to the utilitarian principle of happiness and the promptings from deep within himself (and in human nature) of an even higher value. Thus, he qualifies this altruistic idealism by subordinating it to happiness as means to end, as in the *Logic* passage and again in *Utilitarianism*:

The utilitarian morality does recognise in human beings the power of sacrificing their own greatest good for the good of others. It only refuses to admit that the sacrifice is itself a good. A sacrifice which does not increase, or tend to increase, the sum total of happiness it considers as wasted.[20]

However, despite these avowals of orthodoxy the doubts linger. Is happiness or is love (*agape*) the dominant value? If the height of ethical attainment for one individual is nobility of character rather than happiness, is it not so for all? And in that case what meaning remains for 'the general happiness'? For if each for the sake of the other pursues the nobility of his own character as the highest virtue, the notion of 'general happiness' would seem either to disappear or to be merged with the ideal of altruistic love which each seeks to realize in himself.

Moreover, Mill himself explicitly affirms the possibility of intrinsic goals distinct from happiness. The utilitarian doctrine, he argues, 'maintains not only that virtue is to be desired, but that it is to be desired disinterestedly, for itself'. Utilitarian moralists, while admitting that virtue (however they may agree to define it) is the principal means to the ultimate end of happiness, nevertheless 'recognise as a psychological fact the possibility of its being, to the individual, a good in itself, without looking to any end beyond it'. Such disinterested virtue is in no way contrary, Mill insists, to the fundamental principle of utility; without it 'the mind is not in a right state, not in a state conformable to Utility, not in the state most conducive to the general happiness'. He continues:

The ingredients of happiness are very various, and each of them is desirable in itself, and not merely when considered as swelling an aggregate. . . . They are desired and desirable in and for themselves;

besides being means, they are a part of the end. Virtue, according to the utilitarian doctrine, is not naturally and originally part of the end, but it is capable of becoming so; and in those who love it disinterestedly it has become so, and is desired and cherished, not as a means to happiness, but as a part of their happiness.[21]

The ambivalence is clear—indeed more than ambivalence, for doubts arise concerning the consistency of Mill's ethical thinking; certainly he raises difficult problems, not only of psychology (as he hints) but also of logical relationship by thus including within happiness components which are both ends in themselves and means to that which, in a more final sense, is an end in *itself*.

Whatever one's answer to these problems, here are two goals which give substance to Mill's notion of improvement; but they are not the only ones. Three others emerge from his writings as competitors for the intrinsic status of ends-in-themselves and as criteria for the assessment of human betterment: individuality, freedom, and truth. Mill's concept of individuality, together with some of its associated problems, is examined in chapter 5. It is argued there that for Mill individuality is the freely chosen expression, in growth and development and in diversity of activity, of one's distinctiveness as a unique being; the crucial items of the concept are potentiality, development, distinctiveness (the uniqueness of one's own self in its differentiation and differences from other selves), variety in self-expression, and choice. It is suggested too that he writes of it in a manner that seems to elevate it from something valuable as a means (for instance, to economic enterprise, to the enrichment of society, to testing the worth of different forms of life) to something valuable in its own right (pp. 82–4), as if he were hovering on the edge of commitment to belief in the essential worth of individuals as such. Again, when Mill asserts in *Logic* VI that every practical art has 'one . . . general premise . . . which enunciates the object aimed at', it seems likely that what he had in mind for education was individuality conceived as it is described above.[22] Whether or not he saw it as a rival to happiness in claiming intrinsic or ultimate status, he evidently regarded it as a value of the highest order of importance, an essential ingredient in his concept of improvement, and an obvious goal, therefore, for the educator. He was also aware—and this is a vital point which is emphasized below (pp. 81–2, 101ff.)—that individuality has potential for evil as well as good, for brutality and lust as well as benevolence. Development must therefore be *selective*, guided by deliberate value choices towards 'ideal nobleness of character'.[23]

Freedom is another value which Mill esteemed so highly that he seems at times to confer on it the intrinsic status of being a goal in its own right. No one who has read *On Liberty* can doubt his passionate commitment to the principle of freedom, conceived primarily, and negatively, as non-interference, but embodying more positive suggestions in serving as the soil (Mill's own metaphor) for the roots of individual growth and of cultural progress.[24] In this latter, more positive role freedom is, of course, powerfully instrumental, a means to desirable ends beyond itself, and he clearly intends it to be so understood. For instance, it not only enables release of potential and therefore growth and improvement in individuals and society; without it choice is restricted and there can be no genuine morality; nor can there be experiments in different forms of life which may enrich society and, so long as mankind remains imperfect, are indispensable to its progress; moreover, it is a protection against that tyranny of the majority which he so greatly feared—the debasing of standards of taste, probity, and achievement to a common level of mediocrity; not least, it is vital to the discovery of truth, which, whether it springs from the inspiration of genius or emerges more gradually from the dialectic of discussion, requires for its genesis the unfettered activity of intellect.

However, as with altruism and individuality, so here there are indications that freedom had for Mill something more than instrumental significance. In chapter 3 of *On Liberty* he writes thus:

If it were felt that the free development of individuality is one of the leading essentials of well-being; that it is not only a co-ordinate element with all that is designated by the terms civilisation, instruction, education, culture, but is itself a necessary part and condition of all those things, there would be no danger that liberty should be undervalued.[25]

Now freedom and the free development of individuality are not identical; nor is either of them the same as 'individual spontaneity' to which in the following sentence Mill ascribes 'intrinsic worth . . . on its own account'. But in these passages he comes close to equating all three and thus to bestowing on freedom itself the same intrinsic value that he gives to the last (and elsewhere to individuality). In pleading for the equality of the sexes he praises the 'life of rational freedom', the attainment of which, made possible by legal independence of their husbands, would bring to women 'an unspeakable gain in private happiness'. 'The free direction and disposal of their own faculties', he asserts, 'is a source of individual happiness'; and, perhaps recalling his own restricted childhood and the emotional release that terminated his mental crisis:

Let any man call to mind what he himself felt on emerging from boy-hood—from the tutelage and control of even loved and affectionate elders—and entering upon the responsibilities of manhood. Was it not like the physical effect of taking off a heavy weight, or releasing him from obstructive, even if not otherwise painful, bonds? Did he not feel twice as much alive, twice as much a human being as before?[26]

Again, in his comparison of communism and socialism as forms of social organisation the question he asks is 'which of the two systems is consistent with the greatest amount of human liberty and spontaneity'. For after the means of subsistence 'the next in strength of the personal wants of human beings is liberty' and it is a want that increases with the development of intelligence and the moral faculties. Hence, he continues:

The perfection both of social arrangements and of practical morality would be, to secure to all persons complete independence and freedom of action, subject to no restriction but that of not doing injury to others; and the education which taught or the social institutions which required them to exchange the control of their own actions for any amount of comfort or affluence, or to renounce liberty for the sake of equality, would deprive them of one of the most elevated characteristics of human nature.[27]

What he seems to be saying here is not so much that freedom is instrumental to happiness and well-being (though he would, of course, grant that it is), but rather that it is *constitutive* of them; that freedom is among the essential components of happiness (each of which, he states elsewhere, is desirable in itself and as 'a part of the end')[28]—a necessary though not a sufficient condition of being happy; that without freedom these other components are so depreciated that they no longer constitute happiness.

   Mill's concern for truth is apparent throughout his writings, and not only for truth but for rationality and what he calls 'cultivated intelligence',[29] between all of which there are close conceptual associations. 'Truth and the general good', he writes in 'The

Utility of Religion', 'are the two noblest of all objects of pursuit.'[30] In his early essay, 'Civilisation', he asserts that 'an education intended to form great minds' must 'call forth the greatest possible quantity of intellectual *power* and . . . inspire the greatest *love of truth*'[31]—even though the pupil should thereafter contradict his teachers; but not only 'great minds', for Mill was convinced that truth and a resolute commitment to it by the whole body of citizens are fundamental to democracy—hence his conviction of the necessity for universal education as at least a step towards that ideal. Concern for truth is the basis of his plea for freedom of thought and discussion in *On Liberty*—and again, not only for the 'great thinker': 'it is as much and even more indispensable to enable average human beings to attain the mental stature which they are capable of',[32] and so to contribute to the proper functioning of society. It underlies his impassioned championing of the Platonic dialectic in its exposure of ignorance and falsehood and its endeavour to clarify such concepts as justice and virtue, good and evil; and though the results may be inconclusive, it is 'no small benefit to expel the false opinion of knowledge, to make men conscious of their ignorance of the things most needful to be known'.[33] He writes of it with no less fervour in the *Inaugural Address*, commending both Plato and Aristotle for their 'noblest enthusiasm . . . for the search after truth and for applying it to its highest uses'. Here too the value of truth forms part of his case for science education: 'The most incessant occupation of the human intellect throughout life is the ascertainment of truth'—truth for political, legal, technical, personal, and moral *decision*, not merely for speculative or theoretical interest. 'To know the truth', he adds significantly, 'is already a great way towards disposing us to act upon it.'[34] At a more personal level he writes to Florence Nightingale

of the responsibility that lies upon each one of us to stand steadfastly and with all the boldness and all the humility that a deep sense of duty can inspire by what the experience of life and an honest use of our own intelligence has taught us to be the truth.[35]

It is a gospel that he practised as well as preached; for when, during his Parliamentary candidature, he was presented with the words, 'The lower classes, though mostly habitual liars, are ashamed of lying', and was asked if he wrote them, he replied unequivocally, 'I did'. (The response from his working class audience was tumultuous applause!)[36] Indeed, Mill's transparent and undeviating honesty of intellect and intention is among the most conspicuous (and to our own age, wearied even more than his by evasive sophistries, refreshing) aspects of his character. Now Mill was clearly aware that truth is important as a means—to happiness, of course, to justice, to democracy, to personal stature and 'the dignity of thinking beings',[37] to the progress of science, and other desirable ends; but here once again his concern for it seems at times to transcend the merely instrumental and become a passion for truth itself as an object worthy of pursuit in its own right.

By pointing to these goals as desirable ends of human endeavour —indeed more than this, as essential constituents of the good life— Mill fills out his concept of improvement with determinate content. Individual human beings, particular societies, and mankind as a whole are changed for the better in so far as they approach and embody the ideals of happiness, altruism, individuality, freedom, and truth. Whether one chooses to call them goals, aims, values, ideals or to describe them by some other conative or aspirational term is immaterial for the purpose of this chapter; certainly there are conceptual distinctions here, nuances of differentiation in usage and logical relationship which need to be thoroughly explored; but this is not the place to explore them. One must, however, pause to acknowledge that in these goals Mill presents us with an area of conceptual geography (to use Ryle's analogy in *The Concept of Mind*) in which there is an intriguing complexity and mutuality of relationship. One becomes free not simply by aiming at freedom and throwing off restriction, but by being educated into individuality, altruism, and love of truth; likewise, individuality is advanced towards its fulfilment by absorbing into itself the other goals within a situation of minimum interference; truth contributes to and is enlarged by the growth of individuality towards an autonomous moral maturity, and that maturity, expressed in altruistic concern for one's fellow men, is itself nourished by growth towards the other goals. What, then, of happiness? Does it remain a goal in its own right and superior to the rest, 'the grand central point', as James Mill expressed it, '. . . by their bearing upon which the value of all other things is determined'?[38] Or is it in some way absorbed into the totality of the other four, an activity *in accordance with* these excellences (as Aristotle might have put it) or perhaps a *by-product* of their attainment? These questions we must leave as more relevant to a different kind of inquiry from the present, while acknowledging both their fascination and also their importance in determining 'what is the real object to which education is pointed'.[39]

However, it may well be objected to this account of the content of improvement that it overlooks other values which Mill regarded as important, for instance, beauty, justice, equality, courtesy, self-discipline, and more tangible objectives like health and sensory pleasure. Mill's delight in beauty, both natural and man-made, is noted and illustrated below (pp. 33–4, 106); it could produce in him an intensity of emotion which was well nigh unendurable; and though the artist's 'endeavour after perfection in execution'[40] was for him a means to truth, human sympathy, and moral insight, as well as contributing to individual fulfilment and social improvement, it was also, as he conceived it, an experience to be valued for itself. Why not, then, include it with happiness and the four others as a major component of improvement? It is difficult to answer this, save by simply stating the present writer's conviction that in his mature thought Mill implies a priority for these five, regarding beauty as a subordinate though still immensely desirable goal. As for justice, he seems to have regarded it as an essential component of any society which seeks the happiness of *everyone*, as a means therefore rather than an end in itself. The same may be said of equality and the values mentioned after it, save that self-discipline and health contribute primarily to the well-being of the individual and only through him to that of society as a whole.

Clearly, though some values, some goals may be deemed superior—for instance because they are more general than others, or have greater inspirational attraction, or are more satisfying to a 'cultivated intelligence'—yet they presume the support of a substructure of more restricted goals and values: happiness, freedom, and individuality, as Mill understood them, depend on the prior satisfaction of human needs like health and security and, beyond these basic survival values, on social and ethical values of which justice and equality are obvious examples. Mill was well aware of this: the higher values he envisaged could flourish only where they found the necessary support in a substructure of contributory values. This applies equally to individuals and to societies: it is men, women, and children who, in the reality of their own experience, must be granted the foundation values of health, security, justice, equality, and others as an essential step to higher levels of improvement; and it is society, through its political organization, its laws, and the principles embodied in its social and economic life that must provide the opportunity of experiencing them, and thus of raising its corporate life to a fuller expression of higher values. This suggests two questions: what kind of individual and what kind of society did Mill think most likely to secure the realization of his chosen values? The answer to the first will be found in the extended examination of individuality in chapter 5; the second is the subject of chapter 2.

# 2

# What Kind of Society?

VALUES ARE generated in the choices and commitments of individuals, by whom they are then communicated to other individuals and thus absorbed into society. It is principally from these values, established and perpetuated in it, that a society derives its character. Further, by embodying these values in itself—in its laws, its institutions, its moral, political, and economic principles, its art, science, literature, and intellectual life—it educates successive generations into accepting them. There is thus a circular (or perhaps spiral) process of mutual influence and response: values are injected into society by the activities of its individual members; society in its turn, by the formative influence which it inevitably exerts on those who live in it, moulds other individuals, notably children, into the same patterns of commitment. It follows that the promotion of chosen values requires not only individuals who are dedicated to them, but a society which is permeated by them and which exhibits them both in its publicly declared policies and in the multitudinous facets of its corporate life.

Mill was fully aware of this process of value transmission. He also recognized that choice has implications which are both logical and practical: logical, in that commitment to truth or freedom, for example, implies a further commitment to such values as tolerance, respect for evidence, self-restraint, and rationality; practical in that sincerity requires the living out of these values in one's personal life and their implementation in the life of the community. He formed for himself, therefore, a clear picture of the kind of society required by his five primary values—happiness, individuality, freedom, truth, and altruism; it was a picture whose materials were supplied mainly from sources outside himself—his father and Jeremy Bentham, the Philosophical Radicals, Coleridge, Comte, de Tocqueville, and others—but whose artistry and inspiration came from his own (and to some extent Harriet's) impassioned, yet critically perceptive, zeal for human improvement. However, he offered no utopia, no short-cut to perfection; he was neither a visionary nor a revolutionary. His wise insight into the realities and practicalities of human nature and human communities precluded him from any facile expectation of too much and too quickly; human improvement, he recognized, must be a long and difficult task which could be accomplished, if ever, only by bringing to bear upon it all the resources of education, skilled government, and economic expertise. To present his picture in its details is impossible within the compass of this chapter; it would be difficult in any case, demanding a close examination of Mill's ideas in their chronological development; for while its outlines remained virtually unchanged throughout his life, within those outlines there was modification in response to new ideas and to changes in social and political circumstances. It is the broad features, therefore, that concern us here.

Mill had no doubt that it must be a democratic society. It is true that he accepts as a historical fact the existence of other forms of government; he even admits their necessity at certain levels of cultural and political immaturity—'despotism is a legitimate mode of government in dealing with barbarians, provided'—he is careful to add—'the end be their improvement'; monarchy too may have advantages in 'the earliest stages of any community'.[1] But as soon as a people can be guided to improvement by rational conviction and persuasion, despotic or bureaucratic compulsion loses its legitimacy; this situation, he somewhat optimistically and myopically assumes, has long since been reached 'in all nations with whom we need here concern ourselves'.[2] He therefore gives no extended consideration to possible alternatives to democracy. His ideal of democracy lay in the past, in ancient Athens, whose citizens, meeting in the ecclesia, engaged directly in discussion and resolutions of public policy ranging from the comparative trivia of civil administration to momentous issues of peace and war. While conceding the limitations of Athenian democracy—for instance, its exclusion of women, slaves, and permanently resident aliens from political rights—he praised it lavishly, indeed immoderately, for its 'practical good government', its freedom of censure and debate, its constitutional checks, its egalitarian disregard of birth and wealth, and most of all for its educational impact on the ordinary citizens: 'the practice of the dicastery and the ecclesia raised the intellectual standard of an average Athenian citizen far beyond anything of which there is yet an example in any other mass of men, ancient or modern'.[3]

Direct political participation of this kind was feasible in the city-states of the ancient world; in the huge and increasingly complex nation-states of the nineteenth century it was obviously impossible at the level of central government, though it was both practicable and highly desirable, Mill thought, at lower levels of local adminis-tration. Evidently, some form of representative democracy was the best alternative; this he argues at length in *Considerations on Representative Government* and confirms in many other writings. He rejects as 'unscientific and incorrect' the view that good govern-ment is measured by the criteria of order and progress (or 'perma-nence and progression in the words of Coleridge').[4] In the narrower meaning of obedience to authority, order is not a criterion of good government but a condition of *any* government; in the extended sense of the preservation of peace and other benefits, order is included in progress, which assumes the perpetuation of what is good and seeks to enlarge it; moreover, order and progress both depend on the same qualities of character in a nation—industry, integrity, justice, prudence, mental vigour, originality, enterprise, courage—though progress requires them to a higher degree. Nor is progress itself a sufficient criterion, for it points to only half of the truth: even to maintain the *status quo* against the constant pressure of human folly, carelessness, and indolence, let alone make head-way against them, requires unceasing effort which in turn depends on such qualities of character as Mill has named. It must be, then, that the prime object (and likewise a necessary condition) of good government is to promote 'the virtue and intelligence of the people themselves'. The essential criterion for which Mill is looking is, therefore, 'the degree in which [a government] tends to increase the sum of good qualities in the governed, collectively and indi-vidually'. A second criterion, dependent on and assumed by the first, is the quality of the machinery of government; this must be 'adapted to take advantage of the amount of good qualities which may at any time exist, and make them instrumental to the right purposes'.[5]

He concludes:

We have now . . . obtained a foundation for a twofold division of the merit which any set of political institutions can possess. It consists partly of the degree in which they promote the general mental advancement of the community, including under that phrase advancement in intellect, in virtue, and in practical activity and efficiency; and partly of the degree of perfection with which they organise the moral, intellectual and active worth already existing, so as to operate with the greatest effect on public affairs.[6]

It is Mill's case for representative democracy that, despite its imperfections and dangers (of which he was keenly aware), it is the form of government most able to satisfy these two criteria. Essentially (and crucially for an understanding of his position) his test is *educational*: the best form of government is that which operates most effectively as 'an agency of national education',[7] eliciting and exercising the talents of its citizens, training them in moral and intellectual virtues, and prompting them continually to higher levels of individual and co-operative excellence. The goal he envisaged was the 'educative society'—a phrase which he did not use himself but whose import and implications he would have recognized immediately as expressing his own social and political ideals. The nature of this goal and the means of achieving it will emerge more substantially during the present chapter; meanwhile we must take a closer look at the educative role of representative democracy.

It is this form of polity, he confidently asserts in chapter 3 of *Representative Government*, which above all others 'promotes a better and higher form of national character'—and he is thinking here, of course, not simply of moral but of intellectual and other qualities. Character is fundamentally of two contrasted types: the passive, 'which bends to circumstances', and the active, 'which endeavours to make circumstances bend to itself'. While the former is commonly preferred (since it is less obstructive and poses less threat to security), it is the latter which contributes most to human improvement: 'The character which improves human life is that which struggles with natural powers and tendencies'—and this is impossible unless men and women are forced to develop their own resources of thought, will, and energy.[8] Democracy encourages such self-reliance by its acceptance of the principle of freedom, by interfering only to the extent demanded by the general good in the individual's chosen activities. Thus it allows him to assert his individuality, to develop the full potential of his 'mental, moral and aesthetic stature';[9] it allows experiment and diversity in mode of life; and by enforcing the necessity (but not the content) of decision in an open, non-coercive society, it leads to that rational autonomy which is essential to the ideal of citizenship. Moreover, it permits discontent, which is a potent source of progress—'improvement in human affairs is wholly the work of the uncontented characters'[10]—and thus stimulates altruistic effort. By encouraging activity and enterprise democracy also fosters intellectual growth, for 'the test of real and vigorous thinking, the thinking which ascertains truths instead of dreaming dreams, is successful application to practice'[11] (a utilitarian and pragmatic view which is none the less true for that, nor necessarily inconsistent with his belief, elsewhere expressed, in the social efficiency of speculative thought). Such growth is fostered also by the free expression of opinion which is an essential feature of democracy; and it is a growth towards truth as well as in intellectual proficiency; for it is by the dialectic of open debate, the antagonism of conflicting views that truth is forged and fashioned into the indispensable instrument of individual and social improvement that Mill believed it to be.

It is not only by freedom that democracy educates but also and very powerfully by participation:

The maximum of the invigorating effect of freedom upon the character is only obtained when the person acted on either is, or is looking forward to becoming, a citizen as fully privileged as any other. What is still more important than even this matter of feeling is the practical discipline which the character obtains from the occasional demand made upon the citizens to exercise, for a time and in their turn, some social function. It is not sufficiently considered how little there is in most men's ordinary life to give any largeness either to their conceptions or to their sentiments. Their work is a routine; not a labour of love, but of self-interest in the most elementary form, the satisfaction of daily wants; neither the thing done nor the process of doing it introduces the mind to thoughts or feelings extending beyond individuals. . . . Giving him something to do for the public supplies, in a measure, all these deficiencies. If circumstances allow the amount of public duty assigned to him to be considerable, it makes him an educated man.[12]

A similar passage in 'Thoughts on Parliamentary Reform' concludes with the assertion that 'the possession and the exercise of political, and among others of electoral, rights is one of the chief instruments both of moral and of intellectual training for the popular mind'.[13] Mill especially emphasizes the moral effect of participation: by involvement in public responsibility the citizen is obliged 'to weigh interests not his own; to be guided in case of conflicting claims by another rule than his private partialities; to apply at every turn principles and maxims which have for their reason of existence the common good'. Where 'this school of public spirit' does not exist, 'there is no unselfish sentiment of identification with the public'; absorbed in himself and his family, a man can think of his neighbours only as rivals to be worsted in competition, not as allies in a common enterprise. 'Thus even private morality suffers, while public is actually extinct.'[14]

Though there is much that is true and valuable in what Mill is saying here, one feels that he is both idealizing democracy (just as he idealized his picture of it in ancient Athens) and understating the potentiality of human nature for unselfishness. Undoubtedly democracy at its best is a great educative force, but (as Mill well knew from his reading of Plato and Thucydides) it is not immune from dishonesty, corruption, and the betrayal of truth.[15] He knew too (again from his historical reading as well as from personal experience) that ordinary men and women are capable of astounding heights of disinterested and sacrificial service to their fellows. However, participation of itself cannot ensure an educated populace. To achieve this a government must actively promote education both through formal institutions—schools and universities and by providing scholarships and the means of research—and by creating a total environment which nourishes in its citizens appropriate qualities of character (see below, pp. 38–41). This too Mill accepted; indeed it placed him in an uncomfortable dilemma arising from the conflict between his claim for the minimum of administrative interference with private life and his urgent desire for human improvement. The latter clearly required a positive initiative on the part of government in raising the educational and cultural standards of the people. This he was forced to admit: in an *Examiner* article of 1832 he concedes that 'the test of what is right in politics is not the *will* of the people, but the *good* of the people';[16] in *Principles of Political Economy* and later in *On Liberty* he grants the need to enforce (though not necessarily to *provide*) universal education; and while insisting on the general principle that 'the great majority of things are worse done by the intervention of government than the individuals most interested in the matter would do them or cause them to be done if left to themselves', he allows intervention at numerous points to safeguard and improve the conditions of life. He even goes so far as to admit that 'in the particular circumstances of a given age or nation there is scarcely anything really important to the general interest which it may not be desirable, or even necessary, that the government should take upon itself, not because private individuals cannot effectually perform it, but because they will not'.[17]

'Government is at once a great influence acting on the human mind, and a set of organised arrangements for public business.'[18] We have examined the first of Mill's criteria and must look now at the second, the quality of the machinery of government. By this he means not only legislative and executive efficiency but, more broadly, the utilization of human and economic resources to secure the greatest benefit to individuals and the community. Success in this dual task requires an identity of interest between rulers and ruled which is most likely to be secured by representative democracy; for here ideally the rulers are, by election and proxy, the same as the ruled and their interests therefore indistinguishable. Clearly this was not the situation in Mill's time:

The state of society and manners in Great Britain almost compels the electors to make their selection from persons in whom it would not be natural that they should confide; persons to a great degree corrupted by aristocratic institutions. The *leisured class*, the class which ought to furnish statesmen and philosophers, has been bred in a very different school and trained to far other occupations.

'The evils of centuries are not to be remedied in a day',[19] he continues, but a programme for political reform existed in the policies of the Philosophical Radicals, the political arm of utilitarianism, for which Mill became a prominent theoretical spokesman (his position in the East India Company prohibited him from direct political participation). This included a redistribution of Parliamentary seats and an expansion of the suffrage, in order to shift power from the 'sinister interest'[20] of the aristocracy to the rising middle class; shorter Parliaments; reform of the Lords and limitation of its power; and changes in the ballot, including the introduction of secrecy. (Also included were items like the extension and improvement of education, population restriction, and full employment, which are more social than political.) Certain of these proposals found modified expression in the Reform Act of

1832. However, although 'a good apparatus is always preferable to a bad',[21] the best devised political and administrative structure is not proof against misuse. There were two special dangers, Mill thought: incompetence and depravity in the rulers, and (in a democracy) ignorance and selfishness in the ruled—the populace being as prone as an aristocracy to the exercise of 'sinister interest'. The remedy for both was fundamentally the same: an educated administration, intelligent, wise, enlightened, and professionally trained; and an educated electorate.

The need for administrators who have achieved high levels of moral and intellectual education is one of Mill's constant themes; so much so that he risks the charge of élitism (see chapter 4, below). 'The idea of a rational democracy', he writes, 'is not that the people themselves govern but that they have security for good government . . . . The people ought to be the masters, but they are masters who must employ servants more skilful than themselves', relying on 'the deliberately formed opinions of a comparatively few specially educated for the task' and showing 'deference to superiority of cultivated intelligence'.[22] There is an old proverb, he writes in an article in *The Examiner*, that 'some are wise and some are otherwise'; it is his contention 'that the people ought to have the benefit of having their affairs arranged by the wise, rather than by those who are otherwise'.[23] Elsewhere he writes of the need for 'able and educated public servants', claims that 'to see the futurity of the species has always been the privilege of the intellectual *élite*', and commends Plato for his

vigorous assertion of a truth of transcendent importance and universal application—that the work of government is a skilled employment; that governing is not a thing which can be done at odd times, or by the way, in conjunction with a hundred other pursuits, nor to which a person can be competent without a large and liberal general education, followed by special and professional study, laborious and of long duration, directed to acquiring not mere practical dexterity, but a scientific mastery of the subject.[24]

What Mill has in mind here is not only Parliament (which would attract a wider range of ability, he suggests, if Members were paid) but also a professional civil service. This latter, he argues forcibly in a Parliamentary Paper of 1854, should be selected by competitive examination, a proposal which, if adopted, 'would form an era in history' and be inestimable in its effect 'in raising the character both of the public administration and of the people'.[25]

The corollary of an educated administration is an educated electorate; hence the urgency of providing universal education for 'the labouring classes' whose schooling at the time was little or none: 'I regard it as wholly inadmissible that any person should participate in the suffrage without being able to read, write and, I will add, perform the common operations of arithmetic.' Justice therefore demands that the means to these elementary attainments should be available to all, either freely or at a cost which the poorest could afford. However, this was not yet; meanwhile 'universal teaching must precede universal enfranchisement'[26] and Mill accordingly devised a scheme, explained in *Representative Government* and 'Thoughts on Parliamentary Reform' which allowed the vote to all, including women, who could pass an elementary educational test and were not subject to such disqualifications as insanity, bankruptcy, receipt of parish relief, and evasion of tax. But not an *equal* vote: 'One person is *not* as good as another; and it is reversing all the rules of rational conduct to attempt to raise a political fabric on a supposition which is at variance with fact.'[27] Since 'the judgement of the higher moral or intellectual being is worth more than that of the inferior',[28] it deserves to be weighted in favour of his superior qualifications and greater value to society; this could be determined on an educational or an occupational basis, with, say, two votes going to the skilled labourer, three to a foreman, farmer, or manufacturer, and five or six to a doctor or lawyer. This, to us conspicuously undemocratic, proposal Mill later abandoned in favour of a form of transferable voting put forward by Thomas Hare which gave more effective representation to minorities; that he could entertain it at all is an indication of the high value he placed on education, in itself and for its social and political efficacy, and of a certain hesitancy which he felt about giving full reign to democracy. The former is, of course, a central theme of the present book; the latter we shall look at again later in this chapter.

Although Mill was anxious that there should be an educated, trained, and proficient administration, he was acutely sensitive to the dangers of centralisation and the bureaucratic abuse of power. At the end of his review article, 'Centralisation', there occurs a remarkable passage:

If there be an ethical doctrine which more than all others requires to be taught, and has been taught with deepest conviction by the great moral teachers, it is that the love of power is the most evil passion of human nature; that power over others, power of coercion and compulsion, any power other than that of moral and intellectual influence, even in the cases where it is indispensable, is a snare, and in all others a curse, both to the possessor and to those over whom it is possessed; a burthen which no rightly constituted moral nature consents to take upon itself, but by one of the greatest sacrifices which inclination ever makes to duty

—a clear echo in these last clauses of the Platonic Guardians! While the love of liberty is wholly unselfish,

the appetite for power is, on the contrary, essentially selfish; for all cannot have power; the power of one is power over others, who not only do not share in his elevation, but whose depression is the foundation on which it is raised. Accordingly the love of power is the passion of the τυραννικαὶ φυσεῖς—of those in all ages who have inflicted on the human race its greatest miseries.[29]

'There is no such thing in morals', he states elsewhere, 'as a *right* to power over others.'[30] Even the power of the majority, democratically asserting itself through a reformed franchise, is questionable in its consequences (again a reluctance to allow the full implications of democracy); for it may well, through its elected representatives and by the pressures of a despotic public opinion 'seek to control . . opinions and feelings which depart from its standard . . . to shape the education of the young by its model, and to extinguish all books, all schools, all combinations of individuals' which aim at 'keeping alive a spirit at variance with its own'.[31]

Bureaucracy has, of course, its advantages: 'It accumulates experience, acquires well-tried and well-considered traditional maxims, and makes provision for appropriate practical knowledge in those who have the actual conduct of affairs.' It is inimical, however, to 'individual energy of mind'; bureaucratic governments are slaves to routine, which 'goes on revolving mechanically, though the work it is intended to do remains undone', degenerate into 'pedantocracy' and eventually 'perish by the immutability of their maxims'.[32] Mill deplores its effects in the nations of the European continent, France in particular, where 'by regulating minutely whatever it allows to be done by others . . . [it] has dwarfed not only the political, but in a great measure the entire practical capacity of the people, and even their intellectual activity and moral aspirations in every field of mental action except pure theory' and kept them in 'a state of political infancy.'[33] It is no wonder that he castigated Comte's *Système de Politique Positive* with its corporate hierarchy of philosophers, its passion for systematization and unity, as 'the completest system of spiritual and temporal despotism which ever yet emanated from a human brain' (with the possible exception of Loyola) and as marking the 'melancholy decadence of a great intellect'.[34]

Centralized government there must be, Mill agreed, but with proper safeguards, of which the most important, as we have seen, are educational. And it is not only the administrators who must be protected against themselves by 'a liberal mental cultivation' both morally and intellectually elevating:

There cannot be a combination of circumstances more dangerous to human welfare than that in which intelligence and talent are maintained at a high standard within a governing corporation, but starved and discouraged outside the pale. Such a system more completely than any other, embodies the idea of despotism by arming with intellectual superiority as an additional weapon those who have already the legal power. . . . The only security against political slavery is the check maintained over governors by the diffusion of intelligence, activity and public spirit among the governed.[35]

Clearly there must also be devolution of responsibility through local government—'the greatest dissemination of power consistent with efficiency'—though again with due safeguards, for 'any despotism', he remarks with uncanny insight, 'is preferable to local despotism'.[36] Efficiency, however, is not enough; consistently Mill insists that a further aim must be 'the nourishment of public spirit and the development of intelligence'; local administration should include some of the best minds of the locality, who will share with the less gifted both their professional knowledge and 'their own more enlarged ideas and higher and more enlightened purposes'.[37] The proper policy for both central and local administration is always one of minimum interference, though not, as was noted above, to the exclusion of positive initiative in promoting the public welfare. The individual must be left (but also encouraged) to provide independently for his own and the general good; where he fails, there should be no coercion save his own loss and the pressure of public disapproval; government assistance is permissible but 'should be so given as to be as far as possible a course of education for the people in the art of accomplishing great objects by individual energy and voluntary cooperation'.[38]

Though Mill had no doubt that democracy was ideally the best form of polity, his faith in it was not unqualified; in fact he was keenly and increasingly sensitive to weaknesses which (as he saw them in contemporary Britain) posed a threat to his cherished values. There were obvious misgivings about the machinery of representative government: Parliament lacked the knowledge and expertise necessary in a responsible legislative assembly—'a popular body', he describes it, 'not specially educated for the purpose, having served no apprenticeship and undergone no examination, and who transact business in the forms and very much in the spirit of a debating society'; moreover, a bare Parliamentary majority might well represent a clear *minority* of voters, thus giving scope to the 'sinister interest' of class legislation (a situation not un-familiar in present-day Britain).[39] However, these defects were not without remedy: one was a reformed franchise and electoral system, another the institution of a professional civil service, to both of which, as we have seen, Mill was firmly committed; another was the establishment of a 'Legislative Commission' (not so far distant from the modern notion of a 'think-tank') to advise on legislation and re-form.[40] Far more insidious, he thought, were the less tangible dan-gers of democracy: first, there was the threat to freedom arising from the conforming pressure of majority opinion; second, a further threat from the same source to individuality, originality, and diversity of life—itself a danger to the very existence of democracy; third, the mental stagnation and consequent threat to truth resulting from low standards of, and interest in, intellectual attainment; fourth, a uniform mediocrity to which the three previous contributed and which was further strengthened, he thought, by advances in commerce, transport, communications, even education (in its then state of unenlightened instruction); fifth, he also feared the spirit of commercialism, noted by de Tocqueville in America, which, if uncorrected by nobler sentiments, he regarded as the 'most serious danger to the future prospects of mankind'.[41]

Against these dangers he inveighed eloquently and repeatedly in *On Liberty*, in his review of de Tocqueville's *Democracy in America*, in the essay on Bentham and in other writings (not excluding *Representative Government* where, among other infirmities of democracy, he frankly recognized its tendency to 'collective mediocrity').[42] Together they seemed a formidable obstacle to human improvement as expressed in his five major goals; and so forcibly does he attack them that the sincerity of his commitment to democracy has been questioned. Certainly he underwent a shift in view from the optimistic radicalism of his youth to a cautious and conservative liberalism in his middle and later years—a change induced, among other influences, by his reading of Coleridge and de Tocqueville. He came to see that the road to the elevated, rational happiness which he envisaged as the ultimate goal was long, arduous, and beset by numerous perils; he further came to see that, despite Helvetius' dictum and James Mill's over-facile inference from association psychology to the power of education, and despite his own underlying egalitarian assumptions, human beings are not all equal, and are unlikely ever to be, in intelligence, imagination, moral judgement, and administrative ability. In this he was bending to the facts of the human situation: men and women *are* educable, corrigible, possessed of marvellous and varied potential, and capable of co-operative enterprise for the common welfare; equally they are selfish, aggressive, corruptible, and at times painfully blind to their own and the general good.[43] What Mill experienced was not a loss of faith in democracy, but a deeper understanding of human nature and human community, an understanding which, obeying the logic of utilitarianism, led him to place greater emphasis than previously on the *good* of the people as distinct from the *will* of the people (see above, p. 20).

It was not only democracy that Mill wanted, believing it to be the form of government most appropriate to the realization of his ideals; he also desired a society which can broadly be described as socialist. Whether this is the right word to describe it is arguable; one writer has declared categorically that 'Mill was never a socialist'; another allows him the 'qualified socialism' which he attributes to himself in the *Autobiography*.[44] The question will be considered later; meanwhile let Mill speak for himself. His condemnation of much that he saw in contemporary British society led him to hope for 'a renovated social fabric', to achieve which would require a fundamental re-examination of 'the whole field of social institutions'.[45] These words were written late in his life, but they apply equally to his middle years. Describing the 'third period . . . of my mental progress', when he was strongly influenced by Harriet (not yet his wife), he writes:

While we repudiated with the greatest energy that tyranny of society over the individual which most socialistic systems are supposed to involve, we yet looked forward to a time when society will no longer be divided into the idle and the industrious; when the rule that they who do not work shall not eat will be applied, not to paupers only, but impartially to all; when the division of the produce of labour, instead of depending, as in so great a degree it now does, on the accident of birth, will be made by concert on an acknowledged principle of justice; and when it will no longer either be, or be thought to be, impossible for human beings to exert themselves strenuously in procuring benefits which are not to be exclusively their own, but to be shared with the society they belong to. The social problem of the future we considered to be, how to unite the greatest individual liberty of action with a common ownership in the raw material of the globe and an equal participation of all in the benefits of combined labour.[46]

There is a similar passage in his review (written in 1851) of F. W. Newman's *Lectures in Political Economy*:

It appears to us that nothing valid can be said against socialism in principle; and that the attempts to assail it, or to defend private property, on the ground of justice must inevitably fail. The distinction between rich and poor, so slightly connected as it is with merit and demerit, or even with exertion and want of exertion in the individual, is obviously unjust; such a feature could not be put into the rudest imaginings of a perfectly just state of society.[47]

He condemns poverty as the 'first among existing social evils' and deplores 'the condition of numbers in civilised Europe, and even in England and France' as 'more wretched than that of most tribes of savages who are known to us'; yet of all the great positive evils of the world poverty is the one which 'may be completely extinguished by the wisdom of society'.[48] A humane standard of living is the right of all; to achieve this, the better off should be willing 'to submit to a very considerable sacrifice of their own means'; the aim should be the 'diffusion of wealth and not its concentration', and the criterion of wealth should be 'how much the circumstances of society permit to be assigned to [one] consistently with the just claims of others'.[49] Yet he is critical of the pursuit of wealth for its own sake both by individuals and (as will appear later) by the state. In 1829 he complained to the French Saint-Simonian, d'Eichthal, of the English 'disposition to sacrifice everything to accumulation and that exclusive and engrossing selfishness which accompanies it' and condemns 'the pursuit of wealth in a degree greater than is required for comfortable subsistence'.[50] This was in the flush of his youthful extremism; but ten years later he still claims that society must be protected against 'the unbalanced influence of the commercial spirit'; and later still in *Principles of Political Economy* he rejects as 'essentially repulsive' the idea of 'a society only held together by the relations and feelings arising out of pecuniary interests'.[51]

It is not only his ideas on work, wealth, and poverty that give a socialist colour to Mill's thought; at a more fundamental level he had a profound concern for people and their relationships, a concern which sprang not only from his utilitarianism but also from his keen sense of justice and an underlying egalitarianism. The last is finely expressed in a passage in *The Subjection of Women*:

The true virtue of human beings is fitness to live together as equals; claiming nothing for themselves but what they as freely concede to everyone else; regarding command of any kind as an exceptional necessity, and in all cases a temporary one; and preferring, whenever possible, the society of those with whom leading and following can be alternate and reciprocal.

There is little, he adds, in contemporary life that cultivates such relationships—least of all the family which, instead of being, as it should be, 'a school of sympathy in equality, of living together in love', is one of despotism.[52] He had a special interest in and concern for 'the labouring classes', who at that time were far removed from the power, privilege, and standard of living they now enjoy as a result of the work of the trade unions. This is obvious not only in his writings, such as 'The Claims of Labour' and the chapter in *Principles of Political Economy*, 'On the Probable Futurity of the Labouring Classes', but in his active support for their attempts to better their conditions by advocating legal protection against employers, combined action through trade unions (to whose dangers, however, he was no less alert than to their benefits), worker co-operatives, profit sharing, and representation of the working classes in Parliament. Industrial partnership he sees as an essential means of healing the gap between employer and worker, of creating 'unity of interest instead of organized hostility'; for 'the industrial economy which divides society absolutely into two portions, the payers of wages and the receivers of them, the first counted by thousands and the last by millions, is neither fit for nor capable of infinite duration'.[53]

In all this he insists characteristically that the indispensable foundation for the improvement of the condition of the workers is education, intellectual and moral; it is also a protection against the abuse of the political and industrial power they will eventually acquire. In their present mental and moral state they are unfit to wield that power and unable to devise their own betterment. What they need, however, is not charity, patronage, or condescension, but an education designed to help them help themselves; and this includes not merely instruction, whether formally by universal schooling or informally by libraries and newspapers, but the total impact of the social environment whose formative influence is far more potent than any direct teaching. Industrial training there must also be, 'not to improve them as workmen merely, but as human beings'; even as workmen it will enable them to use hand and brain in concert, inducing both manual dexterity and (significantly again) those 'habits of order and regularity . . . which have more to do with the formation of character than many persons are aware of'.[54] No longer are they children to be kept in leading-strings; they are equals with the rest of the population and it is as such that they must be guided and advised; their education must increasingly be self-education and 'to their own qualities must now be commended the care of their destiny'.[55]

It would clearly be a mistake to suppose that Mill objected to everything he saw in the industrial and economic life of the nation. Though he abhorred the evils of capitalism as it then was, he was unwilling to condemn it out of hand in exchange for a thorough-going socialism: the evils and injustices of the present system were indeed great, but they were not, he believed, increasing, and the tendency was towards their diminution. What was needed was 'a calm comparison between two different systems of society, with a view of determining which of them affords the greatest resources for overcoming the inevitable difficulties of life';[56] though he believed it was through injecting into free-enterprise capitalism the intellectual and moral principles of socialism that the former would be given its best chance of improvement. So too with private property: he deplored the inequity of a society in which 'immense fortunes are possessed by a few and coveted by all' and looked for a situation in which 'the greatest possible numbers possess and are contented with a moderate competency which all may hope to acquire',[57] yet he could see advantages in private ownership, notably in stimulating intelligence and encouraging responsibility, foresight, and prudence. Here again his approach is experiential: 'We are too ignorant either of what individual agency in its best form, or Socialism in its best form, can accomplish to be qualified to decide which of the two will be the ultimate form of human society'; but he hazards a guess that decision will depend on 'which of the two systems is consistent with the greatest amount of human liberty and spontaneity'.[58] For *landed* property, however, he sees little justification: land, he argues in approving Coleridge, is 'the gift of nature, the source of subsistence to all and the foundation of everything that influences our physical well-being';[59] further, it is limited in quantity and cannot be increased; the community, therefore, may rightfully appropriate it to beneficial purposes. (In certain cases such purposes might include allocation of land to private tenure, e.g. the Irish peasants, in order to stimulate initiative and self-reliance.) Yet once again, though conceding that land should belong to the nation at large, he thinks it will be 'a generation or two' before progress in intelligence and morality will be sufficient to prevent abuse of public ownership.[60]

Likewise his attitude to competition was a mixture of distaste with practical realism guided by experiential and educational criteria. Basically he was against it:

I confess I am not charmed with the ideal of life held out by those who think that the normal state of human beings is that of struggling to get on; that the trampling, crushing, elbowing and treading on each others' heels, which form the existing type of social life, are the most desirable lot of human kind or anything but the disagreeable symptoms of one of the phases of industrial progress.[61]

The moral arguments against it are powerful, 'as arming one human being against another, making the good of each depend upon evil to others, making all who have anything to gain or lose live as in the midst of enemies';[62] in short it demeans human relationships; in addition it is as conducive to fraud and pretence as it is to excellence. Yet he cannot accept socialist condemnation of competition as solely responsible for current economic ills: it protects against monopoly, reduces prices and, in a situation of labour shortage, may well increase wages. For the present its value as an incentive makes it indispensable: 'Competition may not be the best conceivable stimulus, but it is at present a necessary one, and no one can foresee the time when it will not be indispensable to progress.'[63] Even in the provision of schools it is not unacceptable, for it promotes variety and safeguards civil and political freedom by countering state control.[64]

If, then, one asks, was Mill a socialist? the answer must be yes and no. He certainly regarded himself as one (in some sense of the word), and it is obvious that his ideals of society included elements which are central to any socialist doctrine and others which can hardly be excluded from the broad heading of socialism. Such are his demand for a just distribution of the national product which would eliminate extremes of wealth and poverty, and his insistence on the disabling and demeaning effects of poverty and on the need for an assured minimum standard of living; such too are his proposals for co-operation, profit sharing, and industrial partnership, and his (not uncritical) support for trade unionism; and underlying all these are the twin principles of equality and respect for persons which are socialism's essential moral foundations. Moreover, he examined in detail and with obvious sympathy the various socialist schemes proposed by the St. Simonians and Fourierists in France and by Robert Owen and his followers in Britain. By the first of these he was deeply and permanently influenced; though he doubted the practicability of their proposals, he was confident that they must 'tend to give a beneficial direction to the efforts of others to bring society . . . nearer to some ideal standard'.[65] Communism too, in a non-Marxist form, he discusses sympathetically in *Principles of Political Economy*; but while allowing that 'the restraints of Communism would be freedom in comparison with the present condition of the majority of the human race', he questions whether in such a system 'there would be any asylum left for individuality of character; whether public opinion would not be a tyrannical yoke; whether the absolute dependence of each on all, and surveillance of each by all, would not grind all down into a tame uniformity of thoughts, feelings and actions'.[66]

Mill himself distinguished two kinds of socialist. There are the 'revolutionary socialists', predominantly Continental, who wish to take over the entire productive resources of the nation (including, some of them, all private property) and place them under a central administrative control for the general good. The other kind are gradualists; they wish no less than the previous for a new order of society where 'private property and individual competition are to be superseded'; but they plan to achieve their ideals by applying them first 'on the scale of a village community or township' and extending them 'to an entire country by the self-multiplication of such self-acting units'.[67] Mill allies himself with the latter; he rejects the notion of class warfare, fears the possibility of 'bursting society asunder by a socialist revolution' with its trail of 'bloodshed and misery', and prefers small-scale experiment and trial before plunging into nationwide socialization.[68] He was not in principle averse to some degree of central planning; for despite his advocacy of *laissez-faire* he believed, as has been shown, that government intervention was justifiable in certain circumstances and for certain purposes; but he regarded as intolerable the detailed bureaucratic regulation of life which was entailed by the more extreme socialist schemes.[69]

What Mill desired was not simply economic and administrative efficiency; nor was it a strict practical implementation of the logic of socialist or even utilitarian ideals. At a profounder level altogether he was concerned to secure a certain quality of life. This is apparent in passages already quoted on power (p. 24), on equality in human relationships (p. 29), and on the scramble for wealth (pp. 28–9). It appears also in his comments on work and leisure in his letter/article on 'The Negro Question': there is no value in work for work's sake, he argues, in the proliferation of 'work upon work without end'; rather he would assert 'the gospel of leisure and maintain that human beings *cannot* rise to the finer attributes of their nature compatibly with a life filled with labour'. In the same article he condemns, in words as apt now as when they were written, 'those fopperies of so-called civilisation which myriads of hands are now occupied and lives wasted in providing'.[70] While personal enjoyments are not to be scorned, since, with due safeguards and if they are of the right kind, they are conducive to benevolence, one should cultivate 'the habitual wish to share them with others'.[71] There is need too for solitude and meditation:

It is not good for man to be kept perforce at all times in the presence of his species. A world from which solitude is extirpated is a very poor ideal. Solitude, in the sense of being often alone, is essential to any depth of meditation or of character; and solitude in the presence of natural beauty and grandeur is the cradle of thoughts and aspirations which are not only good for the individual, but which society could ill do without.

This is part of his argument against a policy of continuous econ-omic growth; he continues in a passage so prophetically apposite to our own situation that it is worth quoting at length:

Nor is there much satisfaction in contemplating the world with nothing left to the spontaneous activity of nature; with every rood of land brought into cultivation, which is capable of growing food for human beings; every flowery waste or natural pasture ploughed up, all quadrupeds or birds which are not domesticated for man's use exterminated as his rivals for food, every hedgerow or superfluous tree rooted out, and scarcely a place left where a wild shrub or flower could grow without being eradicated as a weed in the name of improved agriculture. If the earth must lose that great portion of its pleasantness which it owes to things that the unlimited increase of wealth and population would ex-tirpate from it, for the mere purpose of enabling it to support a larger, but not a better or a happier population, I sincerely hope, for the sake of posterity, that they will be content to be stationary, long before necessity compels them to it.

(He insists, however, anticipating an obvious misunderstanding, 'that a stationary condition of capital and population implies no stationary state of human improvement'.)[72]

There is much that is valuable in Mill's picture of the society he hoped for, and much that we, at a later stage in the development of democratic socialism, can profitably take to heart. Fundamental is his emphasis on values: though he did not attempt the kind of analysis that is familiar now in educational philosophy, exploring semantic subtleties, sifting logical relationships, and trying to establish an axiological geography, the emphasis is apparent none the less. He was convinced that to create a certain kind of society requires the injection into it, and the continual nourishing within it, of a core of values generally accepted and practised by its citizens and embodied in its formal institutions.[73] We have seen what the chief of these were for Mill. Significant here is his rejection of an absolute stance: staunch utilitarian though he was, he saw that the ideal of the general good, if too rigidly pursued, can lead to loss of freedom, individuality and personal altruistic initiative; conversely there are occasions when individual freedom must yield to govern-ment intervention for the individual's and the common good; like-wise ideal distributive justice, reducing all to a common level of possessions, may extinguish those excellences of individuality which wealth may permit (without, of course, guaranteeing); truth too, in its implementation if not in its discovery, may be forced to wait on circumstances and is in any case always modifiable by further experience. Instead of a situation of dominance, with one value pre-eminent over others, he inclines to one of flexible and adjustable tension, sensitive to experiential test, but always firmly oriented towards 'human improvement'. Such tension is more difficult to maintain in practice, and also perhaps to justify theoretically, than an absolute position; moreover, it risks misinterpretation and explains how, according to the viewpoint taken, Mill can be seen variously as an apostle of liberty and a moral totalitarian, a forerunner of modern socialism and an upholder of aristocratic élitism.[74]

Valuable too is his constant championing of individuality and diversity—an aspect of his thought which will receive detailed examination in chapter 5. It was his fears for these that made him hesitant to approve communist schemes of social organization; he doubted whether they

would be consistent with that multiform development of human nature, those manifold unlikenesses, that diversity of tastes and talents and variety of intellectual points of view, which not only form a great part of the interest of human life, but by bringing intellects into stimulating collision and by presenting to each innumerable notions that he would not have conceived of himself, are the mainspring of mental and moral progression.[75]

In Britain today our danger may be almost the reverse of this— an over-indulgence of individual freedom to the point of losing our sense of community, of responsible obligation to a society larger than each of us and demanding at least a minimum of conformity to common values and purposes. Yet what Mill feared is conspicuous enough elsewhere and constitutes, as he rightly judged, a danger to the richest expression of man's humanity. Nor is it wholly absent from ourselves; for in education an over-hasty and often improvised implementation of egalitarian ideals has led, one suspects, to a decline (it is to be hoped only temporary) in intellectual and moral standards and a step towards a mediocrity of conformity to something less than excellence. We should do well, too, to heed Mill's warnings about power and bureaucracy, about the 'less acceptable face of capitalism' shown in its addiction to competition, to growth and the pursuit of wealth, about class warfare and the possibility of violent social disruption. This last is especially timely in its relevance to our present situation of increasing resort to violence and unreason as expressions of dissent; it is not thus, Mill believed, that truth emerges, but from the open clash of opinions, freely voiced and freely, but rationally, opposed. Nor can we be too often reminded that it is the quality of life that makes life itself worth living; that such acknowledged goods as pleasure, knowledge, 'virtue', and aesthetic activity do not, even at their most desirable, sufficiently or necessarily constitute happiness; that there must be in addition supervenient considerations of what kind, how, to what end, and in what pattern of human relationships. 'Where', Mill might well ask with T. S. Eliot, 'is the Life we have lost in living)'.[76]

Most significant of all for the theme of this book is his idea of the educative society. This is not (to repeat) his own phrase; nor does he identify it as a distinctive concept and unravel its implications; nevertheless it is a constant underlying assumption of his argument for a representative democracy embodying the principles of equality and social justice. Without an educated electorate democracy is impossible, for it requires of its citizens an alert, informed, critical interest and, as far as possible, participation in the processes of government; moreover, 'the worth of a state, in the long run, is the worth of the individuals composing it', and if the latter is impoverished, the most perfect machinery lacks 'the vital power', for effective operation.[77] Further, individual excellence, it should be remembered, is something that Mill believed should be cultivated also for its own sake. Clearly there is mutual obligation here—on the citizen to cultivate his talents, on the government to enable him to do so. The heaviest obligation, however, is on the government, to promote the education of its citizens by all possible formal and informal means, including participation and the provision of a favourable total environment; it must, as we have seen, be 'an agency of national education', 'fostering the virtue and intelligence of the people themselves' (p. 18 above). Socialism too requires an educated populace, nurtured to an enlightened rational autonomy, capable of rising above the 'sinister interest' of whatever class, and contributing unselfishly its work and its wisdom to the common good. We have, then, the picture of a society involved in a reciprocal and self-perpetuating educational process, constantly replenished by an inner initiative, conforming to principles of reason and morality, and moving steadily towards the goal of qualitative enrichment.

No doubt Mill would agree that in the century since his death Britain has advanced a little nearer to that goal, and that the potential for further advance is greater than he could have imagined. But the dangers he envisaged are still with us, not only the threat to freedom, individuality, and truth (by, for instance, extremism, violence, and intimidation), not only mental stagnation, mediocrity, and the spiritual mortification of affluence, but principally a failure to grasp two fundamental truths: first, the supreme importance of values in determining the nature and quality of a nation's life; second, the need for unrelenting educational effort in promoting these values. The two truths are not dissociable: they are linked in the concept of the educative society, in which government and people, formal and informal institutions are united in a common educational enterprise.

# 3

# The Role of Education

IN THE two previous chapters we have examined, first, the dominant aims and values to which Mill was committed in the pursuit of
'improvement', second, the kind of society which he thought was
implied by and also conducive to them. The theme of the present
section is the role he assigned to education within society in
promoting both social stability and social change, in fostering
individual growth and excellence while at the same time contributing to the efficient operation of government and to the total welfare
of the community. Mill habitually thought of education in a
narrower and a wider sense; the distinction is clearly made in the
opening paragraph of the *Inaugural Address*: education includes
not only

whatever we do for ourselves and whatever is done for us by others for
the express purpose of bringing us somewhat nearer to the perfection of
our nature; it does more: in its largest acceptation it comprehends even
the indirect effects produced on character and on the human faculties
by things of which the direct purposes are quite different; by laws, by
forms of government, by the industrial arts, by modes of social life, nay,
even by physical facts not dependent on human will, by climate, soil and
local position. Whatever helps to shape the human being, to make the
individual what he is or hinder him from being what he is not, is part of
his education.

And a very bad education this often is, he comments, 'requiring all
that can be done by cultivated intelligence and will to counteract its
tendencies'. For the purpose of the *Address* he chooses the narrower
sense, describing it a few sentences later (from a rather different
angle) as 'the culture which each generation purposely gives to
those who are to be its successors in order to qualify them for at
least keeping up, and if possible for raising, the level of improvement which has been attained'.[1] This distinction between formal
and informal education, between deliberate, organized instruction
or training and the total impact of environment (often, but not
necessarily, random) is important for an understanding both of

Mill and of our own educational situation. In the present chapter 'education' occurs in both senses, with sometimes the wider, informal, and sometimes the narrower, formal, predominant; the social role of education, Mill believed, required both of them in intimate association and mutual support—indeed this was an essential part of his concept of the 'educative society'.[2]

Such a society, it was suggested above (pp. 18–21), is one where government and people co-operate in an educational enterprise which utilizes education in its widest meaning to promote improvement and (a utilitarian must add) increase the sum of human happiness. For its success the enterprise requires a harmony of formal and informal influences; if the two conflict—and Mill clearly recognized that they could and often did—the desired impact is diminished, effort is wasted, and improvement retarded. Such, unfortunately, is the situation which prevails at the present time: the work of schools, and to a less extent of colleges and universities, is impeded by counter-influences emanating from a variety of sources in society at large; these include not only the 'sinister interest' of hidden (and not so hidden) persuasion in commercial advertising and political propaganda, but also the constant pressure of values and attitudes, expressed through the media, in home life, and in peer-group culture, which contradict those conveyed through formal educational institutions—honesty, integrity, respect for persons, tolerance, industry, and the like. Such conflict is never wholly eradicable, and it is undesirable that it should be; in an open, democratic society it arises inevitably from the co-existence of different modes of life and from the 'generation gap'; and, as Mill would willingly admit, it can stimulate a dialectic which leads to new truths and expanded experience. But when the conflict is too severe, the educational enterprise is nullified; and there is evidence—in truancy, vandalism, rejection of authority, and the demand for de-schooling—that we are approaching this predicament in Britain today. It is a premise of the educative society and a presupposition of Mill's thinking that such conflict is reduced to a level sufficient to maintain a dialectic without obstructing educational purposes, that the environment outside formal educational institutions is deliberately structured to support what is done within them; the result will be a self-generating, self-nourishing educational process which moves by its own momentum towards improvement. Of course there are problems here: what

values should be fed into the process? who will select them? may
not the educative society degenerate into a totalitarian monster,
manipulating by indoctrination and pruning freedom to fit the
blue-prints of social engineering? Mill's answer to the first
question appears in chapter 1; the second and some of its
implications as Mill saw them are discussed in the next chapter,
'Élitism'; aspects of the third arise in Chapter 6, 'The State and
Education'.

Bearing in mind, then, Mill's distinction between formal and
informal educational influences and his assumption that they will
contribute harmoniously, or at least with no more than a healthy
discord, to common purposes, we turn now to his view of the social
role of education. A primary function of education in any society is
to promote the cohesiveness and continuity of that society, its
distinctiveness as an on-going, organized community. Education
is not alone in serving this end: military and police forces are
necessary for physical security; the legal system, the machinery of
government and administration, welfare and transport services all
contribute to maintaining the integrity of a society (indeed from
Mill's panoramic perspective all of these could well be regarded as
*educational*—the boundary is indeterminate). But these are likely
to be ineffective if there is lacking a core of commonly accepted
values and purposes to which the majority of citizens subscribe,
even at possible detriment to their personal interests; without such
a common ground of accepted loyalties a society is liable to a
degree of internal strife which may destroy its validity as a community and lead to revolution or subjugation. Education—formal
institutions working within a supporting environment—is a necessary means, and in a secular state the principal means, of ensuring
the integrity and permanence of a society. It performs this function
by initiating children into the values, ideals, attitudes of mind, and
modes of relationship which belong characteristically to a particular society and make it the kind of society it is—distinguishing, for
instance, Englishmen from Scots or Germans and even more
markedly from West Indians or Pakistanis.[3] The process of initiation begins in the home and extends into social life, reinforced in
both by the impact of the media; it is further reinforced by selective
concentration in the curriculum and community life of formal
institutions—for schools, and to some extent colleges and universities, can and do *choose* the rules and values they live by and the

subjects they teach with a deliberateness of purpose contrasted sharply with the often random influences outside.

Although Mill did not formulate it in precise terms, he clearly understood the need for social cohesion and continuity and for an education which promotes them. In his essay on Coleridge he charges French philosophers of the previous century with overlooking three essential conditions which he thought necessary if a nation were to maintain respect for law and government without impairing the manly vigour of its citizens. First is the capacity for self-restraint, 'the power of subordinating . . . personal impulses and aims to . . . the ends of society; of adhering, against all temptation, to the course of conduct which those ends prescribed'. Where, historically, such restraint was missing or relaxed,

the natural tendency of mankind to anarchy reasserted itself; the State became disorganised from within; mutual conflict for selfish ends neutralised the energies which were required to keep up the contest against the natural causes of evil; and the nation, after a longer or briefer interval of progressive decline, became either the slave of a despotism or the prey of a foreign invader.

Where it has existed, its source has been 'a system of *education*, beginning with infancy and continued through life, of which, whatever else it might include, one main and incessant ingredient was *restraining discipline*'. (It is Sparta chiefly, but not solely, that he has in mind—'the entire civil and military policy of the ancient commonwealths was such a system of training'.)[4]

The second condition is a sense of attachment, a 'feeling of allegiance or loyalty'; there must be present 'in the constitution of the State *something* which is settled, something permanent and not to be called in question; something which, by general agreement, has a right to be where it is and to be secure against disturbance'. It is this to which the loyalty attaches itself, and it might be a deity, or a group of persons acknowledged by tradition or achievement as 'rightful guides and guardians' (another Platonic echo?); or it might be laws, ordinances, or ancient liberties; or, finally, the loyalty 'may attach itself to the principles of individual freedom and political and social equality'. Only when there exists such loyalty to 'the fundamental principles of the system of social union' can a society preserve its integrity against inevitable dissensions and collisions of interest. Then third, there must be 'a strong and active principle of cohesion ... a principle of sympathy, not of hostility; of union, not of separation ... a feeling of common interest among those who live under the same government and are contained within the same natural or historical boundaries'.[5] It is the special merit of Coleridge and his fellow philosophers of 'the reactionary school' that they have disclosed these three conditions and, still more, have seen 'in the character of the national education existing in any political society at once the principal cause of its permanence as a society and the chief cause of its progressiveness'.[6] And by 'national education' Mill does not, of course, mean simply the formal system of educational institutions, but also (and thinking again of the city-states of the ancient world) the totality of influences emanating from family, laws, government, tradition, the arts, and the acknowledged values and principles of social life.

This conception of education as an instrument of initiation and conservation, though expressed here indirectly in a critical and expository essay, certainly represents Mill's own view and is substantiated by what he writes elsewhere. He affirms in *Comte and Positivism* the need for disciplined self-restraint, acquired through education, in order to serve the common good; and he looks forward to the day when children will be taught 'as in antiquity to control their appetites, to brave dangers and submit voluntarily to pain, as simple exercises in education'. 'Something', he adds, 'has been lost as well as gained by no longer giving to every citizen the training necessary for a soldier.'[7] In *On Liberty* there occurs a passage whose clear implication is the need to initiate children into appropriate moral standards; society has the duty and the power to accomplish this: 'The existing generation is master both of the training and the entire circumstances of the generation to come', and it must expect to suffer if it allows its children to grow up incapable of 'rational consideration of distant motives'.[8] So too in chapter 3 of *Utilitarianism*: concern for others as equals, he claims there, is a fundamental principle of human association; if it is incorporated in the social environment and 'nourished by the contagion of sympathy and the influences of education' it can be rooted in the individual as 'a thing naturally and necessarily to be attended to'.[9] Already noted (p. 17) is his claim in *Representative Government* that permanence and progress in a society require certain qualities in its citizens: industry, integrity, justice, and prudence contribute to the former, and mental activity, enterprise and courage to the latter.[10] He may be mistaken in his choice of qualities, but there is no mistaking his intention that there *are* qualities which must be instilled by early training to ensure that a society persists and develops as a coherent association of human beings. Finally, in his discussion of the education of the working classes in *Principles of Political Economy* he insists that 'modern nations will have to learn the lesson that the well-being of a people must exist by means of the justice and self-government, the δικαιοσύνη and σωφροσύνη, of the individual citizens'.[11] The intention of these passages is clear: among the primary tasks of education is the perpetuation of a nation's life by initiating its children into the qualities which characterize and nourish that life.

However, the role of education is not confined to 'permanence'; it includes also 'progressiveness', the movement of society towards improvement, the promotion of which (as we have seen) Mill deemed an essential task of government. The originating source of improvement lay, he believed, in the individual, in the gifted intellect, the sensitive, searching imagination, the thrust of altruism 'beyond the point of absolute moral duty'.[12] 'The initiation of all wise or noble things', he writes in *On Liberty*, 'comes and must come from individuals.'[13] The generality of mankind are incapable of the vision and prescience which probe the future for its unrevealed possibilities: 'To see the futurity of the species has always been the privilege of the intellectual *élite*, or of those who have learnt from them; to have the feelings of that futurity has been the distinction, and usually the martyrdom, of a still rarer *élite*.' So he asserts in *The Subjection of Women*; he enlarges on this in a later passage, attributing such originality of insight to 'an unusual degree of nervous sensibility', which is capable of '*sustained* excitement', of 'lofty enthusiasm' which lifts the individual above 'his everyday character'.[14] The truths of science, he suggests in the *Logic*, are 'seen as it were instinctively by superior minds in some comparatively simple case'; and industry too needs its men of higher intelligence whose 'greater perspicacity enables them . . . to see probabilities of advantage which never occur to the ordinary run of men'.[15] Such persons not only originate new truths, new ideals, new standards of excellence; they also, of course, set an example which uplifts their fellows and raises the quality of society as a whole: the 'sacred fire' of a few minds is diffused among all (if circumstances are so devised to make this possible); cultivated, as

they should be, to a high degree of excellence, they enable civilization to 'rain down its influences upon the remainder of society'.[16]
Particularly is this true of a nation's authors:

Events might have spoken or even cried aloud, but they would have
spoken a foreign language; mankind could not have profited, and do not
profit, even by the lessons of their personal experience, until a man of
genius arises to construe those lessons for them. . . . Since the discovery
of printing, books are the medium by which the ideas, the mental
habits and the feelings of the most exalted and enlarged minds are
propagated among the inert, unobserving, unmeditative mass.[17]

But how is greatness to be cultivated and its potential released?
One obvious condition is freedom; this is the reiterated message of
chapter 3 of *On Liberty*: without freedom it is impossible for
human beings to grow to full stature, for talent to display itself;
without freedom there can be no individuality, no diversity, no
novelty. Mill's view of individuality and the conditions of its
nurture is central to his educational thought and will be considered
in Chapter 5 below. A second essential condition for the unfolding
of greatness is 'liberal' education, an education which liberates and
enlarges mind and spirit and makes a man more serviceable to
himself and to others. This is the central theme of his *Inaugural
Address*, delivered in 1867 but expressing (with something of the
nostalgic fervour of the elderly) ideas and ideals to which he had
been committed throughout his life. The point to be stressed here
is the necessity for education if greatness is to contribute the full
measure of its potential to social progress; and Mill intends
education in both senses: a nurturing environment which, through
freedom, ease of personal communication, and a relaxation of class
distinctions, encourages growth and the spread of beneficent
influences, and at the same time a formal education which, by
rigorous intellectual and moral training induces the qualities required for leadership. (It is worth noting that he does not, any
more than did Plato in the *Republic*, confine such education to an
exclusive upper class. In his article on endowments he commends
the suggestion that such funds should be put to educating the
élite (Mill's word) of the poor, who have proved their capacity for
higher education but cannot afford to pay for it. The consequent
gain would be inestimable, not only in extending the reserve of
ability, but also in abating 'the just dissatisfaction which the best of
the poorer classes of the nation feel with their position in it'.)[18]

Especially important in Mill's view was the development of 'the speculative faculties'. This was partly because, in the movement towards democracy (both in Britain and, as described by de Tocqueville, in America) he saw an acute need for intellectual authority in guiding the as yet ill-educated and ill-informed majority; partly, too, because he regarded trained intelligence as a principal instrument in the discovery of truth; partly, again, because he regarded 'intellectual speculation' as 'a most influential part of the productive labour of society' and 'fruitful of applications to the purposes of outward life';[19] but especially because he was convinced that intellect, inquiry, and the state of knowledge and opinion were of fundamental importance to social progress. The evidence of history and of human nature, he affirms in *Logic* VI, points to their being the predominant factors in social change; although 'speculation, intellectual activity, the pursuit of truth' are not 'among the more powerful propensities of human nature', their influence is paramount in the advance of science, morality, and the arts, and in creating the climate of thought which is the essential causative context of all social advance.[20] In the *Autobiography* he makes the confident assertion that 'no great improvements in the lot of mankind are possible until a great change takes place in the fundamental constitution of their modes of thought'.[21] It is because he attached such importance to 'the speculative faculties', 'cultivated intelligence', and 'the instructed minority' in creating the intellectual conditions of social advance, that he was attracted to Coleridge's scheme for a 'clerisy', 'an organised body set apart and endowed for the cultivation and diffusion of knowledge'.[22] He recognized clearly enough (p. 25 above) the dangers of an isolated intellectual oligarchy and of exclusive separation of wise from ignorant. Yet he firmly believed that for the foreseeable future a highly cultivated intellectual and cultural leadership was a necessary requirement of the human situation; it was also of special importance in nineteenth-century Britain, both as a guarantee of improvement and as a defence against the threat of mediocrity. And, of course, it is education that must establish it; *not* education as he then saw it, but a rejuvenated, disciplined, enlarged education such as he outlines in the essay 'Civilisation' and expounds at length thirty years later in the *Inaugural*.

Although Mill believed that the originating source of progress was in the gifted individual and that improvement must be fostered from above by a highly educated élite, he believed no less firmly that it must be prompted also from below: there must be deliberate effort to raise the standards—economic, intellectual, and moral—of the mass of the population, especially of the working classes; and in this task education was equally indispensable. The condition at that time of what Mill for convenience's sake calls the labouring classes (see above, p. 30 note 53) was hardly comparable with what it is today; the trade unions, the welfare state, universal education, and a deep change in social attitudes have improved that condition to an extent he would rejoice to see (though leaving him still dissatisfied). What he saw around him was a poverty that crippled human potential, an ignorance that debarred from effective political participation, and a crushing burden of work that left neither time nor energy for the flowering of humanity. Part cause and part effect of this situation was a moral inertia and ineptitude which robbed the labouring classes of the dignity, self-respect and independence he believed was rightly theirs, and at the same time seriously impeded their economic advance.

Much, of course, could be achieved by direct government action, particularly in alleviating poverty and the conditions of work; much more could be done indirectly by providing appropriate education: 'the first thing needful' is 'an effective national education of the children of the labouring class', though concurrently with this must be 'a system of measures which shall . . . extinguish extreme poverty for one whole generation'.[23] Indeed, education is not merely 'the principal, but the sole remedy, if understood in its widest sense'; and he goes on to remind us once again of the totality of educational influence: 'Whatever acts upon the minds of the labouring classes is properly their education. But their minds, like those of other people, are acted upon by the whole of their social circumstances; and often the part of their education which is least efficacious as such is that which goes by the name.'[24] In the process of amelioration Mill saw that there was a complexity and interaction of contributory factors. Educational improvement obviously depends partly on economic advance: 'until they are well fed, they cannot be well instructed', he wrote in his *Black Dwarf* article on population; and 'a man who is compelled to work fourteen hours out of the twenty-four to obtain bread has no time to instruct himself and is too much harassed and fatigued to turn his attention to important affairs'.[25] But economic advance is itself a result of improved education which, by increase of knowledge, skill, and intelligence, raises the level of productivity and of pecuniary reward. The effect of greater knowledge and skill was manifest, he asserts, in the industrial progress of the time; but

a thing not yet so well understood and recognised is the economical value of the general diffusion of intelligence among the people. . . . The deficiency of practical good sense which renders the majority of the labouring class such bad calculators—which makes, for instance, their domestic economy so improvident, lax and irregular—must disqualify them for any but a low grade of intelligent labour and render their industry far less productive than with equal energy it otherwise might be. The importance, even in this limited aspect, of popular education is well worthy of the attention of politicians, especially in England.

Further, 'the moral qualities of the labourers are fully as important to the efficiency and worth of their labour as the intellectual'—not only such qualities as temperance, prudence, and reliability, but simple honesty: 'The advantage to mankind of being able to trust one another penetrates into every crevice and cranny of human life: the economical is perhaps the smallest part of it, yet even this is incalculable.'[26] 'Human improbity', he continues (and here, surely, extending his comment to the population as a whole) is a vast expense to the community, an expense which is correspondingly diminished as standards of integrity rise. Especially did Mill hope that moral improvement would contribute to economic betterment by limiting the size of families; for he saw in the unrestrained growth of population a principal cause of the poverty and misery that afflicted the labouring classes. The remedy lay partly in themselves, in cultivating the moral qualities of restraint, prudence, and responsible foresight; partly in a formal education which assisted them to do this by developing intelligence and training character; partly in changing the climate of opinion (itself, of course, a powerful educational influence) from acquiescence in excessive breeding to enlightened acceptance of control.

Thus, the education he envisaged for the labouring classes was not one confined to simple literacy and numeracy, though he thought these essential, and more besides: 'There are certain primary elements and means of knowledge which it is in the highest degree desirable that all human beings born into the community should acquire during childhood'—hence the need for compulsory education. Nor was it to be 'an education of mere words', the kind of crammed instruction by rule and rote that he regularly deplored (as, for instance, in the essay 'On Genius'). 'The aim of all intellectual training for the mass of the people', he explains, 'should be to cultivate common sense; to qualify them for forming a sound practical judgement of the circumstances by which they are surrounded. Whatever in the intellectual department can be superadded to this is chiefly ornamental.' It must be 'an education directed to diffuse good sense among the people, with such knowledge as would qualify them to judge of the tendencies of their actions'.[27] Thus he writes in *Principles of Political Economy*, echoing his 'Speech on Perfectibility' of twenty years earlier: 'Such a system of education should exist as will give to the mass of mankind not learning but common-sense practical judgement in ordinary affairs, and shall enable them to see that a thing is wrong when it is wrong.'[28] The moral orientation is obvious; and it was no doubt his intention that this elementary training in common sense and judgement should be extended to specific instruction (but *practical*, not theoretical) in the moral principles fundamental to all human association—honesty, justice, and the like. There is a further point already noted above (p. 30): it must be an education offered to the labouring classes *as equals* and for which they must progressively assume responsibility themselves. What the poor need, he writes in a letter of 1852, is not to be indoctrinated nor fed with other people's opinions, 'but to be induced and enabled to think for themselves' (and this, he adds, is equally true for the rich).[29] Indeed there is already 'a spontaneous education going on in the minds of the multitude, which may be greatly accelerated and improved by artificial aids'. Progress may be slow, he adds cautiously, but the prospect is hopeful.[30]

Mill's emphasis on the moral aspect of education is characteristic: he believed profoundly that quality of life is more important than any quantitative criterion, and that a major factor in achieving it, both for individuals and for society, was the prevalent conception of and attitude to right and wrong, to personal relationships and obligations—in short, moral character. This clearly links with his commitment to the five basic values discussed in chapter 1; for it is these that serve as criteria of right and wrong and obligation, that give content not only to improvement (itself largely a moral concept) but also to morality. In his own time he saw a special need for a firmer attachment to these values and the principles of conduct that flow from them, and this for the whole nation, not just its poorer classes. He charges Bentham with overlooking the importance of national character, which is the very thing 'which causes one nation to succeed in what it attempts, another to fail', which inspires one to achieve lasting greatness, and 'dooms another to early and rapid decay'.[31] In the *Autobiography* he condemns the self-interest of employers and workers which prevents their co-operation for 'generous, or at all events for public and social purposes'; there is in society a 'deep-rooted selfishness', fostered by the institutions and practices of public life, which inhibits devotion to the general good.[32] He makes the same point in 'Chapters on Socialism' when examining the pros and cons of communism: in society as it now is personal interest and private gain are the dominant motives instead of public spirit, conscience, and the honour of work well done.

However, this should not and need not be so; the current situation is due to an 'imperfect degree of moral cultivation', the fault in turn of 'imperfect education', and the remedy is therefore obvious—a general moral improvement through education backed by good government (which, as we have seen, means for Mill a government which is in itself an educative force).[33] Morality, he writes to Harriet, is central to education: 'Admitting the omnipotence of education, is not the very pivot and turning point of that education a *moral sense*—a feeling of duty, or conscience, or principle, or whatever name one gives it—a feeling that one *ought* to do, and to wish for, what is for the greatest good of all concerned?' However, he does not underestimate the difficulties: again to Harriet—'I cannot persuade myself that you do not greatly overrate the ease of making people unselfish'; and in 'Chapters on Socialism':

The education of human beings is one of the most difficult of all arts, and this is one of the points in which it has hitherto been least successful; moreover improvements in general education are necessarily very gradual, because the future generation is educated by the present, and the imperfections of the teachers set an invincible limit to the degree in which they can train their pupils to be better than themselves.[34]

A true statement indeed, which strikes a chord in the hearts of all who have laboured in the classroom! Despite these hesitations Mill had no doubt that education has a vital role in elevating the moral sense and practice of the community, in habituating the people to acceptance of fundamental moral principles and to a concern for the common good. Although he wrote primarily for the social context of his time, his views have universal significance, not least for the Britain of a century later.

Education has a further important role in cultivating the skills and attitudes necessary for the successful operation of a form of government (which is closely related to a form of *society*). If a democracy is to work, its citizens must not only approve, but also be practised in, the methods of its working; not that everyone can participate directly in government—obviously an impossibility in the modern world; but democracy depends for success on the active and lively interest of the whole community, on full spectator-participation, as it were, though with sufficient respect for the rules to prevent invasion of the pitch. Partly this is a question of values, of habituation by the totality of educational influences to the ideals of individuality, freedom, truth, etc., which are fundamental to the democratic way of life; this was the theme of chapter 1 above, and it implies, further, the moral purpose within education which has been considered in the preceding paragraphs. Essential too is a minimum level of literacy, numeracy, and intellectual maturity, without which there cannot be an informed and critical populace, able (as and for whom opportunity offers) to share in the task of governing itself. In addition to all this, however, there is needed a more specific education into the modes of democratic citizenship. This includes, for example, some knowledge of the nation's history, of its constitution and the workings of central and local government; training in clear thinking and the critical assessment of opinion; practice in discussion and reasoned argument—involving, of course, respect for evidence and the ability to discover it; and instruction in techniques of persuasion, both to combat them and (consistently with democratic values) to use them. Such an education would also seek to foster a feeling of community, of living with others in a situation of mutual obligation, and following from this a sense of responsibility (and respect) for others; a readiness for voluntary service, for co-operation towards the common good, and a willingness to eschew violence and settle disputes by appeal to reason. These, and no doubt many others, are the skills and attitudes required in the democratic citizen.

Education for citizenship (or political education, as it is sometimes called) is not a conspicuous feature of British education. The importance of it, however, was recognized long ago by Aristotle:

The citizens of a state should always be educated to suit the constitution of their state. The type of character appropriate to a constitution is the power which continues to sustain it, as it is also the force which originally creates it.[35]

Nor was it lost on Mill (who knew his Aristotle but had no great regard for the *Politics*, which he saw as 'a philosophic consecration of existing facts');[36] in one or another of his writings can be found all the items mentioned in the previous paragraph. Ideally he would require such education for all; but for the time being it might be necessary to be content with less, ensuring a minimal amount for every citizen—enough at least to justify an extension of the franchise—and educating a substantial minority to the summit of democratic leadership, whence their skills and qualities would gradually permeate and elevate the rest (which is what he hoped of the liberal education outlined in the *Inaugural*). Mill does not formulate a specific programme of education for citizenship, but the shape of his intention is clear. He acknowledges in *Representative Government* the need to prepare a people for the particular form of its institutions and 'to kindle a desire for them [as] a necessary part of the preparation'. He continues:

To recommend and advocate a particular institution or form of government, and set its advantages in the strongest light, is one of the modes, often the only mode within reach, of educating the mind of the nation not only for accepting or claiming, but also for working, the institution.

And those who undertake the task, he adds, must clearly understand what are 'the capacities, moral, intellectual and active' necessary for working the institutions they advocate.[37]

In chapters 1 and 4 of the same book he explains the conditions necessary for the success of representative government: there must, first, be a favourable attitude in the people, who should, second, be ready to work for its preservation, and, third, have the will and the ability to perform the duties it imposes on them. To reach this favourable state there must be a process of 'political education',[38] by which in this context he means principally an education through political institutions and the devolution of authority within, initially, a different form of government (preferably a wise and benevolent monarchy); but it is clear from what he writes elsewhere that he would wish this to be augmented by other means of education, formal and informal. For there is a recurrent implication in his writings that a people must be educated into democracy, and not simply once for all, but as an on-going process which continually expands and enriches the possibilities of their communal experience. Thus in his review of de Tocqueville education is essential both to the working of democracy and to protect against its dangers—mediocrity, the commercial spirit, and the diminution of individuality. It can be found in his proposals for the future of the labouring classes in *Principles of Political Economy*, in his recommendation of plural voting (above, p. 23), and in his suggestion that by appropriate education women can be raised to equal status with men in effective, participating citizenship.[39] Again, in his 'Speech on Perfectibility' he goes on after the lines quoted above (p. 48) to require of education that it should enable people to 'despise humbug, see through casuistry and imposture . . . to judge of men by the manner in which they act, not by the manner in which they talk'.[40] He is thinking here primarily of a morally educated public opinion, but it is clear from the closing lines of the speech that he has in mind also a political control exercised by the restraining force of an educated electorate. Finally, in *On Liberty* (which might well be sub-titled 'Education for Democracy') he specifically includes within the purpose of a 'national education'

the peculiar training of a citizen, the practical part of the political education of a free people, taking them out of the narrow circle of personal and family selfishness and accustoming them to the comprehension of joint interests, the management of joint concerns—habituating them to act from public or semi-public motives and guide their conduct by aims which unite instead of isolating them from one another. Without these habits and powers a free constitution can neither be worked nor preserved.[41]

Mill saw a special task for education in providing able entrants to the Civil Service; reference was made earlier to his support for competitive examination of candidates as a major advance towards efficient administration (p. 22). The need for a reorganization of the Civil Service and the means of recruitment to it was becoming increasingly urgent in the mid-nineteenth century; the growing complexity and specialization of its work required more obviously than before a high level of intelligence and character; and democratic pressures were demanding greater equality of opportunity for admission to its ranks. Mill's paper of 1854 assumes 'as requiring no proof' that 'it would be a public benefit if the Public Service, or all that part of it the duties of which are of an intellectual character, were composed of the most intelligent and instructed persons who could be attracted to it'; mediocrity has no place here.[42] Equally he assumes for candidates a wide-ranging education—intellectual, moral, and aesthetic of the kind presented as 'liberal' in the *Inaugural Address*. It must not, he insists, be solely a literary education; science and its practical applications must also be included; in addition he would allow for examination any kind of specialized knowledge which might be valuable in some area of public service. Nor must it be an education professionally orientated, but rather one which aims at 'mental cultivation' for its own sake, one which tends to enlarge and elevate the students' minds and 'adds to their worth as human beings'.[43] It need not even be an education at school or college—a condition which would contradict the principle of equality and would, of course, have excluded Mill himself (as he points out). The need for an enabling education extends beyond the Civil Service to Members of Parliament. In an article, 'Paper Currency and Commercial Distress', in his review of the Parliamentary session of 1826 (written, be it noted, at the age of twenty) he complains of Members' lack of expertise in the matters at issue; he distinguishes between the quack politician 'who, ignorant of principles, generalises upon the few particular instances which his own narrow experience has presented to him' and the scientific politician 'who knows and applies the general principles, the theory, of his art' and who has learnt 'what *causes*, in the field of his enquiries, are followed by what *effects*'. As things are, education does nothing for the 'scientific statesman', who must therefore be self-taught:

He who is destined to direct the government of a nation finds nowhere any adequate provision for teaching him the causes which determine the good or ill condition of the *political* body. In few countries do the laws of human thought and human action, the principles of legislation, government and political economy form any part of the established course of education

—least of all in Britain, where the education of the upper classes deliberately avoids any such intention. It is no surprise, he concludes, that a legislature so inadequately prepared for its task, both by education and subsequent experience, 'should scarcely ever be

**54**     *The Role of Education*

*able*, even when it is *willing*, to legislate for a great nation as the wants of a great nation require'.[44]

Though principally concerned with the role of education in Britain, Mill was no less alive to its importance elsewhere, particularly in countries which were young and developing, like India and Australia, or economically depressed, like Ireland. In India he had, of course, a special interest; within a few years of his appointment to the service of the East India Company he was, he tells us, virtually in charge of correspondence in the department of the Native States, and remained so until he became Examiner two years before the Company's demise.[45] The records of the Company contain a number of letters and other items for whose drafting Mill was solely or chiefly responsible (most of them noted in his own list of his writings), and many of which refer to matters of educational principle, organization and practice. In composing these drafts Mill was expounding the policy of his superiors, and what he wrote was subject to their scrutiny and correction; nevertheless it is reasonable to assume that he helped to shape that policy, was in general agreement with it, and that the opinions expressed in the drafts reflect his own. Certainly there is a clear similarity between their educational recommendations and the functions which Mill attributes to education independently in his own writings.[46]

For instance, there is in the drafts a repeated insistence on moral purpose in education, both for State appointees, who must be 'distinguished by moral as well as by intellectual superiority', and for the populace as a whole, whose education must aim not only at the acquisition of 'useful knowledge' but also at 'the improvement of their moral character'. There is emphasis, too, on the need for an educated class (of native Indians) both to undertake the tasks of administration and to diffuse a civilizing influence throughout the population:

The improvements in education . . . which most effectually contribute to elevate the moral and intellectual condition of a people are those which concern the education of the higher classes, of the persons possessing leisure and natural influence over the minds of their countrymen. By raising the standard of instruction among these classes you would eventually produce a much greater and more beneficial change in the ideas and feelings of the community than you can hope to produce by acting directly on the more numerous class

—a statement which entirely accords with Mill's views, already noted, on the educative function of a highly trained and gifted élite. The drafts also display a conception of the curriculum which is broadly 'liberal' (though not, as we shall see, to the exclusion of essential technical objectives): for the education of the administrative class 'we rely chiefly on their becoming, through a familiarity with European literature and science, imbued with the ideas and feelings of civilised Europe'; this, the draft continues, 'we wish you to consider . . . as our deliberate view of the scope and end to which all your endeavours with respect to the education of the natives should refer'.[47]

There is much else in these drafts which points to a firm and enlightened conception of the role of education in a developing country and which can be taken as representing Mill's own views as well as the policy of the India Office. There is concern for medical, legal, and technical training, and for a 'general scientific education' which is broader than vocational purpose; there must be an increasing flow of qualified teachers—particularly, and with immense ultimate benefit, into the 'indigenous schools'—and a system of inspection to ensure standards; there must be, where appropriate, regular examinations, efficiently organized and impartially conducted; books too are essential, both in English and in the native languages, and 'it is of the highest importance that the books selected should be instructive in their matter, adapted to the capacity of the scholars and calculated to inspire a taste for further acquirements'.[48] Nor are the underprivileged forgotten: there must be scholarships and allowances for the children of the poor; and in the summary of educational advance in India, of which Mill was 'partly the author and partly the editor', it is noted with approval that 'an inroad has begun to be made upon native prejudices even in the department of female education . . . and it is hoped that progress will be gradually made in its diffusion'.[49] Finally, these prescriptions for a far distant land (which Mill, of course, had never visited and knew chiefly from his father's book and his own professional work) are not without a certain sensitivity towards a culture very different from that of Britain. The vernacular languages and literature, though they can offer no substitute for the 'more complete education' of European science and literature, are recommended as the necessary vehicle of elementary education and to be utilized at higher levels for whatever of literary or informational value they contain.[50]

It is obvious from Mill's writings that he had a clear and coherent conception of the role of education in a nation's life, and moreover that he was able to adjust this conception to situations as different as those of Britain and India. Over and above the satisfaction of basic needs like literacy, numeracy, and the provision of technical, executive, and administrative skills, he saw in education (always in both formal and informal meanings) a principal instrument in preserving a nation's identity by initiating its citizens (children and adults alike) into the values and practices which give it that identity; it was equally potent, he believed, as an instrument of progress by injecting into society the insights and aspirations of gifted individuals, by diffusing into the mass of the population the elevated standards of a highly educated élite, *and* at the same time by raising the economic, intellectual, and cultural levels of the labouring classes. Education was thus an agent not only of 'permanence and progression', of cultural transmission and cultural change, but also of growth towards a more homogeneous and egalitarian society.

Especially important for Mill (and for ourselves too, if we would heed him) was the contribution of education to morality and to responsible citizenship. Comment has already been made on these aspects of the role of education; but there is a further point of possible adverse criticism, which is worth noting. It can be argued that Mill's educational prescriptions were designed to enforce a certain social structure; that his emphasis on discipline, on the conservation of traditional values, on respect for well-founded authority, on the value of highly cultivated intelligence, was not so much the expression of disinterested educational purpose as a disguised piece of social engineering specifically aimed at securing the compliance of the labouring classes with political and industrial policies imposed on them from above. This, it might be further argued, would be in line with the thought of *Logic* VI (where he outlines a behavioural science of 'ethology' to be linked with education in shaping human character and conduct) and would add substance to Sir Karl Popper's criticism of Mill as a 'historicist' and 'social engineer'.[51] It is impossible in these concluding sentences to make any adequate defence against this charge. Suffice it to say that, in the present writer's view, such an intention would be contrary to Mill's demonstrable honesty of purpose and to the unquestionable sincerity of his desire to improve the lot of the underprivileged of his time. There is little doubt that much of the (often reluctant) assistance given to English education by nineteenth-century governments was politically motivated by a desire to 'tame' the working classes, to forestall trouble, to provide a compliant work force for industrial expansion. However, this was not the purpose of the utilitarians in general or of J. S. Mill in particular; for the latter, certainly, the impelling motive was none other than his profound and ingenuous concern for human improvement.

# 4

# Élitism

THERE IS present in Mill's writings an unmistakable vein of what may be described as 'élitism'; sometimes more, sometimes less conspicuous it can be traced from his earliest articles and essays right through to the *Inaugural Address* of 1867. Just what is meant by 'élitism', both in Mill and more generally, is something which requires careful examination; but before attempting this, and to prepare the way for it, quotation from Mill himself will help to indicate broadly what it is that has to be examined and what questions need to be asked.

Hints of élitism have been noted already in Mill's demand for a highly educated administration and his emphasis on the fundamental importance of the speculative faculties in securing social progress (pp. 22 and 45 above.) The passages there quoted suggest that he had in mind a class apart, highly endowed if not by nature, certainly by education and training, with the intellectual and moral qualities requisite for leadership in a democracy. The same suggestion appears in the following passage from the essay 'The Spirit of the Age' (1831):

It is right that every man should attempt to understand his interest and his duty. It is right that he should follow his reason as far as his reason will carry him, and cultivate the faculty as highly as possible. But reason itself will teach most men that they must, in the last resort, fall back upon the authority of still more cultivated minds, as the ultimate sanction of the convictions of their reason itself.[1]

'Civilisation' (1835) carries a similar message. Here Mill is complaining of the diminution of individuality by the pressures of a mass society:

It is not solely on the private virtues that this growing insignificance of the individual in the mass is productive of mischief. It corrupts the very fountain of the improvement of public opinion itself; it corrupts public teaching; it weakens the influence of the more cultivated few over the many.[2]

In the review article, 'The Rationale of Political Representation' (1835), he insists

that political questions be not decided by an appeal, either direct or indirect, to the judgment or will of an uninstructed mass, whether of gentlemen or of clowns, but by the deliberately formed opinions of a comparatively few, specially educated for the task. This is an element of good government which has existed, in a greater or less degree, in some aristocracies, though unhappily not in our own, and has been the cause of whatever reputation for prudent and skilful administration those governments have enjoyed.[3]

Commending Hare's scheme of representation in *Representative Government* (1861) (p. 23 above, and note 28), he looks for 'a supplement, or completing corrective, to the instincts of a democratic majority' and finds it in 'the instructed minority' who in the ordinary system of voting are under-represented or not at all. Hare's scheme would allow their knowledge and moral power to have their due weight:

A democratic people would in this way be provided with . . . leaders of a higher grade of intellect and character than itself. Modern democracy would have its occasional Pericles and its habitual group of superior and guiding minds.[4]

It is part of the argument for freedom in *On Liberty* that the discovery of new truths and the origination of new ideas and practices are tasks of which only a few are capable, 'the salt of the earth' who both 'introduce good things which did not before exist' and 'keep the life in those which already existed'.[5] This was written between 1855, when the essay was mentally conceived on the steps of the Capitol in Rome, and 1859 when it was published. In the *Inaugural*, written for delivery in 1867, he argues a case for wide general knowledge coupled with expertise in a limited area:

It is this combination which gives an enlightened public: a body of cultivated intellects, each taught by its attainments in its own province what real knowledge is, and knowing enough of other subjects to be able to discern who are those that know them better. . . . The elements of the more important studies being widely diffused, those who have reached the higher summits find a public capable of appreciating their superiority and prepared to follow their lead.[6]

To these longer passages one can add the recurrent phrases (some already quoted) which point towards the same conception of an élite few whose greater skill and wisdom distinguish them from the inferior levels of the mass of the population: 'superiority of cultivated intelligence', 'authenticated superiority of education', 'instructed and cultivated minds', 'persons of distinguished originality', 'the more intelligent and active minded few'.[7] It should be noted too that Mill himself uses the word 'élite', for instance in the passage quoted above (p. 22) and in the article 'Endowments', where he recognizes the need for a superior education for the élite of the poor.[8] It is, surely, a reasonable conclusion not only that this vein of élitism existed in Mill's thought, but that it was present (though not necessarily in the same form) throughout his life. It is least conspicuous, perhaps, in the *Logic* and *Political Economy*, but even here it can be found in the importance he assigns to 'the agency of eminent individuals' and to 'cultivated intelligence' in industrial management.[9]

What, then, did he understand by it? Clearly, neither the word, on the few occasions that he used it, nor the idea had for Mill the pejorative overtones which it has for us today (apart, that is, from its strictly sociological use).[10] In present usage 'élite', 'élitist' and 'élitism' suggest and are meant to suggest exclusiveness, privilege, a rejection of popular values, and a leadership from above which is inconsistent with democracy. Thus, no compliment is intended when, in educational discussion, the public schools are described as 'élitist establishments' or Plato's ideal state in the *Republic* as 'an élitist blueprint'. However, Mill's conception of an élite, though it included leadership and a commitment to what he deemed superior values, had no pejorative slant—in fact quite the reverse.

Mill's élitism is not a simple concept (as might be said, for instance, of Plato's philosopher-kings or a hereditary aristocracy), nor does it refer to one particular area of activity or to a single quality or skill; it is complex and comprehensive, its dominant aspect varying with the focus of attention. Sometimes he means by it a source of authority, whether intellectual, moral, or cultural, which is vested in the few whose education and experience (and also perhaps their innate ability) have given them a knowledge and wisdom superior to those of the majority. Such would seem to be his intention in the passages quoted from 'The Spirit of the Age' and the *Inaugural Address*; it is a '*natural* state of society', he goes on to say in the former, where 'the opinions and feelings of the people are, with their voluntary acquiescence, formed *for* them by the most cultivated minds which the intelligence and morality of the times call into existence'; and he contrasts this 'natural state' with the 'transitional' situation then obtaining in which 'there are no persons to whom the mass of the uninstructed habitually defer'.[11]

Closely linked with the notion of authority is that of influence, which appears in the 'Civilisation' and *Inaugural* passages: by their example the élite few raise the masses to higher levels of aspiration and achievement; they are a potent *educative* force, a 'spiritual power' who shed a beneficent rain on those less endowed with talent or opportunity.[12] There is an eloquent passage in one of Mill's *Examiner* articles which illustrates in a particular area, namely literature, this conception of educative influence. In it he refers to a class of authors, by implication few in number, whose aim is not simply to please or advise, but to educate:

> to batter down obstinate prejudices; to throw light on the dark places; to discover and promulgate ideas, which must be meditated for years before they will be appreciated; to form mankind to closer habits of thought; to shame them out of whatever is mean and selfish in their behaviour; to elevate their tastes; to inspire them with nobler and more beneficent desires; to teach them that there are virtues which they have never conceived, and pleasures beyond what they have ever enjoyed.[13]

But of course it is equally true in other spheres: government, both national and local, requires leadership by 'a specially instructed Few', 'the very best minds', whose dialogue with the many educates them in political understanding; so too in morals, where the altruism of a minority leavens the rest with generosity of purpose; and in intellectual life, where the scholarly ideal of truth percolates to the common man as a stimulus and a standard for his thinking.[14]

Mill also thinks of an élite who are the source of originality, of novelty, of experiment; they are the cultural explorers who probe the confines of experience and return with new ideas, truths, values to illuminate and expand the horizons of their fellow men:

> There is always need of persons not only to discover new truths, and point out when what were once truths are true no longer, but also to commence new practices and set the example of more enlightened conduct and better taste and sense in human life.

Only the few are capable of this; they are the indispensable 'salt of the earth' without whom, he continues (changing the metaphor) mankind would lapse into stagnation; they are 'the uncontented characters', who undertake 'different experiments of living', test 'the worth of different modes of life', and thus supply 'the chief ingredient of individual and social progress'.[15] Socrates and Jesus, Luther and Newton are among their number, and a host of lesser persons, the élite of every generation, without whom human improvement and the growth of knowledge would have been grievously and permanently retarded.

He thinks too of an élite of political and administrative expertise; this was noted in an earlier chapter (pp. 22–3) and is evident in *Representative Government* and 'The Rationale of Political Representation'. Apart from the passages quoted, there are numerous others which carry the same message; for instance in the former he states as one of the necessities of government 'to obtain in the greatest measure possible, for the function of government, the benefits of superior intellect trained by long meditation and practical discipline to that special task'. He saw it as one of the advantages of aristocracy as a form of government that it could provide just such an expertise, and he commends the aristocracies of ancient Rome and Venice for 'the systematically wise collective policy and the great individual capacities for government, for which history has deservedly given them credit'.[16] Their purpose, however, was not the greatest good of the whole community but the aggrandisement of the state (and themselves with it); and since the propensity of human nature is always to self-interest, this is the inevitable outcome in the absence of popular control. Indeed this was for Mill the crucial problem of politics, 'to combine the greatest amount of the advantage derived from the independent judgement of a specially instructed Few, with the greatest degree of the security for rectitude of purpose derived from rendering those Few responsible to the Many'.[17]

These four aspects, then, are clearly discernible in Mill's élitism—authority, educative influence, originality, political and administrative expertise. He did not envisage them as isolated functions and sharply distinct; in practice each might be combined with any or all of the others; educative influence would follow from any of the other three and could scarcely exist without justification in at least one of them. Élitism, it has already been pointed out, is a misleading term in view of its twentieth-century accretions of meaning; in order, therefore, to protect Mill against its pejorative insinuations and thus to understand him better, we must turn from the positive to the negative and consider what he did *not* mean by it. For reasons stated in the previous paragraph he rejected the idea of an aristocratic élite whether of birth or of wealth; efficient though it might be as an organ of administration, it lacked identity of interest with the mass of the people. No less unacceptable was an élite of bureaucracy or power; his condemnation of these was noted above (pp. 23–5). There was some attraction for him in the notion of a leisured class, a cultural élite such as existed in the slave-supported democracy of ancient Athens; provided, that is, it submitted itself to the restraints of firm moral or religious principles (which he thought improbable). He rejected it, however, in favour of the more democratic diffusion of culture throughout the people: 'Whatever is valuable in the traditions of gentlemanhood', he writes to John Austin in 1847, 'is a *fait acquis* to mankind . . . grounded on the combination of good feeling with correct intellectual perceptions'; its diffusion depends on 'the extension and improvement of education'. He continues:

I have even ceased to think that a leisured class, in the ordinary sense of the term, is an essential constituent of the best form of society. What does seem to me essential is that society at large should not be over-worked, nor over-anxious about the means of subsistence

—and this means a thorough reform of society, including population control and the distribution of wealth.[18]

Far more attractive was Plato's scheme of philosopher-rulers, the deeply learned, highly trained administrators of his ideal state, whose government they founded on their vision of eternal Good. There are many echoes of such an élite in Mill's writings, for instance 'superior intellect trained by long meditation and practical discipline' (above, p. 62), which precisely fits the highly selected top-level rulers who are permitted to govern only after fifteen years of mathematical and philosophical studies and another fifteen of administrative experience.[19] But however attractive this might seem to him in his more Platonizing moments, it was incompatible with democracy and freedom and also, he felt, impracticable, not to say dangerous. So in *On Liberty* he condemns government interference and control, arguing that 'the evil would be greater the more efficiently and scientifically the administrative machinery was constructed—the more skilful the arrangements for obtaining the best qualified hands and heads with which to work it'.[20] Similarly in *Principles of Political Economy* he declares, 'There cannot be a combination of circumstances more dangerous to human welfare than that in which intelligence and talent are maintained at a high standard within a governing corporation, but starved and discouraged outside the pale';[21] the danger is increased by the association of intellectual superiority with legal power. He therefore rejects utterly Comte's scheme for a supreme moral and intellectual authority, 'a corporation of philosophers', 'charged with the duty of guiding men's opinions and enlightening and warning their consciences'; as an organized body this would 'involve nothing less than a spiritual despotism'.[22] He was more favourably disposed to Coleridge's 'clerisy', 'an endowed class for the cultivation of learning and for diffusing its results among the community'; though organized and endowed, it would lack legal and administrative powers and was therefore consistent with his own élite of authority, influence, and originality.[23]

Thus Mill did not think of his élite as a specially privileged class —except in so far as privilege is constituted by advanced education (from which the majority are debarred by lack of talent, if not of opportunity) and by freedom from a confining drudgery of toil; nor as an exclusive class, for he clearly believed that opportunity should be extended to the able in any area of society, and that by diffusion of culture both from above and from within themselves the many could and should be raised towards the condition of the few. Moreover, the conditions he required for the existence and leavening function of his élite were in themselves a defence against exclusiveness, namely, the free interchange of ideas in a continuing dialogue between all sections of the community, and a more equitable distribution of work and wealth which would afford greater leisure and the means to enjoy it (see pp. 69, 74–5, and ch. 2). Nor was it an authoritarian élite; *authoritative* certainly, but not the other: the obedience of the many was to be a voluntary acceptance, not an imposed acquiescence, a willing deference to an authority which was justified by its superior knowledge and expertise. Nor, finally, was it an élite in the etymological sense of 'chosen' —except for those who submitted to a selective examination for a specific task like the Civil Service; in the free, open, educative society which Mill envisaged the members of the élite would select themselves by the unfolding and disciplined exercise of their talents in a nurturing environment.

There were many influences which prompted Mill towards this élitist position; some were personal, others arose from the political and social circumstances of the time, others again sprang from his observation, both historical and actual, of the human situation. His own education made him intellectually a man apart ('an advantage of a quarter of a century over my contemporaries')[24] or at least the co-equal of but few; in boyhood and youth he was privileged to associate with men of talent in various spheres of activity; and throughout his life he belonged (and was conscious of belonging) to a highly educated, cultured middle class, many of whom were energetically devoted to human improvement. Thus, Mill was himself a member of the élite he was proposing, and it could be argued, therefore, that his élitism is in part (but *only* in part, surely) a rationalization of this. Plato, too, was an obvious influence, and though he rejected the 'pedantocracy' of an organized intellectual class exercising close cultural and political control, there were other features of the *Republic*—government by trained professionals, prolonged philosophical and practical education, and dedication to truth—which he could see no reason to relinquish.[25] Others who contributed were the St. Simonians and Comte (despite Mill's rejection of his 'spiritual despotism'), Carlyle's aristocratic conservatism (briefly, until the mutual recognition of their disagreements put an end to their friendship), Coleridge, and the utilitarian educational reformer, John Roebuck. The last of these (a close friend until Mill's affair with Harriet) proclaimed in Parliament that 'the great object . . . in any plan of general education would be to make the most instructed classes the guides . . . . Do what we will, say what we will, this class must guide and govern.'[26]

In addition to these external influences there were two others of a personal kind which swayed him towards an élitist view. First was his passion for truth and his belief that new truths in whatever sphere are initially accessible only to a few or even to the one far-sighted genius (see above, pp. 61–2, and below, chapter 5).[27] Second, he believed with no less fervour that there are higher and lower qualities of experience, and that the former are preferable to the latter; further, that there are men and women more 'highly endowed', possessed of 'higher faculties' than others, and therefore capable of more exalted forms of experience; it is on their judgement and example that the rest of mankind rely for discrimination between higher and lower, better and worse.[28] Thus, however enthusiastically he once accepted the associationist view of universal educability and his father's conviction of the power of education, he came eventually, it seems, to the more realistic view that men differ widely in intelligence, judgement, sensitivity and moral insight, and that in these respects some are manifestly superior to others. On these more gifted persons depends all possibility of progress and improvement, and they must, therefore, be given every opportunity in education and social environment to develop their superior potential.

Mill was also influenced by the circumstances of his time. It was a simple fact that, given the condition of society and the methods of production as they then were, the mass of the population could have little leisure for self-improvement; and their formal education was little or none (the first state grant for education, it should be remembered, was made in 1833, and it was only in the last years of Mill's life that education became universal and compulsory). Inevitably there was a great gulf between them and the educated few, and they must therefore look to these few for authoritative guidance. Even if there were to be the social transformation that Mill hoped for, the human situation being what it is, 'as long as the day consists but of twenty-four hours, and the age of man extends but to three score and ten, so long (unless we expect improvements in the arts of production sufficient to restore the golden age) the great majority of mankind will need the far greater part of their time and exertions for procuring their daily bread'.[29] For this reason, in addition to his recognition of differences in human potential, he thought it reasonable, indeed inevitable, that the majority should defer to the authority of the few. Moreover, Mill greatly feared the pressures of mediocrity and conformity which he believed would come from an extension of democracy (see above, pp. 26–7, and below, pp. 95–6)—a fear which was later accentuated by his reading of de Tocqueville's *Democracy in America* (which he reviewed in 1835 and 1840); and he came to the conclusion that effective resistance to such corrosive pressures must come from the minority 'whom the circumstances of society, and their own position in it, permit to dedicate themselves to the investigation and study of physical, moral and social truths as their peculiar calling'.[30] In a 'rational democracy', he wrote later in his first review of de Tocqueville, 'the omnipotence of the majority would be exercised through the agency and at the discretion of an enlightened minority accountable to the majority in the last resort'.[31] Finally, the deficiencies which he saw in government and in Parliament reinforced in him the conviction that to rule effectively men must be educated for the task; this required not only a broad liberal education (such as he outlines in the *Inaugural Address*), but a specific training in administrative and executive skills; only a few were qualified by ability and opportunity to profit from the education and to undertake the task.

Élitism was a constant but by no means unchanging element in Mill's thought. He describes himself in the opening paragraph of the *Autobiography* as one whose mind 'was always pressing forward, equally ready to learn and to unlearn either from its own thoughts or from those of others'—and this is no exaggerated self-appraisal. The modifications in Mill's élitism, his reaction against Benthamism, and his continuing endeavours to balance democracy with the claims of excellence and expertise are convincingly set out by J. Hamburger in *Intellectuals in Politics* and more briefly by R. P. Anschutz in *The Philosophy of J. S. Mill* (chapter 3 in each work). The development of his thought, as the present writer interprets it, may be stated very summarily thus. His emotional crisis of 1826, with its revelation of the need for 'the internal culture of the individual',[32] both created in him a dissatisfaction with the attitudes inculcated by his upbringing and laid him open to new influences which included Comte, Carlyle, Coleridge and the St. Simonians; he was thus more readily persuaded by Macaulay's attack (in *The Edinburgh Review* of March 1829) on his father's article, 'Government'. In this Macaulay accused James Mill of failing to appreciate the realities of human motivation and so of exaggerating the possibility of identity of interest between government and people and of a genuine popular control; he had, further, overestimated the capacity of the populace for judging the best interests of society. John Mill found in Coleridge and the St. Simonians what seemed to be the proper corrective of his father's views, namely, an educated, responsible élite exercising an authority which was willingly accepted because derived from acknowledged superiority of judgement and expertise. At the same time the patent realities of illiteracy, poverty, and economic exploitation undermined his confidence in the associationist doctrine of the omnipotence of education; to lift such a depressed mass of

humanity as he saw about him to the level of intelligent, principled
democratic citizens was not, he now realized, an immediate goal but
the protracted task of generations; meanwhile wise government
and civilized culture must be upheld—with proper safeguards—by
the élite few.[33]

In the 1840s, fired by the ardour of Harriet Taylor (with whom
he was now in the closest intellectual intimacy) he 'completely
turned back from what there had been of excess in my reaction
against Benthamism'; though less of a democrat, he was more of a
socialist and looked for the abolition of privilege and with it an
aristocracy based on birth or wealth. Yet his fear of 'the ignorance
and especially the selfishness and brutality of the mass' made him
chary of extending its influence and power (hence, for instance, his
scheme of plural voting); most of all he dreaded 'the tyranny of
society over the individual'[34]—a dominant theme of *On Liberty*
which was later to crystallize these fears in a massive plea for
individuality. On the other hand he distrusted no less the selfish
class interests of the ruling aristocracy of his time; it would be long,
he believed, 'before the superior classes could be sufficiently
improved to govern in the tutelary manner supposed', by which
time 'the inferior classes would be too much improved to be so
governed'.[35] There was still need for an élite, therefore, but it must
be one of merit, in which (as he had described it in 'Civilisation')
'the only road open to honour and ascendancy [would] be that of
personal qualities';[36] it would be an aristocracy in the strict sense
of the Greek—'rule of the best'; an aristocracy of personal achievement in which moral, intellectual, political, and cultural leadership
would grow naturally as individual talent was nourished by a
favourable social environment. Increasingly, however, its function
of tutelage would shift to that of co-operative dialogue with an
autonomous populace willing to defer to superior intellect and
knowledge and able to judge for itself to whom such deference is
due.[37]

Essential for progress to this ideal was, of course, education—
liberal education for all to whom it could be made available
(including the élite of the poor by means of scholarships and
endowments) and elementary education for the rest; the former
would provide a reservoir of potential leaders, the latter would
enable the populace to choose its leaders wisely and to assume
increasing control of its own affairs. (Mill had now a renewed faith

in education, having established in his *System of Logic*, as he believed, the basis of a science of society and human nature which could provide an efficient educational practice.) Essential also was the co-operative dialogue already mentioned, a continuous inter-change of views between leaders and led—indeed throughout the whole population—so that truth might be known, disagreement voiced and argued, and policies established by mutual consent; for this, too, education was indispensable. Freedom was a further requisite, for in its absence there could be neither uninhibited dis-cussion, nor authentic choice, nor full development of potential talent. And encompassing all must be a situation of social justice, 'a renovated social fabric' pervaded by a sense of community and shared interest, without which co-operation would be impossible and dialogue no more than a sparring for position.[38]

Such seems to be Mill's final statement of his élitism, reached in his middle years and persisting through to the *Inaugural Address*. He has sometimes been regarded as a forerunner of the élitist theories which have been formulated in modern political studies; but this is to misunderstand. For Mill's élitism was never shaped into (or intended as) a precise pattern or formula, whether as an explanatory hypothesis or a prescriptive programme; it was a flexible concept, adaptable both to new influences and to the circumstances of his time. One modern political philosopher, Geraint Parry, has put it thus: 'Mill's aim was neither to predict nor to justify élite rule, but the liberal goal of raising the level of culture and enlightenment in a democratic society.'[39] This is a correct assessment, but it needs both amplifying and spelling out in greater detail. Mill was faced with the problem of marrying his ideals with the social and political reality of nineteenth-century England; he looked for human improvement in terms of progress towards happiness, freedom, individuality, truth, and moral elevation; he saw around him on the one hand a largely illiterate populace brutalized, as it seemed to him, by the conditions of their life and work and sadly needing enlightened leadership, on the other hand an effete aristocracy with no vision beyond its own class interests. Further, it was clear to him that some men are in fact 'better' than others—by nature more intelligent, more sensi-tive, more inventive, by upbringing more disciplined and more informed, and by experience and training more skilled in particular areas of human activity. The problem was therefore complex: to promote his values and protect them against the corrosive influences of democracy; to combine administrative expertise with responsibility and popular control, authority in leadership with self-determination in the led; to ensure in fullest measure the emergence of excellence and its educative impact from the few upon the many; to raise the many to progressively higher levels of intelligent and informed management of their affairs. Though partly political, the problem is predominantly educational and this, even when considering it from the former aspect (as in *Representative Government*) is how Mill consistently saw it. Its solution lay in creating and maintaining an élite, neither privileged nor exclusive, whose wise administration and sustained example of excellence in a situation of freedom, dialogue, and expanding education, would promote the self-fulfilment and happiness of the whole community. The education of this élite, or at least the foundation of its education, he sets out in the *Inaugural*; that of the masses he nowhere describes in detail, but something of his intention can be pieced together from his writings and this will be attempted in chapter 6, 'The State and Education'.

Mill's élitism has been attacked on numerous grounds: it is authoritarian and contradicts the freedom and individuality of *On Liberty*; it is a rationalization of middle class morality and intellectualism, an attempt, however innocent, to perpetuate middle class tutelage of the masses; it is a paternalistic intellectual patronage which is inconsistent with democracy; it entails a privileged and divisive form of education; it overlooks such practicalities as the selection of leaders, the qualities desired in them, and the means of their dialogue with the populace; it postulates in the élite a measure of unanimity unwarranted by human and historical evidence, notably the observed fact of disagreement among experts. Much of this criticism is unfounded, the more so when the word 'élite' is stripped of the emotional vesture which it has acquired in the vocabulary of class prejudice. The first ignores the distinction between 'authoritarian' and 'authoritative' and the development in Mill's thought from youth to middle life (see pp. 67–8); the second, while containing an element of truth (for no human argument outside pure logic is wholly free of rationalization, and no man can shed off the environmental context of his thought) ignores Mill's declared purpose to educate the masses from 'leading-strings' to informed autonomy; the third is an emotive rephrasing of the second and suffers the same objection; the fourth assumes that the education of Mill's élite must be élitist in the pejorative sense—Oxbridge, Eton and the old school tie—but Mill had little good to say of the public schools and English universities of his day and no doubt would have approved of a comprehensive system of schooling so long as it guaranteed excellence and maximum achievement for the most able (and the rest). The last two criticisms are more substantial; the former involves two matters, leadership and communication, which will be examined in the following paragraphs; the latter justly points to a weakness in Mill's position. For he did assume in his élite a unanimity of the best minds which would give them persuasive authority; now a measure of consent is essential, since total disagreement is no possible platform for a plausible policy; but the élite cannot be exempt from Mill's own dialectical principle whereby truth is forged in the clash of openly argued differences of opinion.[40]

Rather than pursue these criticisms it will be more profitable to consider briefly certain problems which are central to democracy, in our day no less than in Mill's, and which his élitism attempted to answer: they concern authority, leadership, and communication. These problems are both political and educational (though there is no clear dividing line), and Mill was equally interested in each aspect; here we shall concentrate on the latter.

In considering the problem of authority Mill was not thinking primarily of coercive authority—the maintenance of civil order by government, law, and police (or in schools by the sanction of punishment); what he had in mind was a relationship of willing deference on the one side to self-authenticating excellence on the other. By 'self-authenticating' is intended an excellence, whether intellectual, moral, aesthetic, practical, or any other, which relies for its authoritative force on nothing but its own manifest superior knowledge and skill—an authority of merit, not of privilege or power. There was a time when, as Mill writes in the early draft of the *Autobiography*, he 'identified deference to authority with mental slavery and the repression of individual thought'.[41] It was Comte, apparently, who weaned him from this opinion by pointing to the acceptance by the uninformed majority of the agreed conclusions of science; and if in science, Mill asked, why not also in politics, morals, and other areas? In the end he persuaded himself that deference to superior knowledge and expertise was not only entirely reasonable but inescapable; thus in 'The Spirit of the Age' he concludes that it is 'one of the necessary conditions of humanity' that the majority 'must place the degree of reliance warranted by reason' in the authority of others.[42] There is no contradiction here with individuality: it is a man's right and duty to develop his own powers, to question the views of others and to assert his own; but there comes a point where, if he is honest with himself and with the human situation, he must submit to the guidance of those who know better. Nor with freedom: among the essential conditions of autonomous self-direction are, first, ready access to factual information, for which one is necessarily dependent on others; and, second, the self-restraint which recognizes the necessity of such dependence—the alternative being restriction imposed by ignorance. Nor with democracy, which in the modern world even more inevitably than in the ancient, requires delegation of power, under suitable control, to the acknowledged expert.

The problem of authority for Mill does not lie, therefore, in such supposed contradictions; it consists rather in determining the *kind* of authority that is acceptable in a free, open, democratic society (which is also an *educative* society) and establishing the *conditions* in which it is reasonable to accept it. It is a problem of eliciting and training talent, of raising levels of achievement, of encouraging self-restraint and a reasoned deference to superior knowledge; a problem of human relationships, of mutual trust, mutual enlightenment, of a sense of community and common responsibility in pursuing the general happiness, of adjustment between persons, interests, and ideas. Thus, though it has obvious political implications (which Mill discusses in *Representative Government*), it is in essence, and in the broadest sense of education, an educational problem. It is for the politician to set the stage by providing a situation of freedom, equality, participation, and social justice, and by devising institutions which are themselves educative; the rest must be the work partly of formal education but even more of that creative ferment of ideas, experiments, influences, and personal interaction which characterizes the educative society. Within such a ferment focuses of authority will assert themselves according to the demands of the occasion and the contribution their acknowledged expertise can make to the furtherance of the common good.[43]

Mill has little to say, and this mainly incidental, about authority within formal education. There are, of course, obvious differences between schools and adult society: for instance, children are minors, for whom teachers have legal and professional responsibility, a fact which clearly gives the latter an authority of a special kind. Yet one can justifiably assume that here too he viewed authority as presenting not so much a conflict with freedom and individuality as an educational challenge to create an environment in which talent—of teachers and pupils—can express itself and win the acceptance due to its acknowledged merit. Thus, the teacher's authority would rest, not so much on his status as a member of staff, his legal position *in loco parentis*, or the order he managed to impose on his classes (though all these contribute to it), but as possessed, for the time being at least, of greater knowledge (e.g. in Latin or chemistry), greater skill (in music or athletics), as representing an authoritative discipline or body of learning, and as a person whose quality of relationship with his pupils facilitated their acceptance of his authority. His pupils would share this authority to the extent that they too became experts, however limited, in whatever knowledge and skill they were able to master. As in adult society, so here the essential conditions of authority so conceived would include dialogue, participation, justice, a due measure of freedom, and an absence of unearned distinction.

Leadership is a related problem; Mill does not discuss it specifically, but his élitism is in effect an attempt to solve it. The need for leadership in society is obvious and in the past has rarely been disputed; recently, however, the concept itself has been questioned; it has acquired pejorative overtones by its association with Fascist and Nazi 'leadership' and by its alleged incompatibility with the prevalent emphasis on freedom, individuality, and egalitarianism. Yet the need exists no less: the complexity of modern civilization, the increasing demand for specialized knowledge, the intricate and far-reaching decisions that have to be made—all these point to it; so too does the decline in religious and moral commitment and the consequent permissive scepticism (which were not without parallel in Mill's time), a situation which, as Lord James pointed out a generation ago, requires 'the existence of a minority of individuals capable of securing, by the respect which their own qualities evoke, the adherence of the majority of men to higher standards than those they would create for themselves'.[44] Granted, then, the need for leadership (which Mill would certainly not dispute, either for his own time or ours—his élitism is an obvious plea for it), the crucial questions would seem to be: What kind of leadership is needed, and what qualities in the leaders? By whom should leadership be exercised? How should leaders be trained?

To the second and third of these questions Mill had clear answers. Leadership belongs to those whose ability, education, and moral probity enable them to exercise it and secure for them the necessary deference of the majority; in society as it then was these could only be few, but he hoped for a time when economic justice and the extension of education would thrust up leaders in increasing numbers from all areas of the population. As for their training, it consists in a broad liberal education at school and university and beyond, followed by preparation for a specific area of expertise. He is less definite in regard to the first question and seems to have given it little explicit consideration. True, he mentions 'cultivated intelligence', 'originality', 'spirit', 'nervous sensibility', 'moral power', 'lofty enthusiasm', and (though he does not use the word) expects in some the charisma of outstanding personality, the 'occasional Pericles'.[45] But these attributes, though emotionally persuasive, are lacking in precision (perhaps inevitably, psychology being the inchoate discipline it then was); nor do they present a complete picture. Leadership needs also the quality of humility which, to quote Lord James again, 'is prophylactic against the disease of leaders, love of power'; it needs 'wide sympathy and a keen sense of human value'; it needs courage, stability, tact, perseverance.[46] Instead of exercising power *over* others, 'the democratic leader creates power with them'; instead of *giving* orders, he must learn 'to take orders—from the situation'.[47] Leadership, according to another writer, is a fluid concept which requires 'a *real interplay of persons* who have learnt when to speak with authority and when to keep silence'.[48] Thus might Mill's tentative sketch be strengthened and enriched—and there is nothing in these modern suggestions with which he would disagree.

Indispensable to Mill's conception of authority and of leadership is dialogue, an ongoing intercommunication between those who have authority and those who defer to it, between leaders and led. Without it the influence of the former can never permeate the latter nor the latter's ideas and aspirations be understood sympathetically by the former; the consequence would be an impaired relationship, authoritarian rather than authoritative, obedience rather than deference, and a halt to democracy and improvement.

Mill assumed that such dialogue was possible in the society of his day despite extremes of wealth and poverty, knowledge and ignorance more flagrantly contrasted even than now. But suppose it is *not* possible; suppose that authority is neither acknowledged nor respected, that there is no common ground of understanding in agreed values and purposes, that communication is blocked by language barriers of 'elaborated' and 'restricted codes'. Such, it might plausibly be suggested, is the situation in which Britain finds itself today; hence the divisiveness of politics, the intractability of industrial disputes, the growing malaise of schools manifested in the rejection of discipline, of learning, even of school itself, and in the widening rift between teachers and taught (this last, as some would have it, a conflict between 'middle class' and 'working class' values).

Were Mill alive today, he would acknowledge our difficulties and (remembering the over-optimism of his youthful faith in education) concede that they admit of no quick or easy solution. Convinced as he was of the moulding power of environment, he would insist that schools reflect society (though they can also contribute to improving it), and if schools are to change, so must society itself. Fundamental, therefore, is the need to create a social environment which educates towards the possibility of dialogue: by institutions which promote participation; by the moral force of just laws; by equitable taxation; by co-operation in industry; by a press and other media which stimulate thought and extend mental horizons; by a vast improvement in the quality of home life; by a formal education which fulfils its role of initiation and conservation (pp. 41–3 above).[49] In these and other ways, he would contend, it is possible to establish the conditions of dialogue. Reflected in schools it would increase the potential for dialogue there, though its influence would need deliberate reinforcement by measures within each school to promote understanding, co-operation and community of interests between staff and pupils.

The key to an understanding of Mill's élitism is in its educational intention, as Geraint Parry rightly suggests in the sentence quoted above (p. 69). Political motive is not absent, for the maximization of happiness requires expert and informed administration combined with the highest moral and intellectual qualities; government is the task of a few, but a few whose catchment area will broaden with the extension of educational opportunity. Such at least was his hope—even now only partially realized after a century of compulsory schooling and a provision of education lavish beyond what he could have conceived possible. More important for Mill (and perhaps for us too) is the example of excellence, embodied in the few and elevating society by the infection of its own high quality. The few are an indispensable cultural force, a vital component of the educative society; without them mankind is ensnared in perpetual mediocrity. Moreover, the supporting environment which nourishes the talent of the few into the realization of its potential is beneficial also to the many; freedom, equality, dialogue, and the rest, are equally essential conditions for the achievement even of a minimum of civilized humanity. Thus the élite contribute both directly and indirectly to improvement. Whatever diminishes or disparages this contribution, whether by taunts of privilege, by a spurious egalitarianism, or by denigration of intellectual achievement, Mill would reject as an assault on that vision without which, he believed, the people must ultimately perish.

# 5

# Individuality

THE PRINCIPLE of individuality is central to Mill's conception of
man and of man in society; it contributes decisively to his view of
education and of the state's responsibility in promoting it; moreover, it raises social and educational issues whose importance
remains undiminished and which give it, therefore, a peculiar
relevance and even urgency for the present time. In Mill's writings
it is inevitably a recurrent theme. He argues in *Representative
Government* that the encouragement of individual excellence is the
principal criterion of good government; in *Principles of Political
Economy* he declares that 'originality of mind and individuality of
character . . . are the only source of any real progress' and must be
protected from government intrusion and the tyranny of the
majority; in industry and commerce individual enterprise is more
efficient than state control.[1] The same principle, tacitly assumed,
thrusts a recalcitrant element into the causal determinism of his
'ethology', the theory of the formation of human character which
he expounds in Book VI of his *System of Logic*—causality and
individuality are not the easiest of bedfellows.[2] It appears in his
frequent expression of admiration for the heroic, for the great
cultural explorers and innovators;[3] it is an element in his criticism
of Bentham, in his passionate plea for the equality of the sexes, in
his championship of the oppressed and under-privileged. Again
and again he warns of the dangers of diminishing the individual
and restricting his energies—by despotism, by bureaucracy, by the
dead hand of tradition, by dogmatic orthodoxy, by the pressures of
conformity, by the 'collective mediocrity' of representative democracy, by compulsory state education. Most emphatic and eloquent
of all is the celebrated chapter 3 of the essay *On Liberty*, entitled
'Of individuality, as one of the elements of well-being': 'The
initiation of all wise or noble things comes, and must come, from
individuals' and 'In proportion to the development of his individuality each person becomes more valuable to himself, and is therefore capable of being more valuable to others.'[4] What Mill meant

by individuality, however, is by no means perspicuous, and this is a question which clearly requires examination. It will be considered principally within the context of the essay (and the third chapter in particular), which Mill himself regarded as a definitive expression of his views on freedom and individuality.[5]

The words 'individual' (noun and adjective), 'individually' and 'individuality' occur some one hundred and thirty times in *On Liberty* and the last is a key term in the title of chapter 3; but Mill at no point—nor, so far as the present writer has discovered, in any other of his works—attempts a formal clarification of their meaning. In many instances the noun 'individual' means little more than 'person' (in the neutral sense of any man, woman, citizen, human being)—'the tie which binds every individual to the race', 'the vicious or thoughtless individual'; sometimes it conveys the idea of unitariness, the man or woman as the constituent unit of a social grouping, distinguished from and even opposed to it—'individuals, classes, nations', 'individuals are lost in the crowd'; occasionally it echoes the greatly enriched content which, as will be seen, Mill inserts into 'individuality'—as in the quotation above, 'The initiation . . .' etc.[6] The adjectival use is close to that of the noun: sometimes it means 'personal' in the sense of peculiar, belonging to oneself—'their own individual character'; sometimes 'unitary' or 'specific'—'individual cases', 'individual liberty'; and occasionally it hints at richer ingredients—'wearing down into uniformity all that is individual', 'persons of genius are . . . *more* individual than any other people'.[7] There is nothing especially remarkable in all this, nor in the infrequent adverb 'individually'; but with 'individuality' it is very different. This too Mill sometimes uses in quite ordinary senses: 'Where does the authority of society begin? How much of human life should be assigned to individuality and how much to society?'[8] But this plain descriptive use of the word is in marked contrast to the emotionally charged prescriptive use which is characteristic of Mill's writings.

For Mill 'individuality' concentrates in a single concept his ideal of human character and his hopes for the future of mankind; it is a criterion for appraising the achievements of men and societies, for testing the worth of a culture, a civilization; it embodies a philosophy of life and a theory of education; shaped and refined in the fires of his own experience—his childhood relationship with his father, his mental crisis, his affair with Harriet, and much else beside—it is, in a sense, an epitome of the man himself. What, then, did he mean by it?

Human beings, Mill believes, are possessed of a certain potential for development; they are born into the world with faculties and powers which grow and mature according to the opportunities afforded them. This belief, though lacking precise formulation, is implied again and again by what he writes in *On Liberty*. 'Human nature', he affirms,

is not a machine to be built after a model and set to do exactly the work prescribed for it, but a tree which requires to grow and develop itself on all sides according to the tendency of the inward forces which make it a living thing[9]

(the imagery is borrowed from the German von Humboldt whom Mill has quoted both in the preceding pages and on the title page of *On Liberty*). He complains against Calvinism that men are cramped and dwarfed by its doctrines like trees 'clipped into pollards or cut out into figures of animals' rather than allowed to grow 'as nature made them'. Surely, he continues, it is more consistent with belief in divine providence that he endowed us with faculties

that they might be cultivated and unfolded, not rooted out and consumed, and that he takes delight in every nearer approach made by his creatures to the ideal conception embodied in them, every increase in any of their capabilities of comprehension, of action, or of enjoyment.[10]

Desires and feelings, he argues against a supposed critic, are part of 'the raw material of human nature'; in each of us they must be encouraged to 'unfold'—though 'properly balanced' and subject to the discipline of conscience and moral values—into a character which is the genuine 'expression of his own nature'; genius, where it exists, must be allowed to 'unfold itself freely both in thought and practice'.[11] (It may be noted in passing how often Mill uses the imagery of organic growth—trees, 'unfold', 'rooted out'; his principal recreational interest was botany, but apart from this there are clear indications of the influence of Rousseau and Pestalozzi, whose educational ideas based on 'nature' and 'natural growth' were becoming increasingly well known ; in the *Autobiography* he refers specifically to 'the vein of important thought respecting education and culture' derived from 'the labours and genius of Pestalozzi'.)[12]

So far, then, we have the ideas of potentiality and development: 'individuality', he says, 'is the same thing with development'.[13] Now although Mill believed that human beings shared certain general characteristics which could be inferred from observation and gave a degree of predictability to behaviour, he also believed— certainly by the time he wrote *On Liberty*—that they were not merely different but distinctively different, each having his peculiarities of endowment which required for their development differences in opportunity and provision: 'To give any fair play to the nature of each, it is essential that different persons should be allowed to lead different lives.' It is for each man 'to find out what part of recorded experience is properly applicable to his own circumstances and character'. And finally:

Such are the differences among human beings in their sources of pleasure, their susceptibilities of pain and the operation on them of different physical and moral agencies that, unless there is a corresponding diversity in their modes of life, they neither obtain their fair share of happiness nor grow up to the mental, moral and aesthetic stature of which their nature is capable.[14]

Moreover, there are some whose distinctiveness amounts to originality, occasionally even to genius; though few indeed, they are 'the salt of the earth; without them life would become a stagnant pool'; from these 'more highly gifted and instructed One or Few' derives the 'initiation of all wise or noble things'.[15] Clearly, then, as he remarks elsewhere in a different context, 'the more scope that is given to the varieties of human individuality, the better'.[16]

Hence there come to be included in the concept of individuality the further ideas of distinctiveness, variety, originality, even eccentricity. To these must be added one more of crucial importance, namely choice. To abandon or be deprived of choice is to be reduced to a second-hand existence of mere imitation, of unthinking conformity; one becomes less than a human being. Not only this, but choice is essential to the development of potential, both that which belongs to us all as human beings—'perception, judgement, discriminative feeling, mental activity . . . moral preference'[17]—and that which is the distinctive possession of each. It is an essential constituent, therefore, of the concept of individuality. To sum up then, one may say that, for Mill, individuality is the freely chosen expression, in growth and development and in diversity of activity, of one's distinctiveness as a unique being; it is to be *oneself* as completely as possible. (With this compare Professor Himmelfarb: Mill's 'idea of individuality was not so much defined as characterised by association with such words as "experiment", "spontaneity", "originality", "variety", "choice", "diversity", "vigour", "desire", "impulse", "peculiarity", and "eccentricity,"'; to these she adds 'development' as a word of special interest for which Mill was indebted to von Humboldt. 'Its antithesis,' she goes on, 'was represented by "custom", "tradition", "obedience", "conformity", "restraint", "law", and "discipline".')[18]

The two words 'as possible' apply a significant limitation which cannot be passed over without comment. It has been a mistake of many modern writers on education (particularly advocates of 'growth' or 'natural development') and even of some official reports to recommend the 'full development' of the child or person as the proper aim of education.[19] The mistake lies in the unqualified 'full', as if every potentiality of human nature should be given equal scope for development—good and bad, benevolence and aggression, aesthetic talent and sexual perversion; and as if any man or women had the time, energy, or opportunity to develop fully the whole range of his or her potentiality. The facts of human existence and the nature of human society require a *selective* development. At first sight it may seem that Mill too is guilty of this error: he writes of 'the free development of individuality', of allowing genius to 'unfold itself freely'; he commends 'individual spontaneity' and eccentricity, and commits himself to von Humboldt's principle of 'human development in its richest diversity'.[20] Would he tolerate, then, the Napoleons and Hitlers, the Great Train Robbers, the compulsive 'stripper' and similar ingenious or self-assertive eccentrics in deference to 'individuality'? Clearly not, In Mill's usage 'free development' is an elliptical and perhaps rather careless phrase which carries a very definite, though unspecified value qualification. There are limits even to individuality: it must respect 'the rights and interests of others'; in so doing it permits a larger growth of the social as against the selfish in human nature; it is 'the best and highest' that must be allowed to grow and thrive; and in the early editions of the *System of Logic* development aims at securing 'conformity of our character to ideal perfection according to some particular standard'.[21] Thus the limits are imposed by reference both externally to society and the rights of others, and internally to standards and values deliberately chosen as higher or better. Mill suggests a further limitation in the accumulated experience of the human race; some activities and experiments are excluded because they 'have been tried and condemned from the beginning of the world until now [as] . . . not . . . useful or suitable to any person's individuality'.[22] This last seems a highly subjective criterion despite its empirical vesture; he gives no instances.

The point may seem obvious, perhaps laboured; but it emphasizes the distinction, so often overlooked in educational (and other) discourse, between the descriptive and the prescriptive, the factual and the normative. Mill's 'individuality' can be represented in purely descriptive terms: unrestrained choice, human distinctiveness, growth, development, variety; but as such it remains a formal pattern, a vessel without content; in part informative, it is nevertheless incomplete as a practical guide. It leaves unanswered such questions as: choice of what? growth towards what? what kind or quality of variety? And these are value questions which lead us from the factual to the normative. This is a step which Mill saw to be necessary and from which he did not shrink: partially in *On Liberty* and more extensively in his other writings he filled out his concept of individuality with the values he believed essential to give it practical meaning—happiness, truth, justice, beauty, and concern for others. In so doing he offers a needful reminder to enthusiasts for 'growth' and 'following nature' that without normative content their theories (if they deserve that name) are idle. 'All human action . . .', he tells us, 'consists in altering and all useful action in improving the spontaneous course of nature.'[23]

This examination of the meaning of individuality suggests a further important question briefly referred to in chapter 1: did Mill regard it as an end or as a means? Had it for him an intrinsic worth or merely a derived worth dependent on its instrumentality in improving society? Is individuality valuable *in itself*? That he regarded it as instrumentally valuable he makes plain beyond all doubt both in *On Liberty* and in numerous passages in other works. The development of individuality, he tells us in the sentence quoted on p. 77, makes man more valuable both to himself *and to others*. It not only ennobles and beautifies the man himself but as the works partake the character of those who do them, by the same process human life also becomes rich, diversified and animating, furnishing more abundant aliment to high thoughts and elevating feelings, and strengthening the tie which binds every individual to the race by making the race infinitely better worth belonging to.

It offers opportunity for testing 'different experiments of living', of proving the 'worth of different modes of life', and this too is an important factor in human improvement. It is an essential 'counterpoise and corrective' to the mediocrity that Mill believed to be stifling English society. Originality is vital to the discovery of truth and to 'set the example of more enlightened conduct and better taste and sense in human life'; without it 'human life would become a stagnant pool'.[24] The same message rings clear in *Representative Government*: because it quells individual energy, bureaucracy develops into a 'pedantocracy' and perishes 'by the immutability of [its] maxims'; representative government, by contrast, preserves its vigour by allowing 'the conceptions of the man of original genius . . . to prevail over the obstructive spirit of trained mediocrity'.[25] Democracy alone preserves individuality, and in turn is preserved by it. Underlying much of his economic thought is a belief in individual enterprise as more productive than state control; and because at the same time it educates by personal involvement in decisions and planning, it contributes to raising the general level of intelligence; competition, though it has its dangers, is a stimulus to activity and indispensable to progress.[26]

There are also, however, strong indications that Mill came very close to a belief in the intrinsic value of the human person, a conviction that men and women are valuable in themselves and that this is one reason for respecting and fostering their individuality. He complains that 'individual spontaneity is hardly recognised by the common modes of thinking as having any intrinsic worth or deserving any regard on its own account'. Again, a man who is over-protected or over-directed by external authority may well be kept to the straight path of virtue, 'but what will be his comparative worth as a human being?' Granted a 'tolerable amount of common sense and experience' his self-chosen mode of life is the best, 'not because it is the best in itself, but because it is his own mode'.[27] No one, he asserts in *Principles of Political Economy*, 'who professes the smallest regard to human freedom or dignity' can deny 'that there is, or ought to be, some space in human existence . . . entrenched around and sacred from authoritative intrusion'.[28] A certain reverence for the human being as such would also seem to be implied in his 'religion of humanity', so eloquently defended in 'Utility of Religion'. This religion consists in a devotion to the 'ideal excellence' of the whole of humanity as something worth pursuing for its own sake; but the excellence of the whole, as Mill often insists, is constituted by (and surely consists in) the excellence of its parts, and if the former is valuable *per se*, so too is that of each part.[29] None of this amounts to an explicit avowal of the intrinsic worth of the individual man or woman, and Mill nowhere commits himself to such; but this, clearly, is the tendency of his thought. One is forced to ask, therefore, whether belief in the intrinsic value of the individual is compatible with utilitarianism, 'the creed which accepts as the foundation of morals Utility or the Greatest Happiness Principle'.[30] If Utility is the primary ethical principle, then presumably happiness, whether of the individual or of the greatest number, must take precedence over the worth of the individual as such. On the other hand it seems scarcely sensible to place a higher value on happiness than on the person who embodies the happiness; we value happiness, one might argue, only derivatively—*because* we first value persons.

Two further questions arise: is Mill consistent in this view of the individual? and what is his justification of it? There is a passage in 'Thoughts on Parliamentary Reform' which does suggest an inconsistency:

> If it is asserted that all persons ought to be equal in every description of right recognised by society, I answer, not until all are equal in worth as human beings. It is the fact that one person is *not* as good as another; and it is reversing all the rules of rational conduct to attempt to raise a political fabric on a supposition which is at variance with fact.[31]

However, the inconsistency is more apparent than real. Mill is thinking here in terms of political responsibility and political judgement; he is arguing for plural voting on the grounds that in these respects men differ because of their education and that these differences should be acknowledged in a system of weighted voting —the better educated the more votes. Moreover, he would allow as obvious to common observation that some men are more intelligent than others, more talented in one or another direction—human potentiality is not equal from the start; this is one source of the vein of élitism which runs through his thought. There is an important difference, however, between equality of potential and equality of worth; Mill could consistently deny the former as an observed fact while acceding to the latter.[32]

As for justification, it must be said at once that there is no logical justification for judgements of intrinsic value. Instrumental value one can, and Mill does, logically justify by such aims as social improvement; intrinsic value is an act of judgement, faith, commitment which issues from the heart as well as the intellect. And so it is with Mill: he believed in the worth of human beings, not as the conclusion of reasoned argument, but as a conviction which sprang partly from his own nature, partly from the impact of profound experience, partly from his education and subsequent intellectual growth. The inconsistency, if it exists, is rather between this belief and the neutrality, value-wise, of his association psychology and of his account of human nature as subject to scientific law. As all of us must at some time, Mill thought with his heart as well as his head; individuality, with its value implications, was a premise assumed in all his thinking, which strict logic could neither justify nor compel him to forgo. (He could have found a justification in the doctrines of the Christian Church, had he been able to assent to them—each person a separate and unique object of God's love and the redemptive activity of Christ; but despite his profound admiration for Jesus and his moral influence, he found them intellectually untenable.)[33]

The passion and persistence of his plea for individuality suggest a derivation from deep emotional sources. Self-help and initiative in learning were part of his father's educational technique; it is true that there was also a great deal of careful and detailed instruction, even drilling—a word which John himself uses to describe his grounding in formal logic; but the boy was forced by the very circumstances of his education, as well as by his father's deliberate policy, to rely on himself for much of his learning: 'Anything which could be found out by thinking I never was told until I had exhausted my efforts to find it out for myself.'[34] Individual initiative, thus early rooted in him, was an idea (and an ideal) to which he clung by habit and by emotional association with his childhood. A further outcome of his father's training was an attitude of nonconformity, of critical resistance to commonly accepted beliefs and linguistic usage; to these he was encouraged to apply the Socratic *elenchus*; and Socrates himself, the arch-nonconformist, the individual *par excellence*, was held up to him as an ideal of human character. Indeed his classical training as a whole was a force impelling him in the same direction; he writes in *On Liberty* of 'a Greek ideal of self-development'; he expresses his admiration for the outstanding statesmen of Greece, such as Lycurgus and Pericles; and he writes eulogistically of Athenian culture as conducive to individual genius.[35]

At least as important as these influences were the two most profound experiences of his life, his "mental crisis" and his passionate attachment to Harriet. The first, though possibly triggered off by nervous exhaustion and overwork, was basically the revolt of his own nature against the habit of analysis and the quantitative emphasis of orthodox utilitarianism, both of which had been drilled into him by a dogmatism he had been unable to resist, and both of which, it was now revealed to him, were destructive of individuality in its qualitative and affective aspects. The revolt was intensified by the discovery, on his own pulse, as it were, of the emotive power of poetry, first in Wordsworth, then in Coleridge and other Romantics (including Goethe); hence for the first time he 'gave its proper place among the prime necessities of human well-being to the internal culture of the individual'.[36] The second, however innocent (and both Mill and Harriet insist on this), was to say the least unusual, and was inevitably interpreted as an outrage against conventional morality.[37] It can reasonably be assumed that the fervour of Mill's support of individualism was in part a defensive reaction against their critics and an assertion of a man's (and a woman's) right to make his own decisions according to his own conscience.

There were intellectual as well as emotional sources for Mill's 'individuality'; most important among these were Bentham, de Tocqueville, and association psychology.[38] Bentham taught that what is called 'society' or any community within it is 'a fictitious entity'; its reality consists only in the individual men and women who are its members. This is his principle of 'individualism', as distinct from 'individuality', from which it is crucially different. Moreover, the happiness of each member, he maintained, is the sum of its constituent pleasures and pains which can be precisely measured by a 'felicific calculus'. Mill, instructed in Benthamism from his early years, was inevitably influenced by this emphasis on the individual unit; but he came to give it a wholly new meaning and direction as a result of his own growth and experience (and, no doubt, his own character). Alexis de Tocqueville, the French critic of American democracy, was another influence and one more congenial to Mill's later mode of thinking. Reviewing his book, *Democracy in America*, Mill underlines the danger, emphasized by de Tocqueville, of 'the growing insignificance of individuals in comparison with the mass'; it is happening, he affirms, not only in America but in England, and here 'because the mass . . . has grown to so immense a size, that individuals are powerless in the face of it, and because the mass, having by mechanical improvements become capable of acting simultaneously, can compel, not merely any individual, but any number of individuals to bend before it . . . Hardly anything now depends upon individuals, but all upon classes.'[39] As for association psychology, this was the formal psychological basis of utilitarianism: mental content and character are formed by the accretion of 'ideas', initially single sensory items of experience, which are attracted to each other by associative links such as contiguity and similarity; individuality, in the form of these discrete sensory items, is thus central to our being.

This suggests a further problem: what kind of entity is the subject of these experiences, the self, and what meaning is possible for 'personal identity'? Mill gave no prolonged consideration to it and was inclined to dismiss it as philosophically insoluble. He mentions it briefly in his *Examination of Sir William Hamilton's Philosophy*, in chapters, 8, 9, and 12 on consciousness and the mind, and again in a note to the later edition of James Mill's *Analysis of the Phenomena of the Human Mind*. In the former he is attacking Hamilton's intuitionist view that the self is directly known, that (quoting him) consciousness is 'the recognition by the mind or ego of its own acts or affections', that we simply 'perceive' ourselves as persisting subjects of experience just as we perceive an external world of persisting objects.[40] Mill could not accept the intuitionist view; he was a phenomenalist and held the position that knowledge and experience can be explained or interpreted in terms of phenomena, or, more accurately, sense data; the material world is what we actually perceive at a given moment or what, as a result of earlier perception, is accepted as 'a permanent possibility of sensation'. The self and our consciousness of self can be explained in the same way. There is no need to construct a hypothetical 'self' by

distinguishing between 'the perpetual flux of the sensations' and
their total and then fabricating this latter into an imaginary ego:

It is . . . true that our notion of Mind, as well as of Matter, is the notion
of a permanent something, contrasted with the perpetual flux of the
sensations and other feelings or mental states which we refer to it. . . .
This attribute of permanence, supposing that there were nothing else
to be considered, would admit of the same explanation when predicated
of Mind, as of Matter. The belief I entertain that my mind exists when
it is not feeling, nor thinking, nor conscious of its own existence, re-
solves itself into the belief of a Permanent Possibility of these states.

Unconsciousness is a suspension of the combination of conditions
which would call that 'permanent possibility' into action. But Mill
is honest enough to admit that problems remain which seem
'beyond the power of metaphysical analysis to remove'—hence his
qualification in the passage above, 'supposing that there were
nothing else to be considered'. If the mind is a series of feelings and
possibilities of feelings, it is also, quite patently, 'a series of feelings
which is aware of itself as past and future', which consists not only
of present sensations but also in part of memories and expectations.
This brings us back to the intuitionist version of the ego and, as
Mill admits, the 'final inexplicability [of] . . . ultimate facts'.[41] He
makes the same admission in a note to his father's book:

There is a bond of some sort among all the parts of the series, which
makes me say that they were feelings of a person who was the same
person throughout, and a different person from those who had any of
the parallel successions of feelings; and this bond, to me, constitutes
my Ego. Here, I think, the question must rest until some psychologist
succeeds better than anyone has yet done in shewing a mode in which
the analysis can be carried further.[42]

Another difficult problem for a man of Mill's persuasions was the
freedom of the will; and here, too, he has been thought by some, if
not by himself, to have evaded the final issue and even to have
'bent logic'[43] to maintain his position. It was his purpose in *A
System of Logic* to explicate the foundations of scientific method.
The details of this attempt do not concern us here; suffice it say
that it essentially involved the concepts of uniformity, natural law
and cause: any particular event was explicable (or predictable) if the
circumstances of its occurrence were well enough known and if it
could be subsumed under established uniformities of natural law.
In accordance with these, he tells us,

The whole of the present facts are the infallible result of all past facts, and more immediately of all the facts which existed at the moment previous. . . . If the whole prior state of the entire universe could again recur, it would again be followed by the present state.[44]

Thus his picture of the world is firmly deterministic: under certain known laws and conditions, a and b, then c will ('must') happen. This raises obvious difficulties for Mill's 'individuality', and for his sociological theory, and he was well aware of them.

In Book VI of the *Logic*, 'On the Logic of the Moral Sciences', he raises the issue specifically in chapter 2, affirming by way of introduction his own acceptance of the determinist position, 'which I consider the true one', and by which it seems to be implied that: 'No one who believed that he knew thoroughly the circumstances of any case and the characters of the different persons concerned, would hesitate to foretell how all of them would act.'[45] He is careful to point out first that the objection to the suggestion of *compulsion* involved in the 'doctrine of necessity' is unfounded; there is no compulsion in any normal sense, but rather a uniform sequence, so that if a friend who knows us well knows all the circumstances too, he will confidently predict how we shall act. This is not compulsion; it is not inconsistent with freedom any more than (as theologians have maintained) with divine fore-knowledge. In other words 'necessity' is here a kind of metaphor which is misinterpreted as a compelling force 'too powerful to be counteracted at all' and magnified into Fatalism: all in fact it means is 'uniformity of order' and 'capability of being predicted': 'When we say that all human actions take place of necessity, we only mean that they will certainly happen if nothing prevents.'[46] 'Any *must* . . .,' he says elsewhere, 'any necessity other than the unconditional universality of the fact, we know nothing of.'[47]

This gives Mill the lead he wants:

The causes, therefore, on which action depends are never uncontrollable; and any given effect is only necessary provided that the causes tending to produce it are not controlled.

Moreover, although a man's character is 'in the ultimate resort' formed for him by circumstances, he still has a part to play 'as one of the intermediate agents':

His character is formed by his circumstances . . . but his own desire to mould it in a particular way is one of those circumstances, and by no means one of the least influential.

It follows that 'we are exactly as capable of making our own character, *if we will*, as others are of making it for us'. And even though
our *willingness* depend in part on circumstances (upbringing,
education, accident), we still have the feeling 'of our being able to
modify our own character, *if we wish*'; this is 'the feeling of moral
freedom which we are conscious of' and to complete it requires
mastery over habit and temptation and the achievement of 'confirmed virtue'.[48] Thus does Mill leave room in his account of
cause, effect, and natural law for the freedom of the will and thereby for human improvement. Or does he? One is left with the
uneasy feeling that human volition has been given a special dis-
pensation of exemption from or intervention in the laws of cause
and effect ('his own desire to mould it in a particular way'); that to
include human volition along with purely material factors among
the 'circumstances' which form character is a convenient ambiguity
which by-passes the fact that will and desire also have their place
in the cause-effect process. However, as his biographer writes of
him, 'If logic brought him to conclusions repugnant to the interests
of mankind, he had no hesitation in using his great powers to bend
the logic.'[49]

Although Mill expressly denies it, there is a further weakening
of his determinist stance in his conception of the social role of the
gifted individual. Clearly he was impressed from early in childhood
by what he read of great men and great exploits: this was part of the
attraction for him of ancient Greece and Rome with their outstanding historical figures, of Plutarch's *Lives* and the voyages of discovery. Later, this romantic attachment of childhood developed
into a considered view of the essential contribution of the great
man or women to human progress—an indispensable factor in
man's onward march. Originality or invention, he insists in
*Representative Government*, is necessary both for progress and for
permanence in society; it is a first claim on any government,
therefore, that it should stimulate and foster the qualities that
belong to originality—activity, energy, courage, imagination, and
the rest.[50] Again, in *Logic* VI, countering the view that social progress is subject to invariable laws and cannot be influenced by
individuals or acts of governments, he argues firmly that this is to
confuse causation with fatalism, that the human will is among
the most powerful of causative agencies, and that 'exceptional

individuals in important positions' have contributed vitally to the improvement of mankind:

> If Newton had not lived, the world must have waited for the Newtonian philosophy until there had been another Newton or his equivalent. . . . Eminent men do not merely see the coming light from the hill-top; they mount on the hill-top and evoke it; and if no one had ever ascended thither, the light, in many cases, might never have risen upon the plain at all. Philosophy and religion are abundantly amenable to general causes; yet few will doubt that had there been no Socrates, no Plato, and no Aristotle, there would have been no philosophy for the next two thousand years, nor in all probability then; and that if there had been no Christ and no St. Paul, there would have been no Christianity.[51]

It is the same message that we have seen in *On Liberty*, where, apart from the quotation that heads the book—'human development in its richest diversity'—there is Mill's own statement of faith in the manifold wealth of human genius and its power of origination.

A nineteenth-century critic has charged Mill with a 'violent exaggeration of individualism', a 'metaphysical apotheosis of the individual'; and to this he attributes the 'aversion' which *On Liberty* 'inspires in so many minds'.[52] This is unfair, not to say inaccurate. Mill's persistent emphasis on the individual and the need to protect him from impoverishment and diminution is balanced by a due recognition of the claims of society. It is true that he allows the individual a certain primacy. The laws of social phenomena, he insists, are derived from those of individual psychology: 'Human beings in society have no properties but those which are derived from, and may be resolved into, the laws of the nature of individual man.'[53] And the excellence and happiness of society as a whole are constituted from those of its individual members: 'May it not be the fact', he asks in his criticism of Comte,

> that mankind, who after all are made up of single human beings, obtain a greater sum of happiness when each pursues his own, under the rules and conditions required by the good of the rest, than when each makes the good of the rest his only object . . . ?[54]

It is true, too, that there is an element of exaggeration—possibly deriving from Harriet's influence—in his claims on the individual's behalf: 'the sole end for which mankind are warranted . . . in interfering with the liberty of action of any of their number is self-protection'; 'the only unfailing and permanent source of improvement is liberty'; 'the family is a school of despotism, in which the virtues of despotism, but also its vices, are largely nourished'.[55] But Mill is perfectly well aware that man is man *in society*, shaped by environmental pressures around him, limited by his own inadequacies (which can be made good only from the resources of the community), restricted even in the enjoyment of freedom to certain fundamental liberties, and owing a debt of obligation to the enfolding society without whose support his own life would be barbarous.

The importance of environment and of man's response to it were not lost on Mill; coupled with the deliberate use of association psychology there lay here, he believed, an instrument of enormous educative potential for human betterment (and equally *mis*-educative if ignored or directed to unworthy goals.) He mentions in the *Autobiography* the impression made on himself by his holidays at Ford Abbey (the country house in Somerset rented for a time by Jeremy Bentham) and by his journey with Sir Samuel Bentham to the Pyrenees.[56] True, he mentions later how he 'ceased to attach almost exclusive importance to the ordering of outward circumstances' and came to give its due place to 'the internal culture of the individual'; but he never abandoned his belief in the moulding power of environment—'whatever helps to shape the human being', he tells us in the *Inaugural Address* is part of his education, and he stresses later the educative importance of home and family.[57] He makes the same point in 'The Claims of Labour': 'Whatever acts upon the minds of the labouring classes is properly their education. But their minds, like those of other people, are acted upon by the whole of their social circumstances.'[58] In Book VI of the *Logic* he both admits, as we have seen, the shaping force of circumstances and also claims that man himself can select the circumstances which shape him—thus making them a self-chosen instrument of his education. Clearly, Mill did not think of the individual as a mere abstraction, nor was he oblivious of man's reciprocal involvement in a context of thought and activity.

Equally he was aware of the need in any society for authority, legal and cultural; aware, too, of society's legitimate claims on the individual and the latter's obligations to the community. This is evident in all his major political writings—*Principles of Political*

*Economy, Representative Government, On Liberty*—as well as such
shorter essays as 'Civilisation', 'Bentham', 'Coleridge' and his
review of de Tocqueville. In the first of these, under the chapter
title 'Grounds and Limits of the *Laisser-Faire* Principle' (Book V,
xi), he discusses at length the proper boundaries between individual
freedom and government intervention. While convinced that 'there
is a circle around every human being which no government . . .
ought to be permitted to overstep', he is equally certain that there
are areas of the national life where intervention by the central
authority is justified. Education is among the foremost of these:
'The uncultivated cannot be competent judges of cultivation' and
'there are certain primary elements and means of knowledge' which
all members of a community must acquire, compulsorily if need
be, during childhood.[59] Protection of children, public charity, and
colonization are further examples. He discusses the same subject,
though with greater emphasis on non-interference, in chapters 4
and 5 of *On Liberty*, and here again, for example, he accepts the
need for intervention in education: 'Is it not almost a self-evident
axiom that the state should require and compel the education, up
to a certain standard, of every human being who is born its citizen?'[60] Civilization, he tells us in the essay of that title, involves
co-operation and therefore compromise, 'the sacrifice of some
portion of individual will for a common purpose';[61] and in *On
Liberty* he reminds us that 'the fact of living in society renders it
indispensable that each should be bound to observe a certain line
of conduct towards the rest':

It would be a great misunderstanding of this doctrine [of personal
freedom] to suppose that it is one of selfish indifference, which pretends
that human beings have no business with each other's conduct in life,
and that they should not concern themselves about the well-doing or
well-being of one another, unless their own interest is involved. Instead
of any diminution, there is need of a great increase of disinterested
exertion to promote the good of others.[62]

Finally, he argues in *Utilitarianism* that there exists a firm natural
foundation for the greatest happiness principle in 'the social
feelings of mankind, the desire to be in unity with our fellow-
creatures':

The social state is at once so natural, so necessary, and so habitual to
man, that, except in some unusual circumstances or by an effort of

voluntary abstraction, he never conceives himself otherwise than as a member of a body; and this association is riveted more and more, as mankind are further removed from the state of savage independence.[63]

All this scarcely suggests a 'violent exaggeration of individualism' or a neglect of obligation to the community; rather, a sane and balanced view of the proper relationship between freedom and authority, between self-regarding and other-regarding attitudes. And even if it were impossible to instance this from his writings, there would be the example of his life, which is a record of continual service to others in the light of his ideals, from the youthful enthusiasm of birth-control propaganda to his denunciation of Governor Eyre for his brutal administration of Jamaica in the 1860s.[64]

It should be noted, further, that Mill places firm limits on individuality and its attendant freedoms where they are incompatible with levels of personal or political maturity. His doctrine of individuality properly applies only to those who can utilize the freely chosen expression of their distinctiveness for their own improvement and that of society:

This doctrine is meant to apply only to human beings in the maturity of their faculties. We are not speaking of children, or of young persons below the age which the law may fix as that of manhood or womanhood. Those who are still in a state to require being taken care of by others must be protected against their own actions as well as against external injury. For the same reason we may leave out of consideration those backward states of society in which the race itself may be considered as in its nonage. . . . Liberty, as a principle, has no application to any state of things anterior to the time when mankind have become capable of being improved by free and equal discussion.[65]

Moreover, Mill's statement of the legitimate sphere of individuality in chapter 1 of *On Liberty*, comprehensive though it is, suggests, if closely examined, the admissibility of important exclusions and exceptions in the interests of society—his hesitation about freedom of expression, and his provisos with regard to freedom of association, 'not involving harm to others' and 'not forced or deceived'.[66] This, coupled with the normative restrictions on individuality mentioned above (pp. 81–2) and with his statement of the legitimate sphere of government in the final chapter of *Principles of Political Economy*, does not leave the impression of an exaggerated individualism. Nor does his account in the *Autobiography* of the development, concurrently with his friendship with Harriet, of the socialist tendencies of his thought: the social problem of the future, they thought, was 'how to unite the greatest individual liberty of action with a common ownership in the raw material of the globe and an equal participation of all in the benefits of combined labour'; the solution would require a transformation of character 'both in the uncultivated herd who now compose the labouring masses, and in the immense majority of their employers', all of whom must combine and labour 'for public and social purposes'.[67] Indeed one student of Mill has found in him strong leanings towards an authoritarianism which would allow individuality and freedom only within the 'rationally binding chains'[68] of his religion of humanity as interpreted by an intellectual élite.

What Mill feared—and this in part explains the occasionally exaggerated tone of his claim for individuality—was the dwarfing of the individual by social or legal pressures, the inhibiting of originality, of initiative. This is a recurrent theme in his writings. One of the effects of the growing complexity of civilization, he complains, is 'that the individual is lost and becomes impotent in the crowd, and that individual character itself becomes relaxed and enervated'; in particular he deplores the diminished 'influence of superior minds over the multitude'.[69] (It is worth noting that one of the remedies he suggests is national institutions of education; another is to ensure that the constitution of the country is such as to invigorate individual character.) He accepts de Tocqueville's charge against democracy that it diminishes the individual; and it is no less true, Mill urges, of England than of the American democracy of which de Tocqueville was writing. It would be difficult, he writes, to show any country in which 'the growing insignificance of individuals in comparison with the mass ... is more marked and conspicuous than in England'; and so great is its combined strength 'that individuals are powerless in the face of it'.[70] The same view is expressed with equal force in the essay on Bentham, where Mill questions the conclusion that it is always 'good for mankind to be under the absolute authority of the majority of themselves'. This, he argues, is a situation which imposes, if not by legal penalty then by 'the despotism of Public Opinion', a conformity of mind and outlook, an identity of 'partialities, passions and prejudices', which makes impossible any correction of human imperfection and stifles improvement in man's moral and intellectual nature.[71] Variety, enterprise, and competition are essential not only for economic and social progress but also and emphatically in the realm of ideas; the worth of a state is the worth of the individuals who compose it, and any state which 'dwarfs its men . . . even for beneficial purposes, will find that with small men no great thing can really be accomplished'.[72] Most especially did Mill fear the suppression of genuine greatness. His admiration for men of outstanding achievement and his conception of their social role were noted above; these, reinforced by his study of Plato's *Republic* and of Comte and Coleridge, encouraged in him the élitist leanings examined in chapter 4.

It is pertinent to this consideration of Mill's doctrine of individuality to ask what was his view of man. What conception had he of human beings, of the human situation? Much of the answer has become apparent in the preceding pages of this chapter, and with little addition it is possible to complete a reasonably clear and compact picture. Man, for Mill, is part of nature, subject to natural laws and the operations of cause and effect; this, as has been seen, raises the problem of determinism and presents him with a conflict between two sides of his own personality. As logician and philosopher of science he was impelled towards determinism; but the poet, the artist, and the moralist in him rebelled against it and drew him towards spontaneity, choice, creativity, and freedom. It was to these last, despite logical inconsistency, that he was ultimately and essentially committed; as Sir Isaiah Berlin contends in his lecture, *John Stuart Mill and the Ends of Life*, 'He believed that it is neither rational thought, nor domination over nature, but freedom to choose that distinguishes man from the rest of nature; of all his ideas it is this view that has ensured his lasting fame.'[73]

Because man is part of nature  he is shaped (though not necessarily *determined*) both by endowment and by environment; the endowment is a potential for development  and because man is not necessarily good his development requires education, a selective fostering of potential using as a major instrument the other shaping influence, environment. Although his emphasis on the two components of the process shifted as he grew older, education remained essentially for Mill a selective development of potential by a selective manipulation of environment. Fundamental, therefore, to human nature is its educability; it responds to training; it is corrigible;  and because it is *rational*, it is amenable not only to formal education but also to the informal, but no less powerfully educative, impact of discussion and reflection on experience. It follows that man is (or can be) progressive, not simply in the sense of forward movement, but of change for the better; both man and society are capable of improvement. Later in life, after the disappointment of his early enthusiasms, he came to accept that the improvement must be gradual; but that it is possible he never doubted.[74]

That human beings are in certain fundamental aspects equal and should be granted equality of consideration was also a part of his creed—though in the final count it was subordinate to his utilitarianism. It was an assumption of his social and political thinking that each man's individuality is equally deserving of respect and of the conditions which enable its development; these include his freedom and his participation (albeit qualified) in democratic government. Unlike many of his contemporaries Mill saw the logical indefensibility of restricting this to one sex—hence his lifelong battle for women's rights, expressed most powerfully in *The Subjection of Women*. For reasons of utility, however, he was prepared to limit equality (at least for the time) by allowing plural votes to the better educated and restricting the franchise of the illiterate and the immoral (see above, p. 23). Though inclined at first, it seems, to a belief in equality of natural endowment amenable in all alike to the educative influence of environment, he moved to a pragmatic acceptance of differences in ability, as actually observed to exist, and so, as already indicated, to an élitist stance. *Variety* of endowment and its need for expression were central to his argument for liberty; this suggests a further belief, never expressly stated, in the uniqueness and intrinsic value of each human being (pp. 83–4 above).

Man is not only part of nature in the sense stated above; he is also part of history, of society, of the universe. He is part of a historical process by which he is modified, even improved, but of which the final outcome cannot be known; he is a member of society, whose culture he absorbs and to which he owes obligations of service; he belongs to a universe which exceeds his grasp:

Human existence is girt round with mystery: the narrow region of our experience is a small island in the midst of a boundless sea, which at once awes our feelings and stimulates our imagination by its vastness and its obscurity.[75]

Though the outcome of the historical process is unknown, its direction, Mill believed, is towards happiness. Precisely what this is he never makes clear—indeed its nature might well vary from stage to stage of the process; but an answer he might accept is 'that which satisfies the fullness of a man's own nature'—which of course still leaves the question open. Certainly, however, the fullness of human nature included for Mill the intellectual, the moral, the aesthetic and what he calls 'the sympathetic'—reciprocity in love and respect;[76] it included a sense of perfection, of standards of excellence to be pursued for their own sake, and a conscience sensitive to their demands. All this constitutes no ignoble conception of man: rooted in nature he strives to improve upon his natural self by infusing it with ideals supplied from imagination; this task he shares with his fellow men, to whose collective happiness he is committed even at the expense of his own.

There are, of course, weaknesses in Mill's doctrine of individuality, and these must be briefly noted before passing finally to consider its educational significance. The charge that he abstracts the individual into a false isolation from his social context has already been rejected (pp. 91–2). The critic there mentioned affirms: 'Any social philosophy founded upon 'individuals' as such is founded not on real facts and living beings, as we find them and know them, but upon mental abstractions, that is, upon postulates, not on realities.'[77] Indeed, this is true and Mill was not fool enough to overlook it; there is, nevertheless, a genuine sense in which individuals are distinguishable from their context, and he was right to emphasize the fact. Where he was at fault was in leaving this sense indeterminate and in relinquishing without sufficient exploration important issues arising from the distinction. Again, some of the more crucial of these issues have already been mentioned. The problem of personal identity and the nature of the ego he surrenders as finally insoluble, leaving us still wondering whether (as much of his writing suggests) the self is a metaphysical entity possessed of an intrinsic uniqueness and value, or the product rather of social and environmental forces working on some elemental stuff which has been partly structured by organic heredity. What does give to human beings such worth, such uniqueness, originality, genius as they are deemed to possess? What is it that differentiates *my* self from my neighbour's and both of them from the countless other selves in the mass of humanity?

Mill does not give us any certain answers—nor could he, it might be thought, within the terms of his association psychology; but without them the concept of individuality must remain unclear. Nor does he resolve the problem of determinism: with part of himself he wanted human nature to be predictable, subject to natural law, and thus amenable to 'ethological science'; with another he wanted it to be free to choose, to originate, to diverge; he seeks to escape the dilemma by including desire among the *circumstances* which mould character—as if a man could somehow be identical with his environment (pp. 89–90 above); but one is not readily convinced by such conceptual subtleties.

A further weakness, but more excusable, is his failure to clarify the boundaries between individual and society, between freedom and authority; more excusable because the boundaries are inconstant, varying from society to society and from one historical period to another. Of the need for some demarcation of the proper limits of individual freedom and the authority of the community he was certainly aware; but here again he was torn between two sides of his nature, the individualist and the socialist, the apostle of 'inner culture' and the utilitarian. The struggle left him in a position of ambiguity which, despite the persuasive passion of *On Liberty* has enabled some to see him principally as an authoritarian (p. 95 above).

It might also, perhaps, be objected that the indecisiveness of Mill's basic value commitment spills over into his account of individuality, adding to the unclarity of the concept. It was argued in chapter 1 that he was committed to five primary values— happiness, freedom, truth, altruism and, of course, individuality— each of which on the evidence of his writings could be regarded as an end in itself and intrinsically worth while. In situations where these conflict, as sometimes they must, which has priority? For the claims of any, if sufficiently pressed, inevitably compete with some or all of the rest: the full expression of individuality or of truth may prove inconsistent with the freedom and happiness of others; the well-being of the community imposes restraints on freedom and self-expression; and a wholehearted altruism is likely to inhibit the full development and possibly the happiness (depending on what one means by it) of the individual. In what circumstances does individuality take precedence? When is it subordinate? How is it interrelated with the other four? These and the like questions find no clear answer in Mill. Moreover, though he has no doubt that, to be practically useful, the concept of individuality requires prescriptive as well as descriptive content, that development must be *selective* according to chosen standards and rules, one is left wondering (so a critic might argue) in which standard or value especially individuality finds fulfilment. What should dominantly characterize the fulfilled, developed individual—happiness, freedom, truth, altruism, any one of these or all of them in varying emphasis? Again, his answer is uncertain, and perhaps he would claim that a mature individuality finds fulfilment in any or all of these, choosing responsibly as circumstances suggest.

It remains now to consider the significance of Mill's principle of individuality in the context of educational thought and practice. Emphasis on the individual, on the child as the centre of the educational process, is now commonplace, at least in this country; it has become an accepted ingredient of contemporary educational theory. Mill did not develop his concept of individuality into a coherent theory or practical policy of education; but the essential elements of such a theory and policy are clearly present in the concept as he understands it, and its influence is evident in many of his pronouncements on educational topics. For instance, he deplores 'cram', stuffing the memory with 'the results which have been got at by other people'; it is an affront to children's reason and understanding, and he contrasts it with methods of instruction which rely on 'observation, experience and reflection'.[78] Similarly, he recommends as more appropriate to childhood, the learning of foreign languages 'by practice and repetition before being troubled with grammatical rules'.[79] Religious and moral indoctrination he deplores as inconsistent with the independence necessary for children's intellectual development;[80] he commends the 'freer system' of English schools, compared with French, as responsible for 'the superiority of England over France in the love and practice of personal and political freedom'.[81] Liberal education, as he explains it in the *Inaugural Address*, has amongst its aims the release of individual potential, discovery in intellectual exploration, the cultivation of sensitivity, imagination, and mental skills; it is the education of the whole man. 'Real education', he quotes approvingly in one of his letters, depends on 'the contact of human living soul with human living soul';[82] and its purpose is 'not to *teach*, but to fit the mind for learning from its own consciousness and observation'.[83] There is a vein of child-centredness, or at least of individual-centredness, running through all these pronouncements; yet it is an important part of Mill's educational insight that, as has already been noted, he sees the individual not simply as such but as belonging to a social and cosmic context wider than himself.

In this and in other respects Mill avoids the pitfalls that have beguiled not a few educational theorists into distortion and exaggeration of vital truths. It is indeed such a truth that the individual child is the immediate focus of educational effort: it is *his* self, in its difference and distinctiveness, that must be observed and understood as it grows in response to innate forces and the pressures of environment; without such understanding the educator is doomed to frustration—or must resort to the imposition of preconceived patterns of development. It is no less true, however, that children are products of a historical process stretching far into the past; that they belong to a present whose influences, opportunities, and limitations are further shaping them; and that they are makers of a future whose quality will depend on the values they inject into it. Individuality is indeed fundamental, but it is not enough. Education is a means of facilitating the passage from the past, through the present, to a future which is more worthwhile than either; it is, as has been well said, 'a process of shaping society a generation hence'.[84] In this the individual is crucial—it is *his* excellence (or otherwise) which will determine the excellence (or otherwise) of that future; and it is upon him as the dynamic source of growth and change, the inheritor and the creator of values, that the educator concentrates his attention. But the individual is not all-important; he does not stand outside or above the processes of history or social change; he is part of them, and any viable account of education must accommodate itself to this fact.

Now Mill, despite the occasional lapse into exaggeration in *On Liberty*, is keenly aware of the need to balance individuality on the one hand against sociality on the other; insistent though he is on the former, he is sufficiently a student of the past and sufficiently an enthusiast for the improvement of mankind to see the individual in a wider role than one merely of self-nurture or personal growth. The purpose of historical studies, he explains in the *Inaugural Address*, is to encourage a student to take interest in history, 'not as a mere narrative, but as a chain of causes and effects still unwinding

itself before his eyes and full of momentous consequences to himself and his descendants'; and among the principal aims of education, he writes elsewhere, is 'the direct cultivation of altruism and
the subordination of egoism to it, far beyond the point of absolute
moral duty'.[85] Nor is this the only point where Mill corrects the
imbalance of later educationists. The fallacy of 'full development'
and Mill's recognition of the need for normative guidance of
growth were noted earlier. Another fallacy, no longer so prevalent,
has been the demand for 'natural' development. 'Fix your eyes on
nature', advised Rousseau; 'follow the path traced by her.' Left as
God made them, all things are good; but 'man meddles with them
and they become evil'.[86] His advice is persuasive in its romantic
appeal; nor is it without practical value; but because it is incomplete, it is misleading; if literally interpreted and uncritically
obeyed it can be disastrous.

It is incomplete because 'nature' is unexplained and the suggestion is conveyed that the educator need only let things be—as if
children grew of their own accord into the fairest specimens of
humanity. But children do not, any more than trees or roses, grow
to perfection without human intervention; civilization is a record
of man using the 'laws' of nature to interfere with and improve on
nature; and this is as true of education as it is of horticulture. Mill
provides a corrective to the mistaken interpretation of Rousseau's
'naturalism', partly by his careful analysis of 'nature' and *'naturam
sequi'*, partly by his clear recognition that man's duty is not to
*accept* nature (save in the obvious sense of obeying the 'laws' by
which she operates) or to refrain from intervention, but to amend
and enhance nature by injecting into her his own values and ideals:

> What self-culture would be possible without aid from the general
> sentiment of mankind delivered through books, and from the contem-
> plation of exalted characters, real or ideal? This artificially created or at
> least artificially perfected nature of the best and noblest human beings
> is the only nature which it is ever commendable to follow.[87]

Individuality does not, for Mill, mean the unhindered, un-
directed growth of natural potential, but a growth refined and
embellished by the purposive effort of the educator.

Commonly associated with individuality in educational discourse is the concept of freedom: without freedom, it is said, the
child's distinctive potential, the peculiarities of endowment and
circumstance which contribute to his individuality, have no

opportunity for growth and expression. Like other educational concepts, however, it has rarely been submitted to the scrutiny of analysis; the result has been confusion of theory and misdirection of practice. Among the confusions is the belief, less prevalent now, that freedom in education means total non-interference or the least possible interference compatible with life in community; hence has come an under-emphasis on the due role in education of discipline and authority; another is the erroneous distinction, which still bedevils us, between 'freedom from' and 'freedom to'. Non-interference, except in very limited and specifically structured situations such as play-groups, is educationally unacceptable; because children are part of a culture within a historical process, and because education is a means—the most powerful means, many would add—to human amelioration, the process of education involves initiation into a culture, the deliberate direction of children towards certain values and modes of life. As for the supposed distinction between 'freedom from' and 'freedom to', the so-called 'negative' and 'positive' freedoms, this does not survive analysis: freedom is a negative concept implying non-interference, the absence of externally imposed direction, a situation which leaves open the possibility of choice, of self-motivation; but what this situation is used for, what the choice that it enables, is not part of the concept of freedom; it belongs rather to the concept of purpose, of decision; 'freedom to', as the writer has argued elsewhere, is 'freedom from *in order to*'—a purpose clause concealed by abbreviation and assuming 'freedom from' as the ground of its possibility (see above, p. 9 and note 24).[88]

Now Mill, as has already been suggested (pp. 7–10), was not guiltless here: though committed to happiness as the supreme value and to freedom and individuality as means of achieving it, he writes sometimes as if these latter two were end-values in their own right; he never undertook a careful analysis either of the separate concepts or of their interrelationships. Genuine freedom, he asserts in the introduction to *On Liberty* means 'pursuing our own good in our own way'—with the proviso that we allow others to do the same; later in the essay it is 'doing what one desires'.[89] These descriptions are akin to 'positive freedom'—freedom *to* or *for*; but in much of his argument he virtually equates freedom with non-interference, the negative and (in the present writer's view) correct account of the concept. One must grant that Mill is inconsistent here, even muddled. On the other hand he makes it plain—as others have not always been careful to do—that freedom, whether as non-interference or as doing what you like, does not properly belong to children, whose immaturity requires that they 'must be protected against their own actions'.[90] Nor does it escape him that children must be initiated (though he does not use the word) into a culture, and that this too imposes limitations on their freedom: education, in the narrower sense which he adopts for his *Inaugural Address*, is 'the culture which each generation purposely gives to those who are to be its successors' to enable them to maintain and improve upon the existing level of attainment.[91] Such an account of education is incompatible with a policy of strict non-interference.

Equally important is what he has to say on discipline and authority. These too are concepts which Mill made no attempt to analyse; but his use of them, though uncritical, was nevertheless significant. It is altogether good, as Mill would be the first to agree, that citizens of a democracy should assert their individuality, their varieties of character and outlook, should question, criticize, make their own decisions and choices; on this depends the quality of its culture and its progress to a richer experience. But protest and self-assertion can go too far, more especially when they derive from self-interested motives untempered by any appeal to reason or the general good, and are backed by an easy resort to disruption and violence. Educational institutions have not escaped this imbalance of emphasis; indeed they may well have assisted it by pedagogic innovations which have (quite rightly) shifted the initiative from teacher to taught—to teach is not so much to instruct as to facilitate learning. The remedy lies in a recognition of the necessary role in human affairs of discipline (in the sense of order, restraint, and rational control) and authority (in the sense of a respected locus of rules, propriety, rightness or correctness, whether in law, morals, art, or some other area of particular expertise).

This was obvious to Mill, champion though he was of individuality and freedom. Discipline is essential for moulding the raw instincts of human nature into the character of a civilized being:

Nearly every respectable attribute of humanity is the result not of instinct but of a victory over instinct; and there is hardly anything valuable in the natural man except capacities—a whole world of possibilities, all of them dependent upon eminently artificial discipline for being realised.[92]

It is essential for maintaining a society where 'vigour and manliness of character' co-exist with respect for law and government; in such societies (typified for Mill in the city-states of classical Greece) there was always, he affirms, 'a system of *education*, beginning with infancy and continued through life, of which ... one main and incessant ingredient was *restraining discipline*'.[93] He commends an 'ascetic discipline, in the original Greek sense of the word', which will lead to self-control and 'form the habit and develop the desire of being useful to others and to the world'.[94] Finally, commenting on the rigour of his own education, he adds his belief that 'much must be done and much must be learnt by children for which rigid discipline and known liability to punishment are indispensable as means'.[95] One can reject here his somewhat facile reference to punishment without abandoning the genuine wisdom of the rest.

Mill's recognition of the need for authority was noted above (pp. 71–3); civilized life, it was obvious to him, is impossible without it, and he saw as the 'three great questions in government', 'To what authority is it for the good of the people that they should be subject?', 'How are they to be induced to obey that authority?' and 'By what means are the abuses of this authority to be checked?'[96] A further question which constantly perplexed him was where the boundary should be drawn between the authority of the individual over himself and that of the state to interfere. Politically the ultimate authority must be the will of the majority, but this is fraught with danger and it is essential, he thought, for there to be 'a perpetual and standing Opposition to the will of the majority' to ensure that intellectual and moral advance is not crushed beneath a mean and prejudiced uniformity; hence his partiality towards an educated élite to whose 'superiority of cultivated intelligence' the majority would show due deference.[97]

The need for authority is no less in other spheres—the intellect, morality, the arts. The need for deference to intellectual authority is stated in the passage from 'The Spirit of the Age' quoted above (p. 58). In 'Professor Sedgwick's Discourse', he expresses the view that the function of a university is to provide 'the education by which great minds are formed', minds whose superior qualities will lead the mass of their countrymen 'to greater achievements in virtue, intelligence and social well-being', and inspire the leisured classes to appreciate and emulate this very superiority.[98] This claim that there must be deference to intellectual authority was one he never relinquished; even in *On Liberty* he does not reject out-right the suggestion (posed as an objection to free discussion) that 'simple minds', having reached the limit of their capacities, must 'trust to authority for the rest'.[99]

In morals, Mill argues, there must be a supreme ethical principle, 'some standard by which to determine the goodness or badness, absolute and comparative, of ends or objects of desire'; and this standard is, of course, 'the happiness of mankind, or rather of all sentient beings'.[100] The authority of this ultimate principle is backed by secondary rules whose justification is derived from it, but which are normally sufficient in themselves for ethical guidance without further appeal—for instance, honesty, fair dealing, impartiality, tolerance.[101] To assist the individual in obedience to this authority there is the example of the great, in history or in fiction; there is 'the contemplation of an idealised posterity—shall I add, of ideal perfection embodied in a Divine Being'; for those who cannot assent to this latter there is the 'Religion of Humanity', 'the strong and earnest direction of the emotions and desires towards an ideal object, recognised as of the highest excellence and as rightfully paramount over all selfish objects of desire'; and finally there is the prompting of conscience, whose essence is 'a pain, more or less intense, attendant on violation of duty, which in properly cultivated moral natures rises, in the more serious cases, into shrinking from it as an impossibility'.[102] In the arts there is the authority of an ideal beauty exemplified in the great masters. Art is 'the endeavour after perfection in execution',[103] a perfection which is evidenced in all great poetry, music, painting, and even in the mundane products of daily life if they are infused with the earnest desire after this same perfection. Thus, neither in intellectual judgement nor in morals nor in aesthetics does Mill leave the individual to an untutored subjectivity. What precisely constitutes truth or happiness or beauty may still be arguable; but that there are authoritative standards which claim respect and commitment Mill did not doubt.

Individuality is patently a key concept in Mill's thought. There is justification for the criticism that he did not elucidate its content —though it is not difficult to supply that content from his writings; that he was confused about its status—means or end; and that he left unresolved a number of crucial problems such as the nature of selfhood, the extent of its determination by external causes, and the sources of its unique worth. However, by the importance he assigned to it, by his grasp of its limitations unless fortified by normative control, and by his insight into the dangers arising from its too literal practical implementation he has expanded and enriched the thought of subsequent generations. He has pointed to the need to discover and develop potential, to provide an environment which stimulates growth, to protect against those pressures, whether of public opinion or aggressive authority or forms of organization, which induce or permit mediocrity; he is a forerunner, though not a direct source, of modern child-centredness; he anticipates much that is now accepted as of proven value in British education. Perhaps Mill's chief significance for the present time is his clear recognition that without a firm prescriptive element, without a value-orientation, individuality is a merely formal concept which offers little guidance to the educator. What those values should be is for each to decide according to his own view of life and with reference to the society of which he is a member. They may not exactly tally with Mill's, but one can say with confidence that a study of his concept of individuality, in the total context of his thought, is an eminently civilizing exercise in itself and at the same time leads to a richer understanding of the educational process.

# 6

# The State and Education

MILL'S LIFETIME coincided almost exactly with the establishment of a national system of education in England and Wales.[1] In 1806 the state had no part and no interest in education;[2] by the time of his death in 1873 the foundations had been laid for a universal, free, and compulsory system of elementary schooling. Utilitarians played a major part in this process, among them Mill's father, James. In Parliament it was mainly the work of two men, J. A. Roebuck and Joseph Hume,[3] both of whom were Members for most of the years between 1830 and 1850; they were supported by George Grote during the few years of his Parliamentary career. Roebuck's Resolution of 1833, the first attempt to secure legislation for a national system, was explained and argued in a speech notable for its clarity, earnestness of purpose and educational wisdom.[4] His views were typical of utilitarian thinking of that period about education and the state's obligation towards it; as such they were part of the formative context of Mill's opinions (the more obviously since the two men were close friends up to this time).[5] Thus, Mill's educational ideas and recommendations were not those of an isolated thinker (as his strong personal emphases might sometimes suggest); rather, he was involved in a powerful current of thought (not confined to Utilitarians) which was fed by social and economic pressures as well as by moral and intellectual ideals.

Certainly there is much in Roebuck's Parliamentary speeches (and in the article in *Tait's Magazine* which preceded them) that Mill must have acclaimed, and much that is paralleled in his own writings: the firm purpose of improvement towards happiness, the stress on moral education, the flavour of élitism modified by an ultimate egalitarian goal, the fear of indoctrination and loss of freedom, the inclusion of art and music and 'political education' in the curriculum, and the reverence for intellectual achievement. Mill was also committed, hesitantly at first, always with reservations, but in the end conclusively, to some form of national system of education or at the least to state supervision of and compulsory powers over children's schooling. However, state intervention of any kind raised for him a crucial issue which was hinted at above and discussed very briefly in the previous chapter. This we must examine before considering his views on and (to some small extent) involvement in the movement towards a compulsory national system of education.

He was committed to two values, freedom and happiness, which imply contrasting conceptions of the role of the state. Thus, freedom suggests the principle of non-interference, which he emphatically adopts in *On Liberty*; happiness points to a positive role of actively promoting well-being, and this necessitates some intrusion into personal freedom. He nowhere examined this contrast as a philosophical issue of apparently conflicting values; but he was certainly aware of it and, more especially, of the practical difficulties it presented. His most thoughtful treatment of it is in the final chapter of *Principles of Political Economy*, 'Of the Grounds and Limits of the *Laisser-Faire* or Non-Interference Principle'; he considers it again in *On Liberty* and touches on it in 'Coleridge', *Representative Government*, 'Centralisation' and other writings.

In the life of every individual there is an area which human freedom and dignity require to be held 'sacred from authoritative intrusion'; the sole justification for the state's invading it is 'to prevent harm to others. His own good, either physical or moral, is not a sufficient warrant'.[6] Yet 'the ultimate appeal on all ethical questions' is utility—'the permanent interests of man as a progressive being'; 'the test of what is right in politics is not the *will* of the people, but the *good* of the people'; there is therefore scarcely any matter of general interest which, in specific circumstances, may not justify the intervention of authority.[7]

The issue is clear, but Mill does not resolve it—if indeed it is resoluble at either the philosophical or the practical level; *practically* he regards it as a question of balance, of deciding 'how large a province of human life this reserved territory should include'; and he admits the difficulty of assessing this balance, of differentiating between what concerns only the individual and what also concerns society.[8] He admits too that *inaction* can be a source of harm to others, and that restraint may therefore take the form of compulsion to act; he makes a valuable distinction between 'authoritative' interference, which limits and controls the free agency of individuals, and 'non-authoritative', which relies on advice and persuasion and provides a standard and an example by exhibiting them in its own institutions; he considers a number of objections to state intervention, and he allows certain exceptions to the principle of non-interference, of which education is the most obvious practical instance.[9] However, when all is said, one feels that it is implicitly rather than by careful analysis and pointed justification that he slips into acceptance of intervention and a doctrine which J. M. Robson describes as 'the least-government theory'.[10] There was no escaping this conclusion; he was forced into it by the practical implications of utilitarianism and by his own impelling ideal of human improvement; but a deeper analysis might surely have strengthened his case.

In fact his justification is embodied mainly in the 'large exceptions' which he discusses in *Principles*.[11] The state may intervene where 'the consumer is an incompetent judge of the commodity'; in general he knows best what he wants, but this 'market test', adequate enough for the material needs and daily uses of life, is inappropriate in matters of character and culture: 'The uncultivated cannot be competent judges of cultivation. Those who most need to be made wiser and better usually desire it least, and, if they desired it, would be incapable of finding their way to it by their own lights.' Thus a government may reasonably enforce and provide education on the assumption that its moral and intellectual standards are higher than those which the majority of the people would spontaneously demand. Intervention is also justified where men have power over others, as over children and lunatics. Interestingly, Mill also includes animals, 'those unfortunate slaves and victims of the most brutal part of mankind'; to protect them is not, as commonly supposed, 'an interference with domestic life', and he wishes the law were more effective in so doing. It may be necessary, too, in order to give the support of law to collective purposes which would otherwise be ineffective, for instance in determining hours of work and in apportioning land in colonial territories. Colonization itself, 'as an affair of business', is beyond the resources of private endeavour; the state alone can meet the initial cost and recoup it later. Provision for the destitute is another area where the state must act: 'the certainty of subsistence should be held out by law to the destitute able-bodied', but no more than the necessary minimum, leaving private charity to provide more for the deserving individual. Further, there are many valuable public services which are outside the interest or beyond the means of voluntary enterprise—lighthouses and other aids to navigation, scientific and geographical exploration, research and the promotion of knowledge (on these last see also below, p. 121).

Such he judges to be the exceptions to 'the practical maxim that the business of society can be best performed by private and voluntary agency'.[12] Yet he grants that in particular circumstances of time and place

there is scarcely anything really important to the general interest which it may not be desirable, or even necessary, that the government should take upon itself, not because private individuals cannot effectually perform it, but because they will not

—he lists roads, docks, harbours, canals, navigation, hospitals, schools, colleges, even printing-presses. He adds, however, an essential condition, that all such intervention be undertaken in a manner which will 'encourage and nurture any rudiments it may find of a spirit of individual exertion', removing obstacles and providing facilities and guidance. Thus he adheres consistently to his principle of the educative function of government (pp. 18ff., above), insisting that, as far as possible, any assistance should be given as 'a course of education for the people in the art of accomplishing great objects by individual energy and voluntary co-operation'.

Mill's objections to government interference can be summarized as follows. Fundamental was his stand on the principle of individuality and the urgent need, as he saw it, to preserve inviolate the entrenched circle of personal freedom. Closely related was his firm belief that private effort is usually more effective—and shows itself so when in direct competition with public agency; the reasons are clear: the former has superior motivation in personal interest and responsibility, superior knowledge and judgement arising from a more intimate involvement. Even if this were not so, private enterprise, both individual and co-operative, would still be justified by its educative (or *self*-educative) force, which is an essential part of 'the peculiar training of a citizen'[13] (see above, pp. 30–2). Further, while government action tends to uniformity and represents only the average, 'with individuals and voluntary associations . . . there are endless experiments and endless diversity of experience'.[14] Mill's distrust of power and his aversion to bureaucracy have already been noted; since power was suspect in itself, its concentration in government must 'be regarded with unremitting jealousy'[15]—even in a democracy, for the depressive influence of mass opinion and majority rule is as hostile to individuality as any despotism. Moreover, he feared that by undertaking too much the administrative machine (Mill's phrase) might be clogged by its own superfluity so that things were 'ill done, much not done at all because the government is not able to do it without delays which are fatal to its purpose'.[16] Finally, government agency requires compulsory taxation which in turn requires a proliferation of expensive and onerous restrictions to prevent evasion.[17]

Intervention in education is clearly justified by the criteria Mill here proposes—consumer ignorance, protection of the weak, public interest—as well as by the general principle of utility; and in both *Principles* and *On Liberty* he picks it out as an obvious exception to the principle of non-interference, but only, as will be seen, with strict safeguards. We shall now consider in detail his justification of this exception, the dangers he thought it involved, and the limitations he wished to impose on it.

There is no doubt that in the early 1830s Mill gave much thought to education and followed with close attention the attempts to urge Parliament and public opinion towards state responsibility for providing it. He had long been convinced of the importance of education; this, of course, was an important element in the utilitarian creed to which he had been exposed from childhood, but it had now become an integral part of his own thinking. The evidence is clear in his writings of this period, for instance in the essays 'On Genius' and 'Civilisation' where he proclaims the value of education (rightly conceived) as a creative force, a means to truth, to intellectual vigour, to strength of character. The same concern appears in his 'Notes on the Newspapers', contributed to *The Monthly Repository* in 1834, where he comments specifically on educational policy and the discussion of it in Parliament.[18] It is seen also in his letters: 'Nous travaillons toujours à la cause de l'éducation', he writes to Victor Cousin (the French philosopher and educationist for whom he has been trying to procure the Reports of the National and the British and Foreign School Societies), and he commends Roebuck for his 'nouveau discours [of 1834] encore meilleur que le premier'.[19] And already at this time one notes his sensitivity to the religious issues involved and his commitment, lifelong and unremitting, to a sectarian system free from religious tests and denominational control.

At this stage in his life Mill fully accepted the need for universal education; he was inclined also to accept a degree of state involvement, though he was still uncertain, so it would seem, as to what the manner and the nature of that involvement should be. His father had long ago declared himself, tentatively and on balance, in favour of state intervention despite its dangers—'it is still so very great and good to have the whole facility of reading and writing diffused through the whole body of the people, that we should be willing to run considerable risks for its acquirement'.[20] John shared this view of the value of literacy: it was the necessary means to the creation of an informed and critical populace which could counter the abuses of government; moreover, such a populace, educated to greater self-awareness and self-control, would limit its procreative efforts and thus reduce the size of its families and the degree of its poverty; a reduction in crime was another looked-for consequence; further, the spread of knowledge and enlightenment was good in itself as constituting a potential for improving the quality of human happiness, and this (as he had learnt from his nervous crisis) was far preferable to any quantitative proliferation of vulgar pleasures.

For the moment, however, such hopes seemed far from fulfilment; existing provision of elementary education was inadequate in both quantity and quality (and in the latter respect at higher levels too, not least at the universities of Oxford and Cambridge against which Mill directed his most scathing criticism.) 'The diffusion even of merely nominal education', he writes in 'Notes on the Newspapers', 'has been greatly exaggerated; few persons are aware how large a portion of our people are still destitute of any means of instruction whatever.'[21] Nevertheless, in mere number of schools it was not impossible for provision to match the needs of the population if existing funds were intelligently managed; this, at least, is the hope expressed in his review of a report on the state of public instruction in Prussia, compiled by Victor Cousin and translated into English by Mrs. Sarah Austin:

The £20,000 granted by Parliament last year [1833] for building schoolhouses called forth private contributions of nearly treble the amount. Independently of all this, we have the immense endowments which the charity commissioners have brought to light and proved to have been for generations embezzled and wasted. As far, therefore, as *quantity* of teaching is concerned, the education of our people is, or will speedily be, amply provided for.

He continues: 'It is the *quality* which so grievously demands the amending hand of government. And this is the demand which is principally in danger of being obstructed by popular apathy and ignorance.'[22]

He emphasizes the same point in a notable passage in 'Notes on the Newspapers' which follows the sentence quoted on page 113: 'The mere *quantity* of teaching is a secondary consideration to the *quality*; and that we believe to be, for the most part, more thoroughly bad than anyone without facts before him would dare to conjecture. We believe this to be true of all ranks and all branches of education alike.' Lecturers at the newly founded University College, London, have amazed him by their accounts of the ignorance of the youths who go there from the grammar and public schools; even worse are the elementary schools for the children of the working classes:

They scarcely even profess to aim at anything more than teaching words; and words out of a book. No attempt is made to communicate ideas or call forth the mental faculties. The mind of the teacher is never once brought into contact with the mind of the child. An automaton could do all that is done by such teaching, and all that they are qualified to do. . . . School-houses may be had, or money to build them; all the 'properties', the mere instruments of teaching may be complete; even books, though of them there is a sad deficiency, may be provided. . . . But it is not brick walls, nor instruments, nor books, nor dead matter that is wanting; mind must be taught by mind. . . . Even if we were to think with the vulgar that anyone who knows a thing can teach it—even so the bulk of the existing schoolmasters could teach nothing, for they know nothing; no *thing*, no *words* even, except the very words set down in their books. They cannot make their scholars what they themselves are not[23]

—a percipient statement of educational truth whose full import even yet eludes our grasp.

It was the deficiency in quality that especially, in Mill's view, called for state intervention. To remedy this it was necessary to raise up 'an improved race of schoolmasters'; hence he commends the proposal to establish 'Normal Schools' whose work would include the training of teachers. 'This is', he writes, 'at once the most important step towards a national system, and a good in itself of inestimable value.' Even without building any more schools, if 'we educate teachers for the existing schools to a standard greatly exceeding the present average, we shall, by this single measure, change the whole character of the education of the country'.[24] A further reason, again involving a demand for quality, but of life as much as of education, appears in a later item of 'Notes on the Newspapers'. Except for the very poor, people can acquire for themselves the skills necessary for a trade or for family life; professional training can be left to 'the competition of the market', save where the public need protection against incompetence, as with doctors and teachers:

But all instruction which is given, not that we may live, but that we may live well; all which aims at making us wise and good, calls for the care of Government: for the very reason given by the Lord Chancellor, that the majority have neither the desire, nor any sufficient notion of the means, of becoming much wiser or better than they are.[25]

(This pronouncement echoes Roebuck's view that it is the duty of a government 'directly to promote good'; it has profound implications not only for formal education but also for the whole intellectual, moral and leisure life of any community; *prima facie* at least it conflicts with the principle of non-interference which is central to *On Liberty*, and thus raises the problem of crucial importance discussed above, pp. 109ff.).

It is clear from the 'Notes' and from the review of Mrs Austin's translation of Victor Cousin's report that at this period of the 1830s Mill was favourably inclined towards state intervention in education. Already noted in the former is his welcome for the provision of teacher training; in addition he strongly advocates the appointment of a commission to inquire into the state of education and hopes that Roebuck will propose it to Parliament (in fact it was proposed, and carried, as an amendment to Roebuck's proposal of 3 June 1834; see above, p. 108, note 4).[26] 'A State never educates', he avers in the 'Notes', 'except by the general spirit of its institutions. But it can instruct; and by instruction it can not only form the intellect but develop the moral perceptions.' Indeed he knows of 'no branch of the general culture of the mental faculties which is not a fit subject for a State provision'—a bold statement, surely, for his time.[27] The review (published shortly after the appointment of the committee of inquiry) praises Mrs Austin for 'the force and conclusiveness with which [she] combats the shallow opinions and groundless feelings which oppose themselves in this country to a national education'.[28] In an earlier brief notice of the translation he had commended her sensitive handling of the issue of compulsion: 'We English', he writes, 'are great haters of compulsion' except where we are used to it:

To compel a man to toil and fight on board ship is a camel which we can swallow: to compel a parent to have his child instructed is a gnat at which we strain. Habit reconciles us to the one, and our sense of property makes us hate the other. '*My* children shall be taught or not as *I* please.'[29]

National education is the 'highest and most important of all the objects which a government can place before itself', and the value of Cousin's report lies not so much in the details of organization which it describes as in the fact 'that the thing is actually done; done within two days' journey of our own shores'.[30] Unfortunately the spirit which has accomplished it in Prussia is still to be created in England. But it was not only in Prussia that it was actually being done: it should not be forgotten that for several years previously Mill had been closely associated, through his work at the India Office, with the development of an educational structure in India (see above, pp. 54–6); the preparation of his many advisory drafts and the discussion of them with his superiors must surely have sharpened his perception of the educational needs of the populace in his own country and inclined him towards accepting state intervention as the proper means of satisfying them.

There is little that is original but much that is noteworthy in Mill's observations at this time on the state and education. One must commend especially (and there *is* perhaps here a genuine note of authenticity) his emphasis on the quality of education: he is right to insist that it is not primarily buildings and their material contents that impart education (though these do, of course, make their contribution) but men and women—'mind must be taught by mind'. The importance of teacher training (or teacher education, as we now require) follows necessarily from this; again Mill is right in pointing to it as fundamental. Notable also is his demand that the state concern itself not merely with life but with the good life; that beyond the provision of basic educational needs lies a vast potential for personal satisfaction and fulfilment, for intellectual and moral growth which only the resources of the state can make fully available; notable indeed, but also controversial, for although the principle is now widely accepted (for instance, in subsidies to the arts, to libraries and to sport), some would argue, on economic, political, and even strictly educational grounds, against the assumption by the state of such far-reaching responsibility for its citizens' welfare. It might also be argued that his attitude to compulsion as expressed in the review is inconsistent with his resolute defence in *Principles of Political Economy* and *On Liberty* of the principle of non-interference; but the inconsistency is more apparent than real, for in these later works he makes a specific exception of education: it 'is one of those things', he writes in the former, 'which it is admissible in principle that a government should provide for the people. The case is one to which the reasons of the non-interference principle do not necessarily or universally extend.' He makes a similar comment in *On Liberty*: 'Is it not almost a self-evident axiom that the State should require and compel the education, up to a certain standard, of every human being who is born its citizen? Yet who is there', he adds, 'that is not afraid to recognise and assert this truth?' There is no change of view here.[31]

Mill's support for state intervention should not be taken to imply too much. Roebuck's Resolution had called for 'universal and national education of the whole people'—which still left open the extent of the state's responsibility, the manner of its intervention and important questions of how children should be compulsorily educated and to what standard (for which he had his own answers), and 'national education' is a phrase no less elusive and question-begging than is 'comprehensive education' today. Probably Mill had no more in mind for the moment than compulsory schooling for all children, especially the very poor, sufficient to ensure minimum standards of literacy and behaviour; this would be assisted and supervised by the state but *provided* only as needed, that is where voluntary effort fell short; it entailed, of course, a certain indispensable machinery of organization including a minister, grants, supervision of expenditure, and facilities for teacher training, but nothing approaching the complex and enormously costly educational systems of our own age.

Nor should it be assumed that his support for 'national education' was without doubts or reservation. In a letter to Victor Cousin prior to his review of the report on Prussian education he anticipates difficulty in persuading the public to accept compulsion, at least without specific concessions to democratic devolution of power; referring to Roebuck's 1833 speech (a copy of which he is now sending to Cousin) he writes:

Vous verrez qu'il donne à l'élection populaire le choix des instituteurs primaires. Vous mettrez peut-être cela sur le compte du radicalisme; mais radicalisme ou non, je crois que, dans notre pays, où la centralisation n'est nullement dans les moeurs, c'est là le seul moyen de faire accepter par la nation l'éducation forcée.

In the following year he writes of religious opposition to compulsion—'le système coërcitif effraie surtout nos sectaires religieux'— though the public, he can now say, 'l'a assez bien accueilli'.[32] A brief remark in his review of Professor Sedgwick's *Discourse* on studies at Cambridge appears to cast doubt on the very principle of state assistance to education: 'To educate common minds for the common business of life, a public provision may be useful, but is not indispensable: nor are there wanting arguments, not conclusive, yet of considerable strength, to show that it is undesirable.'[33] Competition, individual interest, and the need for effort to secure reward may be more productive, he suggests, than government supervision and security of pay. (However, he may be referring here strictly to the *provision* of schools rather than to financial support and a general superintendence.) To Cousin he repeats the opinion, expressed already in his review of the report, that financial aid is unnecessary if existing funds are properly used: 'En fait de fonds, les anciennes dotations suffisent, dès que le gouvernement les reprend d'entre les mains de mandateurs infidèles, qui les gaspillent sans pitié'—he has in mind the charity schools and those endowments which provide for non-existent schools.[34] Strangely, one fear which greatly troubled him later, namely the possible abuse of a state system to impose indoctrination, seems not to have caused him much disquiet at this time; but the germ of it is apparent in 'Civilisation' where he attacks the conception of education, deep-rooted (as he believes) in the English mind, as a means of inculcating opinions and creating not inquirers but disciples.[35]

Mill's attitude to state intervention remained fundamentally the same for the rest of his life: he accepted its necessity, indeed its inevitability as the government became increasingly and inextricably involved in education; however, there is perceptible on the one hand an extension and consolidation of his reasons for acceptance, and on the other a growing awareness of the dangers of a national system. *Principles of Political Economy*, written in the 1840s shows clearly his conviction of the economic value of popular education: it contributes to a country's wealth by increasing its potential of industrial skill at the middle management and supervisory levels; it improves the quality of labour by elevating it from mere habitual memorized routine to an intelligent activity incorporating some element of imagination and initiative—and thus producing higher output for the same expenditure of energy. No less important is its effect on character in inducing practical and moral qualities—good sense, sound judgement, prudence, and self-restraint, all of which contribute to higher standards of work and productivity. They also contribute to improved labour relations: mental subjection and uncritical obedience to authority have no place in Mill's conception of industrial democracy; the working class must increasingly be regarded, and encouraged to regard themselves, as equals within the industrial (and wider) community, while retaining respect for genuine superiority of knowledge and skill; they must learn, and be equipped, to cooperate with management and among themselves; such a situation requires an informed, self-disciplined, self-respecting working class, 'rational beings' capable of independent judgement. To achieve this there must be 'an effective national education'.[36] The choice is now clear, he asserts: it is 'between interference by government and interference by associations of individuals subscribing their own money for the purpose'. Certainly, nothing should be done through taxation that is 'already sufficiently well done by individual liberality'; but it is his conviction that even in quantity voluntary provision

is, and is likely to remain, altogether insufficient, while in quality, though with some slight tendency to improvement, it is never good except by some rare accident, and generally so bad as to be little more than nominal. I hold it therefore the duty of the government to supply the defect by giving pecuniary support to elementary schools, such as to render them accessible to all the children of the poor, either freely or for a payment too inconsiderable to be sensibly felt.[37]

Such an emphatic statement leaves no doubt of his commitment to state intervention—though with reservations which will be considered shortly. There is a significant new idea, consonant with

Mill's general view of education, which should be noted, namely the *self-education* of the people: it is they who must progressively assume responsibility for their own mental and moral cultivation; it is a process which is already spontaneously at work (encouraged by newspapers, political tracts, lectures, organized discussions, and trade unions), and which can be greatly accelerated by the provision of formal schooling.[38]

Another reason for popular education which assumed prominence in Mill's thinking was the need for minimum standards of literacy and numeracy to justify universal suffrage. Power must lie ultimately in the hands of the people through some form of representative government which, at its best, would grant the vote to all—but *not* unconditionally; the right to power depends on the ability to use it beneficially and this in turn on education:

None are so illiberal, none so bigoted in their hostility to improvement, none so superstitiously attached to the stupidest and worst of old forms and usages as the uneducated. None are so unscrupulous, none so eager to clutch at whatever they have not and others have as the uneducated in possession of power.

He concludes that 'no lover of improvement can desire that the *predominant* power should be turned over to persons in the mental and moral condition of the English working classes'.[39] Political power must therefore be 'the reward of mental improvement':

I regard it as wholly inadmissible that any person should participate in the suffrage without being able to read, write and, I will add, perform the common operations of arithmetic. . . . Universal teaching must precede universal enfranchisement.[40]

As a consequence the vote itself would be held in higher esteem, 'a trust for the public good' rather than an instrument of self-interest.[41] (These words were written in the late 1850s, but Mill had made the same point much earlier in a review article of 1835, 'The Rationale of Political Representation': universal suffrage cannot be seriously considered 'unless preceded by such improvements in popular education as will greatly weaken the apprehensions at present entertained of it'.)[42] It follows, of course, in justice that the minimum educational requirements for the franchise should be readily accessible to all, either freely or at an expense that the poorest can afford.[43]

Mill mentions two further reasons for state intervention and hints at a third; none is as central to his thinking as the two just discussed. In the de Tocqueville article of 1840 he expresses deep concern at the possible dominance in English society of 'the commercial spirit'. It appears to be a fact of human civilization, he argues, that a prolonged and exclusive preponderance in a culture of any one element, however initially beneficent, eventually destroys that culture. Commerce and industry have been a source of unprecedented human improvement, but if they are allowed to dominate unbalanced by other beneficent influences, there will commence 'an era either of stationariness or of decline'. Such a danger exists in England, and it is the duty of politicians and teachers to foster whatever 'in the heart of man or in his outward life' can act as a salutary check on excessive commercialism. There is a special task here for men of genius in all its forms, but Mill also hopes that 'there would also gradually shape itself forth a national education which, without overlooking any other of the requisites of human well-being, would be adapted to this purpose in particular' (he does not say how this might be done).[44] Another desirable area of intervention is assistance to research and learning: clearly there is much valuable scientific research which makes demands in cost and time beyond the reach of all but the very few who happen to combine independent means with the necessary ability and motivation; government has a duty here 'to grant indemnity for expense and remuneration for time and labour thus employed'. It also has a duty to promote scholarship either by direct financial assistance or by the appropriation of endowments:

The cultivation of speculative knowledge, though one of the most useful of all employments, is a service rendered to a community collectively, not individually, and one consequently for which it is *prima facie* reasonable that the community collectively should pay.[45]

Intervention of this kind is, of course, far removed from the promotion of a national system as Mill conceived it; but it is now universally acknowledged to be a responsibility of government. Finally, in his article 'Centralisation' Mill suggests a further role for government in compensating the inequities, both natural and artificial, which handicap the race of life: 'In racing for a prize the stimulus to exertion on the part of the competitors is only at its highest when all start fair'; at present this is not so, and if the state does nothing to help the weaker, the handicap becomes a crushing and dispiriting burden.[46] The implications for education are obvious and (though he does not specifically refer to them) can hardly have been lost on him; a national system of education providing a minimal level of instruction hardly amounts to equality of opportunity as it is now understood, but together with social policies aimed at alleviating poverty and the pressure of toil it would do something, Mill clearly hoped, to create a fairer start to the race.

Thus he found ample justification for excepting education from the general principle of non-interference which he enunciates in *Principles of Political Economy* and *On Liberty*. However, although his conviction of the need for state intervention in education remained unshaken, indeed was strengthened, with the passage of events, he became increasingly sensitive to its dangers and was emphatic in his assertion of them. He admits that government teachers are likely to be 'superior to the average of private instructors', but the latter can also contribute to the common fund of educational skills and wisdom; in any case variety is valuable in schooling and 'it is desirable to leave open as many roads as possible to the desired end'.[47] Experiment too is valuable: in his 'Endowments' article of 1869 he cites Cornell University whose '"eccentric" provision' that every student must work for his living might not have received government endorsement, had this been necessary; and he defends endowments, other grounds apart, as providing opportunity for 'divergence from the common standard', stimulating discussion and forcing a reconsideration of the merits of established practices and opinions.[48] In 'Centralisation' he makes the general point, which he would surely extend to education, that increasing government responsibility curbs voluntary initiative; this latter is both an educative force in itself and is likely to be more successful than government agency which represents only the average; to suppose, he adds, 'that the average of society is better than any individual in it . . . is both a mathematical and a moral absurdity'.[49]

However, his principal fears are of indoctrination and the suppression of individuality; these are forcibly expressed in two notable passages in *Principles of Political Economy* and *On Liberty*:

It is not endurable that a government should, either *de iure* or *de facto*, have a complete control over the education of the people. To possess such a control, and actually exert it, is to be despotic. A government

which can mould the opinions and sentiments of the people from their
youth upwards can do with them whatever it pleases.

And from *On Liberty:*

That the whole or any large part of the education of the people should
be in State hands I go as far as anyone in deprecating. All that has been
said of the importance of individuality of character and diversity in
opinions and modes of conduct involves, as of the same unspeakable
importance, diversity of education. A general State education is a mere
contrivance for moulding people to be exactly like one another: and as
the mould in which it casts them is that which pleases the predominant
power in the Government, whether this be a monarch, a priesthood, an
aristocracy or the majority of the existing generation, in proportion as it
is efficient and successful, it establishes a despotism over the mind, leading by natural tendency to one over the body.[50]

Carried too far, state intervention puts into the hand of government a potent instrument for reducing its citizens to a pliant
servitude of patterned conformity, for exercising a mental and
physical despotism which destroys freedom, initiative and that
diversity which is both an essential ingredient of civilized life and,
with the other two, vital to human improvement. Whether these
fears were exaggerated the reader must judge for himself in the
light of recent history and of contemporary experiments in mass
indoctrination. Nor is Mill's warning without relevance to our
own situation of steadily increasing public control of education
and the elimination by legal or fiscal means of educational institutions which cannot or will not be incorporated into the state
system.

Because of his fears Mill wished to impose strict limitations on
the State's powers and responsibilities in education. He drew a
clear distinction between the right to *enforce* and the right to *direct*
education. The former he did not question: the government is
justified, he writes in *Principles* 'in requiring from all the people
that they shall possess instruction in certain things' (a belief he had
long held, of course).[51] *On Liberty* elaborates the point: essentially
it is the parents' duty to ensure that children are educated for their
part in life; to neglect this sacred trust is 'a moral crime both against
the unfortunate offspring and against society'; but if parents cannot or will not accept the obligation, the state must.[52] Ten years
later, when the 1870 Act was looming into sight, he wrote to a

correspondent: 'a thorough system of instruction for the whole country we must have; and I do not see anything short of a legal obligation which will overcome the indifference, the greed, or the really urgent pecuniary interest of parents'.[53] However, enforcement is one thing, direction is another; the former is acceptable, the latter is not. Thus, though the government may require education, it must not prescribe how or from whom it shall be obtained. To fulfil its obligations (in the absence or failure of voluntary effort and 'as the less of two great evils'), it may need to provide schools and colleges, but 'it must neither compel nor bribe any person to come to them'.[54] It must claim no monopoly of provision at any level: state education 'should only exist, if it exist at all, as one among many competing experiments, carried on for the purpose of example and stimulus, to keep the others up to a certain standard of excellence';[55] and private establishments should not be required to have government authorization. Neither the certification nor the appointment of teachers should be under direct government control: the former could be effected by independent examining bodies the latter by local committees.[56]

His basic position is succinctly stated in the letter of 1868 quoted above: what he understands by compulsory education is

that all parents should be required to have their children taught certain things, being left free to select the teachers, but the sufficiency of the teaching being ensured by a government inspection of schools and by a real and searching examination of pupils.[57]

Public examinations, conducted by or under the supervision of the state, Mill envisaged as the principal instrument for enforcing a compulsory level of educational attainment: starting 'at an early age' and confined initially to testing reading ability, they would be repeated annually and extended in range to ensure not only the acquisition but also the retention (an important point) of a minimum of general knowledge. There would be fines for parents whose children failed the reading test at the prescribed age.[58] But Mill is evidently thinking of something more than simple literacy and suggesting that the state's responsibility extends further to promoting informed citizenship and the desire for knowledge. Beyond the compulsory requirement there should be voluntary examinations in all subjects and certificates of proficiency for those who pass them. Here too Mill is sensitive to the potential dangers;

hence he insists that 'to prevent the State from exercising, through these arrangements, an improper influence over opinion' the examinations must be 'confined to facts and positive science exclusively'. In such controversial areas as religion and politics examiners would be concerned with the truth and falsity not of opinions but of facts, that is 'that such and such an opinion is held, on such grounds, by such authors, or schools, or churches'. With this proviso there need be no bar on the teaching of religion if parents so wished. At the highest academic and professional levels of examination the dangers are so great that the state must be excluded from any part in them.[59] Payment for education Mill regarded as a proper charge on parents who could afford it; this is the view expressed in, for instance, *Principles of Political Economy, On Liberty* and much later in a letter to Henry Fawcett approving his speech at the first conference of the National Education League: 'I, like you, have a rather strong opinion in favour of making parents pay something for their children's education when they are able, though there are considerable difficulties in authenticating their inability.' Economic considerations apart, perhaps he felt (as have others since) that education is, and should be regarded as, a commodity valuable enough to pay for and that what is free tends to be undervalued.[60]

Mill's interest in education did not abate during the later years of his life; that it was a constant part of the under-current of his thought is clear from passages already cited from *On Liberty, Representative Government* and elsewhere; significantly, too, education was the theme of the *Inaugural Address* of 1867. There is further abundant evidence in the *Later Letters* which cover the years from 1849 to 1873. Here we find him commenting and advising on a wide range of educational topics—teaching methods and curriculum, part-time schooling, religious and moral education, indoctrination, punishment, the public schools, universities, the education of the working class and numerous other matters. He writes to Herbert Spencer thanking him for a copy of his *Education* which 'is full of things well worth saying and contains hardly anything with which I disagree'.[61] To T. H. Huxley he writes refusing active support for a proposed International Education Society and questioning its policy on the teaching of theology; there are in any case more urgent improvements required in education, especially (he explains in a later letter) 'improvements in the *mode* of teaching'.[62] In a letter to an unidentified correspondent he praises Thomas Arnold, headmaster of Rugby, for his practical reforms, notably for his attempts to foster 'moral ambition' in his pupils and his example of 'friendly intercourse between masters and scholars'.[63] Acknowledging a pamphlet on spelling reform he deplores the standard of reading achieved in government aided schools: it should not take a child seven years, at the best learning period of his life, to learn to read—'so great a waste of time only proves the wretchedness of the teaching'.[64] To another correspondent he writes on the value of aesthetic education, commenting on the influence upon himself of his holidays with the Benthams at Ford Abbey and of the familiarity gained there with tapestries from Raphael's cartoons 'which peopled my imagination with graceful and dignified forms of human beings'; there is, he adds, 'a great want of this training of the perceptions and taste in our modern societies'.[65]

It is evident from these volumes of *Later Letters* that Mill's views on education were respected and consulted by private individuals both lesser and greater; nor, characteristically, did he refuse his advice save where his ignorance forbade—I am not qualified, he writes to one anxious mother, 'to advise concerning the education of those of whom I have no personal knowledge'.[66] A pleasant example is his reply to a schoolboy who wished to submit an essay on flogging for a competition in the *Boy's Own Magazine* and who sought his advice 'written in your usual clear, lucid manner'. 'To give a proper answer to your question', Mill writes back, 'would be to write the essay which you are intending to write'; he therefore makes two brief points, allowing the occasional need for corporal punishment but preferring 'any other mode of punishment that would be effectual'.[67] A Revd. Stephen Hawtrey, one-time senior mathematics master at Eton, sent him two small books he had published for private circulation; one was about a school at Windsor which he had founded in 1851 and of which he was late warden; the other, *Reminiscences of a French Eton*, was written to supplement (so the author states) Matthew Arnold's *A French Eton*. In the latter (pp. 8–9) Hawtrey expressed dissent from Mill's statement in the *Inaugural* that 'it is beyond the power of schools and universities to educate morally or religiously'. With his customary courtesy Mill thanks him and commends his strictures on the excessive supervision characteristic of French schools and his belief that 'real education depends on "the contact of human living soul with human living soul" '. But courtesy could not deflect him from the truth, and he continues:

> While I applaud both your theory and your practice, I have the less hope of finding my opinion radically altered by them because you seem to me to regard Eton as a favourable specimen of what a school can do in the way of moral and religious training; an opinion from which all that I know of the kind of article turned out annually from Eton into the higher walks of life in this country leads me strongly to dissent.[68]

With this broad and informed interest in education there went a growing concern for and involvement in the movement towards a universal national system. This too is clearly shown in the *Later Letters*. His conviction of the need for compulsory national education, indicated above from a letter of 1868 (pp. 123–4), is confirmed in others. He notes the rapid progress of the National Education League whose two basic principles 'that elementary education should be compulsory and the State Education should be undenominational are striking root deeply into the mind of the nation'; since he has 'held the first opinion for many years and the last always', he is of course delighted.[69] Working class politicians, he writes to Gustave d'Eichthal, suffer from a certain 'étroitesse de vues' which is due to 'le défaut d'instruction générale et surtout de connaissances historiques'; it can be remedied only gradually by 'le progrés de l'enseignement populaire'.[70] He commiserates with an Italian friend who had recently resigned from the Ministry of Public Instruction in protest at cuts in educational expenditure: 'education is the last of the public interests' that should suffer thus, he writes (anticipating a frequent modern complaint).[71] As state intervention became increasingly an established reality so his comments were extended to specific items of schooling, organization and legislation. His friend Edwin Chadwick had submitted to the Newcastle Commission a lengthy report, based on his own inquiries, in which he produced evidence for the advantages, first, of part-time schooling for child workers, second, of what he calls 'administrative consolidation' and the 'combination of local educational means', and, third, of what was known at the time as 'military drill'. After reading the report Mill wrote to Chadwick to say how much he was impressed by the 'irresistible weight of evidence' he had furnished on the first two points, 'the equality, if not superiority, in attainment and intelligence of the short time pupils over the others; and the immense advantage, both in efficiency and economy of large over small school districts'. On military drill he expressed hesitancy in a later letter, fearing that it might 'make the majority of boys wish to be soldiers'.[72]

In February and March of 1862 *The Times* published a number of leaders praising the Revised Code which had been presented to Parliament in the previous year—'an immense and urgent necessity' one of them had called it.[73] This was a revision, as the name indicates, of the system of distributing government grants to schools; it is regularly associated with Robert Lowe, then Vice President of the Committee of Council on Education, the body responsible for formulating the grant regulations. Mill thought well of the leaders; on this issue, he wrote to the American historian J. L. Motley, and on the need for competitive examinations for the Civil Service they seemed to be ahead of public opinion.[74] His support for the Code may well surprise, for it included the principle of payment by results, which educational progress has long since abjured and which one might reasonably suppose to be contrary to Mill's own cherished ideals of individuality and of quality in education. Far from rejecting the principle, however, he positively advocates it: in his article 'Endowments' he admits as just the fear 'that the teacher's duty will be idly and inefficiently performed if his remuneration is certain. . . . But where is the necessity that the teacher's pay should bear no relation to the number and proficiency of his pupils?' This 'real principle of efficiency in teaching', he continues, 'is easily applied to public teaching'.[75] Mill was not blind to the frailty of human nature, nor was he unwilling, in a far from perfect world, to resort to the stimulus of competition and market forces (see above, pp. 31–2).

He comments also on a Scottish Education Bill of 1854, welcoming its introduction by the Government and regretting its rejection by the Commons; in 1869 he deplores the refusal of the Lords to expedite a later Bill—'they are becoming a very irritating kind of minor nuisance' he writes of the Upper House to his friend Alexander Bain.[76] Of special interest are his comments on the 1870 Education Bill which finally established a national system for England and Wales.[77] In a letter to Sir Charles Dilke he describes it as 'the nearest approach now possible to a surrender of English education into the hands of Denominationalism'. If it passes unaltered, he adds (with a significance deepened by subsequent events) 'the effect will be doubly mischievous in Ireland'. To Edwin Chadwick he insists on the importance of 'a skilled central initiative' to balance the influence of the local School Boards which are likely to be dominated by middle class interests. Finally, when the Bill became law, he writes of the great interest excited by elections to the School Boards, noting with delight the election of two women to the London Board and several others elsewhere. One result of the Act, he believes, may well be a great extension of elementary instruction among the children of the poor: 'How much more will be taught or how well time must show; but no real friend of popular education regards this Education Act as a final measure.'

If Mill had still been in the Commons when the Bill was introduced, he would surely have contributed to the debate, commending with the same forthright conviction as in his writings the principle of a national compulsory system but condemning the denominationalism which the Government was forced to concede to the Churches. However, his Parliamentary career which had begun (somewhat unexpectedly) with his election for Westminster in the summer of 1865, ended abruptly three years later. Strangely, he spoke little on education during his years as an M.P., and for the most part indirectly while debating other issues. This was not for lack of opportunity, for a number of Bills relating to education were introduced, including the Elementary Education Bill of 1868 which was withdrawn at the second reading; but for much of his time in Parliament he was deeply preoccupied with the Representation of the People Bills of 1866 and 1867 on which he spoke often and sometimes at length, and later with an Electoral Practices Bill. In one of these speeches he pleaded for working class representation on the grounds that this, more than anything else, would accelerate the provision of popular education; in a very few years, he declared, 'there would be in every parish a school rate, and the school doors freely open to all the world; and in one generation from that time England would be an educated nation'.[78] At the committee stage of the next Bill, in the course of a long speech on female suffrage, he complained of the mere lip-service paid to the education of girls:

We continually hear that the most important part of national education is that of mothers, because they educate the future men. Is this importance really attached to it? Are there many fathers who care as much, or are willing to expend as much, for the education of their daughters as of their sons? Where are the Universities, where the high schools, or the schools of any high description, for them? If it be said that girls are better educated at home, where are the training-schools for governesses? What has become of the endowments which the bounty of our ancestors destined for the education, not of one sex only, but of both indiscriminately?[79]

In a debate on the Civil Estimates in July 1867 he emphasized the need for technical education and commended the practice in other countries of offering it as 'a reward for the good use of the advantages of elementary education'; thus pupils might be induced to work harder at school and remain longer—but not only the abler children, he adds: the less proficient must also be encouraged to stay on and reap the full benefits of schooling.[80]

His most direct Parliamentary involvement was at the committee stage of the Public Schools Bill.[81] This Bill was a consequence of the Clarendon Commission which had been appointed to investigate nine leading public schools; its report, published in 1864, criticized adversely their curricula, teaching methods and administration; the Bill was aimed at remedying the defects of the schools by changes in their constitutions and the application of their endowments. Mill spoke five times during the debates. Three of these contributions were *ad hoc*—a suggestion for including the Head and Provost of Eton among its Governors, a comment on the misuse of endowments by the Fellows of the school, and another comment on a proposal for giving elementary attainment tests to all pupils at the schools included in the Bill (the previous speaker had remarked that 'at Harrow a pupil might go out with honours in Greek and Latin without knowing the multiplication table'). His most significant contributions (albeit brief) were on a theme which concerned him deeply, the proper use of endowments. It was, he said, 'one of the most scandalous abuses connected with endowed schools . . . that the endowments intended for the education of children of parents who could not afford to pay for their education, had been in fact confiscated for the benefit of those who could afford to pay for it'. So patent were the abuses that the working classes were themselves aware of them and were beginning to claim their rights; for although the schools under debate existed to impart 'the highest class of education', an education unsuited to *all* the children of the lower middle and working classes, 'the *élite* of these classes' had indeed a right to that kind of education—and it could be made available to them by a just administration of existing endowments. Mill had further occasion for expressing his indignation on this theme, as we shall see below (pp. 135ff.).

Mill's reputation, his known concern for education, and his special interest in particular aspects—endowments, sectarian issues, the education of women and of the working classes—led to many requests for his advice and practical assistance, not only from private (as noted above), but also from official and semi-official sources. It seems that he was asked by John Chapman, editor of *The Westminster Review*, for an article on national education, but he felt unable to write it 'in the present stage of the discussion' (this was in 1861)[82]. In 1869 he was invited by the Birmingham and Midland Counties Institute to serve as their President for the following year, but since he had no time for writing presidential addresses, he was 'obliged to decline all proposals of that nature' (evidently there had been others).[83] He admits to a single exception in accepting the Rectorship of St. Andrews (to which in fact the students had elected him without his prior consent, and the address was postponed for a year); one can well understand that addresses on the scale of the *Inaugural* could hardly be a frequent exercise. In 1870, after the passage of the Education Act, he received at least two invitations, one from the Southwark Radical Association, to serve on School Boards; but again he was too busy and in any case felt that such work did 'not lie in my speciality'.[84] In one association he had a particular interest, the National Education League, to which reference has already been made (p. 127), and whose principle of 'universal and compulsory unsectarian education' coincided precisely with his own views. In a letter to Sir Charles Dilke (28 February 1870) he expressed himself 'desirous of helping it by some expression of opinion, but I have not yet made up my mind how I can best do so'.[85] The opportunity came a month later when, at a London meeting of the League, he delivered a long speech supporting a motion which condemned the clauses of the Education Bill allowing School Boards to found denominational schools at the public expense and welcomed Gladstone's assurance of amendment (pp. 159–60 below).

Mill's views on religion in education and on the crucial issue of religious teaching will be considered in the next chapter. Meanwhile there are three other topics which, though important to Mill and highly controversial at that time, can be dealt with more briefly. His passionate attachment to equality of the sexes led him inevitably to advocate, both in his writings and (as already noted) in Parliament, the cause of female suffrage and equality of educational opportunity for girls. The two are, of course, interdependent, but Mill gave prior place to the former, believing that, if women achieved access to political power, the demand for unrestricted access to educational resources would follow as a necessary consequence. Thus he argues in a letter to Florence May (later a teacher of music at Queen's College, London, and a student and biographer of Brahms); and writing to Alexander Bain he notes that 'one effect which the suffrage agitation is producing is to make all sorts of people declare in favour of improving the education of women'.[86] The importance of female education is argued in 'The Enfranchisement of Women' (1851) and *The Subjection of Women* (1869, but written in 1861): there are no grounds, he asserts, for supposing that women are constitutionally so different from men as to be unsuited for broadly the same education and the same range of occupations; such natural differences as exist are complementary to, even corrective of, the aptitudes of men; other differences are due to social conditioning by which their nature has been 'greatly distorted and disguised'.[87] He further supports his argument by pointing to the injustice of socially approved male domination; to the moral influence of women both in the family—wives on husband, mothers on children—and in society at large; to the competitive stimulus educated women would exercise on men; to the need for a greater national reserve of intellectual power; to the degradation of the marriage relationship by the existing inequality between man and wife; to the enormous gain in personal happiness and liberation of potential that would come from offering women equality of opportunity with men. He concludes:

High mental powers in women will be but an exceptional accident, until every career is open to them and until they, as well as men, are educated for themselves and for the world — not one sex for the other.[88]

A national system of *elementary* education must clearly include girls as well as boys, as did the schools already provided by the voluntary societies; this was a matter of simple practical logic on which all parties were agreed. Beyond the elementary stage (whose precise age-limits were not yet determined) girls were still, and likely to continue to be, greatly disadvantaged. There was no question yet (in the 1850s) of compulsory *secondary* education or of state provision to ensure its availability; such schools as existed for older pupils were almost exclusively for boys, principally the public schools and the endowed grammar schools. There was however, a strong case for state intervention to stop the mis-appropriation of endowments, many of them originally intended for the education of both sexes and now confined to boys. This was recognized by the Taunton Commission (officially the Schools Inquiry Commission, appointed in 1864), part of whose task was to investigate the use (and misuse) of endowments and whose report formed the basis of the Endowed Schools Act of 1869. It was seized on by Mill in his article in *The Fortnightly Review* of April of that year: common justice requires that endowments be used equally for the education of both girls and boys; since 'in the eyes of the law and of the State, one girl ought to count for exactly as much as one boy', and since 'as members of society, the good education of women is almost more important than even that of men', it is essential that education provided from endowments should be available to both sexes 'without preference or partiality'.[89] (Oddly, this advice was not included in his paper submitted to the Schools Inquiry Commission; on which see below.) In itself secondary education for girls, if it could be secured, was not enough; they must have the same access as boys to educational tests and qualifications, including degrees. Thus in a letter of 1863 he welcomes the admission of girls to the newly established Cambridge Local Examinations. In the previous year he had written to Henry Fawcett (a prominent supporter of women's rights) on the success of a recent conference of the National Association for the Promotion of Social Science at which a paper had been read on 'Female Education, and how it would be affected by University Examinations'; after this, he suggests over-optimistically, the admission of women to degrees is 'almost *une cause gagnée*'. In 1870 he wrote to Alexander Bain of the need to admit women to a full medical education, including the right to graduate in medicine and to practise.[90] Finally, one can find in Mill's letters some interest in co-education as a possible means of bringing together, for their mutual benefit, the complementary natures of the sexes; in one especially, to Pasquale Villari, the Italian Under-Secretary for Education, he seems to suggest that co-education will be the necessary and desirable outcome of the movement for female education.[91]

Among the official requests made to Mill was one for advice on a proposal to introduce selective examinations for the Civil Service; the request was natural in view of his own long and distinguished service at India House, during which it had been a part of his responsibility to advise on establishing a native civil administration (see above, pp. 54–6). His recommendations were published as a Parliamentary Paper in 1855.[92] Although to many this would seem a matter simply of organization and efficiency, for Mill it also involved important educational considerations of which, in his view, the state should take cognizance. There were the obvious advantages, as he saw them, of appointment by proved merit and impartial judgement instead of patronage, and of consequent improvement in competence and efficiency; clearly the public service must gain by the appointment to it 'of the most intelligent and instructed persons'—mediocrity has no place here. But this is not all: competitive examination would provide a great stimulus to 'mental cultivation' which is desirable both on its own account and as enlarging and elevating the students' minds—and whatever does this 'adds to their worth as human beings'. Furthermore, this mode of appointment, by merit instead of favour, would have its impact on the population as a whole, 'a great and salutary moral revolution descending to the minds of almost the lowest classes,' by providing an example at the highest level of impartial recognition of attested ability.

Opponents of the proposal argued that it would transfer patronage from the Crown to a body of examiners; on the contrary, Mill replies, the examiners' decision is not patronage but a judicial act, expert and impartial. Again, they objected that 'Public Offices will be filled with low people, without the breeding or the feelings of a gentleman'; but surely, Mill retorts, gentlemen's sons are as capable as any others of reaching the required standard; if they are not, and if they have neither the energy, nor the public spirit, nor the sense of honour to qualify themselves, they do not deserve the positions they now hold and there is 'a strong case for social changes of a more extensive character'. More significant was the argument that a book-based literary examination would not test the moral and practical abilities required in public servants; but, Mill replies, as well as literature the examination will include science and its applications and a candidate's specialism in any field of knowledge; further, examinations at that level test not only book knowledge but also 'powers and habits of mind'; as for moral qualities, though an examination cannot test them directly, it can do so indirectly by requiring steady application and strength of purpose; in any case, 'a well cultivated intellect will seldom be found unaccompanied by prudence, temperance and justice, and generally by the virtues which are of importance in our intercourse with others'. There is an important difference, he adds, between competitive and non-competitive examinations; the latter require only a minimal competence and, however low this is pitched, 'good nature interferes to prevent it from being rigidly enforced against any but absolute dunces; whilst the other candidates are willing to encourage and applaud this relaxation of duty, and even to connive at frauds on the part of the incompetent'. On the other hand, competition to find the best qualified provides in itself some protection against fraud, favouritism, and laxity. Mill's last point is questionable, but what is important in his argument is its acceptance of educational implications wider than mere efficiency —the moral impact on the populace of an example of impartiality, of substituting merit for favour; the intellectual and moral effect on candidates themselves; the salutary jolt to the privileged classes of applying the principle of equality of opportunity. All this is entirely in keeping with his commitment to a positive role for the state in education, with his conception of the educative function of government, and with his ideal of the educative society.

Another official request came to Mill from the Schools Inquiry Commission (under Lord Taunton), seeking his advice on certain matters arising from their investigation into endowed schools (other than the nine already examined by the Clarendon Commission). He was known to have a particular interest in endowments, and the request, so he wrote to Edwin Chadwick, was not unexpected; his reply, dated 9 August 1866, was included in the Commission's evidence.[93] His interest was far from recent; as early as 1833 he had published an article, 'The Right and Wrong of State Interference with Corporation and Church Property', in which he attacked the abuse and misappropriation of endowments, justified the right of the Government to intervene, and offered his own proposals.[94] Having established his case for intervention and the principles which should govern it, he argued strongly for diverting endowments to educational use: 'The primary and perennial sources of all social evil are ignorance and want of culture', and in remedying this there is 'a wide field of usefulness open for foundations [i.e. endowments]', not only schools and colleges, 'but every means by which the people can be reached, either through their intellects or their sensibilities, from preaching and popular writing, to national galleries, theatres and public games'. Notable in his defence of this proposal is his condemnation of the 'trading' principle in education, that is, the conduct of schools for profit: this, he argues, encourages idleness and deception in teachers and lowers standards by 'the necessity of keeping parents in good humour' and of teaching down to the level of their unenlightened demands. Nineteen twentieths of the unendowed schools, he declares, are 'an organised system of charlatanerie [*sic*] for imposing upon the ignorance of parents' (not, he admits, that most of the existing endowed schools are in much better plight). This should not be understood as an attack on private education as such, which he came to regard as a necessary counter to state intervention in education, but on its perversion by commercialization; 'trading authors' are subjected to the same condemnation.

To uphold *quality* in education it is essential to have at least some educational institutions which are free of the trading principle, and endowments can provide them. Ultimately, the emergence of an educated populace could make endowments unnecessary by conceding the right of a wise government to provide such institutions from taxation; as yet there is no assurance of this; meanwhile 'it is only by a right use of endowments that a people can be raised above the need for them'.[95] The same insistence on quality appears in his 'Notes on the Newspapers' in *The Monthly Repository* of the following year:

Unless we would become a nation of mere tradesmen, endowed institutions of education must exist. There must be places where the teachers can afford to teach other things than those which parents (who in nine cases out of ten think only of qualifying their children to *get on* in life) spontaneously call for. There must be places where those kinds of knowledge and culture which have no obvious tendency to better the fortunes of the possessor, but solely to enlarge and exalt his moral nature, shall be . . . *obtruded* upon the public.[96]

It appears again in his review of Professor Sedgwick's *Discourse*, where he argues for endowed universities as providing (or capable of providing) an education which, because independent of popular demand, can form 'great minds' with 'aspirations and faculties above the herd'; and a few years later, when he praises Coleridge's notion of 'an endowed class for the cultivation of learning and for diffusing its results among the community'.[97] Similar considerations apply to literature: in an *Examiner* article he argues the need to release authors from the pressure of mediocrity by offering them financial subsidy. Some writers seek 'merely to amuse'; for their products there is a ready market and a sure reward. Others there are

who endeavour to educate ...: to batter down obstinate prejudices; to throw light on the dark places; to discover and promulgate ideas which must be meditated for years before they will be appreciated; to form mankind to closer habits of thought; to shame them out of whatever is mean and selfish in their behaviour; to elevate their tastes; to inspire them with nobler and more beneficial desires; to teach them that there are virtues which they have never conceived, and pleasures beyond what they have ever enjoyed.

Since their educative value is great and their financial return uncertain, they deserve public provision—not so much as a reward, but 'to be kept alive while they continue to enlighten and civilise the world'.[98] No doubt Mill would wish to extend such assistance to music and other forms of art just as he does in *Principles of Political Economy* to exploration and scientific research.

There is little space for comment on these earlier views of Mill before moving on to the 1860s. One must applaud his stand for an education which is not bound to simply 'getting on' and which elevates by means of activities and experiences which have their own intrinsic worthwhileness. Also noteworthy is his clear recognition of a state responsibility for education which justifies intervention to the extent of diverting endowments to education and the promotion of cultural activities; having gone thus far he could hardly hold back from committing the state to a wider intervention —which he virtually concedes in envisaging the possibility of supporting education from taxation. Perhaps, it may be objected, he assumes too easily that release from the trading principle and its concomitant parental pressures would achieve the cultural elevation he hoped for. A similar assumption has been made in our own time in the expectation that a state system of schools, and more recently of comprehensive schools, would inevitably raise the general level of education and culture among the populace. As indeed it has; but we have learnt that, as in Mill's day, parents can still, and do, exert a powerful and often anti-educational influence; that the pressures of a malign social environment can frustrate the best endeavours of any school; and that government economies and the resistance of rate-payers can enforce a trading principle as disastrous as that of parents who buy their children's education.

In April 1869 Mill published another article on endowments at a time when the Endowed Schools Bill had already begun its passage through Parliament (the Second Reading was on 15 March).[99] Clearly the situation was now very different: government intervention to secure a proper use of endowments, especially for education, and to enforce universal elementary education was at last generally accepted. Indeed, a danger now was of excessive intervention and government monopoly; he therefore stresses the need for variety and experiment: endowments, if not abused, can supply 'a precious safeguard for uncustomary modes of thought and practice', keep alive discussion, and protect from subservience to conformity (echoes here of *On Liberty*, published ten years before). In education, he again insists as in the earlier article, the essential question is one of *quality*; thus he enlarges his attack on private schools and on the trading principle which subdues them to the level of parental bread-and-butter aspirations; he upholds the role of competition in education, pointing out, however, that there can be competition in fraudulent pretence as well as in excellence; and he concludes by arguing firmly for endowed schools *in addition to* fee-paying schools. 'It must be made the fashion to receive a really good education', and parents must themselves be educated into demanding it; to this end it is essential to provide models of such education within easy reach of all parts of the country; endowed schools, under government supervision, can serve this purpose by supplying 'places of education with the *prestige* of public sanction, giving, on a large and comprehensive scale, the best teaching which it is found possible to provide'. There is an important proviso, however, that endowed schools should not subsidize those who can pay for education but should especially cater for the most able children of the poor, who have proved their capacity for secondary education by their performance at elementary school; such a policy (in line with the proposals of the Taunton Commission), by allowing access to education by merit instead of payment, would be of immense social benefit: 'I believe,' he writes, 'there is no single thing which would go so far to heal class differences and diminish the just dissatisfaction which the best of the poorer classes of the nation feel with their position in it'. And of course, as already noted (p. 133), girls must be included on equal terms with boys.

In contrast with these two articles Mill's evidence to the Commission was brief and restricted to the specific questions put to him:[100] these were, first, the expediency (in endowed schools) of continuing to give free education to the pupils and fixed incomes to the teachers; second, the best method of managing endowments and preventing their misuse; third, the possibility of diverting to educational purposes endowments now being wasted; fourth, the best means of securing sufficient qualified teachers. His answer to the first is clearly predictable from what has already been said: he believed in payment according to results tested by examinations (p. 128 above); endowments should be devoted primarily to assisting the children of the poor, and others only to improve the quality of education beyond what they might otherwise afford. In answer to the second he recommends regular inspection, local school committees working in conjunction with representatives from the Privy Council, and the merging of smaller schools into larger in order to secure more efficient teaching, better qualified teachers, and economies both in inspection and more generally. On wasted endowments he recommends that the many small trusts at present doled out to the supposedly necessitous should be diverted to education, lack of which he believed to be the principal cause of the indigence the trusts misguidedly sought to relieve. Finally, on the supply of teachers, which he acknowledges to be the crux of the whole matter, he accepts the suggestion of the Commission that there should be 'training schools' where teachers would learn 'not only the things they will have to teach, but how to teach them; for which purpose these training schools must of course be connected with schools of the ordinary kind, where the art of teaching may be practically acquired'. He agrees that Holy Orders should no longer be required of teachers in endowed schools, and that teachers should be certificated either by the universities or by some other approved body. He adds a recommendation that a teacher's promotion should depend on proved competence tested by the results of his teaching, the best guarantee of efficiency being 'the assured prospect of removal in case of incompetence proved by experience'; successful reform of endowed schools, he affirms, rests 'upon the degree of certainty which can be given to this expectation'—a somewhat harsh note on which to conclude this survey.

The present chapter began with the statement that Mill's lifetime coincided almost exactly with the establishment of a national system of education in England and Wales (and, it can be added, in Scotland too, where a similar system was introduced by an Act of 1872). An obvious question is how much Mill contributed to this outcome. Directly, not a great deal, if by that is meant political involvement and formal proposals for legislation; from this he was debarred until his retirement from the India Office in 1858, and by that time he had before him an immense programme of writing which he had planned with Harriet before her death. Even during his years in Parliament he was preoccupied with other matters which in his view were prior in importance to universal education because a necessary foundation for its success (notably, of course, a just and representative franchise). However, he can be fairly described as an important theoretical contributor to the practical movement for educational reform, increasing its momentum by his firm pronouncements, in numerous reviews and articles, in major and lesser writings and in his personal correspondence, on the crucial importance of education and on its proper purposes and methods. All this was further enhanced by his growing reputation as a man of outstanding intellect and high integrity. Although inclined at first to rely on the redirection of endowments to supply an adequate educational provision, he yielded to the logic of the situation by conceding and eventually wholeheartedly supporting state intervention in compelling and, as far as need be, providing education. At the same time he assisted clarity of thought and intention by firmly distinguishing the legal enforcement of a minimum educational attainment from total government direction and provision. Of special significance were his attack on unthinking resistance to compulsion simply as such (p. 116 above), his assertion of the social and economic value of education (particularly in regard to the labouring classes) (pp. 119–20) and its necessity for the growth of individual potential (chapter 5), and his exclusion of education from the general principle of non-interference with personal liberty (above, pp. 110ff.). Nor should we overlook his insistence on inspection, teacher training, efficient organization of schools with a due balance of local initiative and central supervision, and his advocacy of equal opportunity for girls (pp. 132–4). In addition there is his constant emphasis on the moral purposes of education and on quality as opposed to mere quantity whether of information absorbed or of schools provided. (A notable and unhappy exception to this otherwise laudable contribution is his support for payment by results as set out in the Revised Code—an error which, excusable at a time when a teaching profession and a professional morality as we know them scarcely existed, he would have quickly acknowledged had he lived to observe its effects on teachers and pupils.) In short, by clarifying issues, by justifying principles, by recognizing the compulsion of fact he did what is to be expected of a good theorist and at the same time gave direction and impetus to the work of others by his own dedicated commitment to education.

# 7

# Religion and Education

MILL IS not uncommonly regarded as a resolute opponent of religion, a freethinking rationalist who was unsympathetic to Christianity and immovably hostile to the Church. This was certainly the opinion of some of his contemporaries: when his *Examination of Sir William Hamilton* was published in 1865, a passage on the deity prompted the editor of one journal to charge him with 'atheism in a form the most revolting' he had ever met with; another described him as 'chief of the Satanic School in England at present'. (In contrast, it should be noted, *The Spectator* wrote of the same passage as 'the true language of prophets and apostles', and Mill himself in a letter referring to these charges claims that there is not a single passage in his writings which 'conflicts with what the best religious minds of our time accept as Christianity'.)[1] In part this view may be due (at the present time, at least) to a failure to distinguish between father and son—the sternly analytical James who distrusted emotion and regarded religion 'with the feelings due not to a mere mental delusion, but to a great moral evil', and the sensitive, imaginative John, whose mental crisis had forced him to acknowledge the necessity of 'the internal culture of the individual'.[2] Partly it arises from ignoring changes in Mill himself: for his attitude to religion was mollified in his middle and later years by the influence of Coleridge and Comte, who made him aware of its psychological and historical aspects, and by the shock of Harriet's death which is reflected, one feels, in the role he assigns to hope and imagination within the perceptibly more reluctant scepticism of 'Theism'.[3]

Superficial justification for this view of Mill can be found in a number of passages throughout his writings. For instance, in the essay on Coleridge he rejects contemptuously the bibliolatry, the 'superstitious worship of particular texts, which persecuted Galileo and, in our own day, anathematised the discoveries of geology'; 'this slavery to the letter' has not only paralysed many an effort to present Christianity as a consistent doctrine, it has resulted also in a sophistical manipulation of the scriptural text 'in order to reconcile what was manifestly irreconcilable'.[4] No less repugnant to him is dogmatism, the ossification of living personal experience into empty verbiage; it is thus that 'so many doctrines of religion, ethics, and even politics, so full of meaning and reality to first converts' have collapsed into lifeless formularies which have no impact on conduct.[5] Especially abhorrent to him was the social and political expression of Christianity, particularly of the Established Church, as he saw it in Victorian England: he condemned the Church for using religion to prop up the *status quo*—'a grand instrument for discouraging all culture inconsistent with blind obedience to established maxims and constituted authorities'; he condemned it, too, for abusing endowments, which, properly regarded, were a trust for 'the spiritual culture of the people of England'.[6] Nor was he convinced that contemporary Christianity was conducive to moral improvement: in a letter of 1850 he asks:

How can morality be anything but the chaos it now is, when the ideas of right and wrong, just and unjust, must be wrenched into accordance either with the notions of a tribe of barbarians in a corner of Syria three thousand years ago, or with what is called the order of Providence —in other words, the course of nature, of which so great a part is tyranny and iniquity?

In another, of 1867, he expresses delight in 'finding an existing Church, or branch of a Church, who are actually Christians'.[7] In the *Autobiography* he deplores 'the obstinate prejudice' that unbelief is necessarily accompanied by faults of character: the best of unbelievers, he unhesitatingly affirms, 'are more genuinely religious, in the best sense of the word religion, than those who exclusively arrogate to themselves the title'.[8]

Utterances of this kind could hardly fail to alienate ecclesiastical orthodoxy. Even more offensive, however, were his strictures on the Deity, which were interpreted (not without reason) as undermining the very citadel of Christian theism. It was Mill's passionate belief, lifelong and consistent, that benevolence and omnipotence were irreconcilable attributes in the creator of such a world as this:

It is impossible that anyone who habitually thinks, and who is unable to blunt his inquiring intellect by sophistry, should be able without misgiving to go on ascribing absolute perfection to the author and ruler of so clumsily made and capriciously governed a creation as this planet and the life of its inhabitants.[9]

His father's scepticism had been founded on the same basis, inexpugnable as it seemed to them both, and as John points out in the *Autobiography*, it was fundamentally a moral, not a logical or intellectual stand.[10] It is a conspicuous fact that the world, both natural and man-made, imposes on its inhabitants a vast amount of suffering; clearly, 'if the maker of the world *can* all that he will, he wills misery, and there is no escape from the conclusion'.[11] There is no defence in the argument that the divine purpose in creation was not happiness but virtue and justice, for in these too the world is notoriously lacking. Surely, then, if God is omnipotent, he is not benevolent; if he *is* benevolent, his power is limited. To pretend otherwise 'not only involves absolute contradiction in an intellectual point of view but exhibits to excess the revolting spectacle of a jesuitical defence of moral enormities'.[12] This was the point forcibly made in the *Hamilton* passage referred to above: that the divine attributes were infinite but beyond our knowledge he was prepared to accept with resignation, but at the same time to reverence such a God in terms 'which express and affirm the highest human morality', this he refused to do:

Whatever power such a being may have over me, there is one thing which he shall not do: he shall not compel me to worship him. I will call no being good, who is not what I mean when I apply that epithet to my fellow creatures; and if such a being can sentence me to hell for not so calling him, to hell I will go.[13]

Some years later, when first standing for Parliament, he was confronted with that final audacious assertion on the hoardings of Westminster: he was elected nevertheless.[14]

This is not the place for a detailed examination of Mill's views on religion, nor of their development (for which see the article referred to in note 3): the purpose of these introductory paragraphs is to sketch out the scene for a survey of his ideas on religious teaching and its place in educational institutions. However, there is a positive and constructive side to these views which has not yet been made apparent. First, he did not wholly reject the possibility of God's existence. In 'Theism', after considering and dismissing three of the common arguments, he presents a fourth 'of a really scientific character';[15] it is the familiar argument from design in nature, but based here, not on analogy (as in Paley's famous watch on the desert island) but, so Mill believed, on a genuine induction. His conclusion is that 'the adaptations in Nature afford a large balance of probability in favour of creation by intelligence'—but, he adds immediately, *only* a probability. Second, he concedes that, 'granting the existence of design, there is a preponderance of evidence that the Creator desired the pleasure of his creatures', for pleasure is the normality of things and pain the intrusion of external interference or accident; but this can hardly have been his sole or dominant purpose—if it was, it has so far proved 'an ignominious failure'. Third, since the combination of benevolence with omnipotence is morally untenable, it can only be that God (if he exists) is a benevolent being, of great, possibly infinite, knowledge, but of limited power—how or by what limited is beyond conjecture. Thus he inclines, like his father, to a dualistic or Manichaean account of the universe as an arena of opposition between good and evil powers, in which man himself can be 'a not ineffectual auxiliary' of the good, 'a fellow labourer with the Highest'; or to Plato's conception of intelligence working with given, resistant materials as in the *Timaeus*.[16]

As for Christ, Mill could not, of course, accept his divinity, but for Jesus the man, his manner of life and his ethical teaching he had the profoundest respect. He would not, he writes in a letter of 1861, 'willingly weaken in any person the reverence for Christ, in which I myself very strongly participate'.[17] In *On Liberty* this reverence is tempered by the assertion, essential for the purpose of the essay, that the interests of truth, ethical no less than any other, 'require a diversity of opinions'.[18] There is qualification too in 'Utility of Religion': the teaching of the Gospels can be paralleled in the *Meditations* of Marcus Aurelius: it is mixed with 'poetical exaggeration' and its maxims are sometimes obscure. Nevertheless, the authentic sayings of Jesus are of such nobility that they surely cannot 'be forgotten or cease to be operative on the human conscience while human beings remain cultivated or civilized'.[19] In 'Theism', however, his praise is virtually without restriction: while still denying that Jesus was God—a claim, Mill asserts, that he never made for himself and would have regarded as blasphemous anyway—he allows the possibility that Christ was 'a man charged with a special, express and unique commission from God to lead mankind to truth and virtue'. For there is in his life and sayings a stamp of personal originality combined with profundity of insight, which . . . must place the Prophet of Nazareth . . . in the very first rank of the men of sublime genius of whom our species can boast. When this pre-eminent genius is combined with the qualities of probably the greatest moral reformer, and martyr to that mission, who ever existed upon earth, religion cannot be said to have made a bad choice in pitching on this man as the ideal representative and guide of humanity.[20]

Mill's view of religion is infused and moulded by the same moral concern which is conspicuous throughout his life and writings. He was convinced that morality was not dependent on religion, either logically or in practice: the utilitarian ethic had a solid foundation in 'the social feelings of mankind, the desire to be in unity with our fellow-creatures', and if these were taught 'as a religion' and reinforced by education, institutions and public opinion, the 'happiness morality' would have all 'the psychological power and the social efficacy of a religion'.[21] What he looked for, therefore, was a secular religion, independent of God and any supernatural accoutrements, and superior to conventional religion in that it was intellectually and morally consistent and untainted by hope of reward hereafter. Thus, assisted by Comte, he was led to the conception of a 'Religion of Humanity' whose motivating force, drawing on emotional sources of sympathy and benevolence, would be the vision of a united and perfected humanity, embracing the best of the past as well as ideals not yet realized. Such would be a genuine religion, embodying the essence of all religion—

the strong and earnest direction of the emotions and desires towards an ideal object, recognised as of the highest excellence, and as rightfully paramount over all selfish objects of desire.

And it would issue naturally in good works.[22]

Increasingly Mill had come to appreciate the value of religion both for society and for individuals, a process which had begun, he tells us in the *Autobiography*, with his reading of a book written by George Grote (under the pseudonym Philip Beauchamp) 'on the foundation of some of Bentham's manuscripts'.[23] Socially religion has in fact been a powerful educative force, though its influence, he suggests, has been due more to its early impact on children than to its being religious: it has also been a source, but not the only one, of authority and moral sanction; but to perform these roles it does not, he argues, require supernatural or metaphysical support. For individuals religion satisfied urgent psychological needs: human existence is a tiny island in an infinity of space and time; the universe is 'girt round with mystery' which baffles all curiosity as to its origin and its destination—'what would one not give for any credible tidings from that mysterious region, any glimpse into it which might enable us to see the smallest light through its darkness?' Further, in the imperfection of life as it is man has 'a craving for higher things'; he needs the satisfaction and inspiration of 'ideal conceptions grander and more beautiful than we see realised in the prose of human life'. Religion meets both these needs, but once again it can dispense with supernaturalism:

Apart from all dogmatic belief, there is for those who need it, an ample domain in the region of the imagination which may be planted with possibilities, with hypotheses which cannot be known to be false; . . . the contemplation of these possibilities is a legitimate indulgence, capable of bearing its part, with other influences, in feeding and animating the tendency of the feelings and impulses towards good.[24]

The Religion of Humanity is enough.

Thus far he takes us in 'Utility of Religion'; but already there is a noticeable softening of his attitude towards conventional religion. In 'Theism', written ten years later than 'Nature' and 'Utility', he moves further in this direction, though still without abandoning his objections to supernaturalism; one reason, no doubt, was the lingering impact of Harriet's death, for her memories still lived for him in the house at Avignon and in the person of his step-daughter and constant companion, Helen Taylor. We have already noted his admission of the probability of creation by intelligence, and even of benevolence in the creator. This concession to probability appears elsewhere in 'Theism'; for instance, in discussing immortality he allows that science provides no positive argument against the separate existence of the soul and its immortality, and he warns against regarding empirical *a posteriori* conclusions as if they had *a priori* validity. So (perhaps with Harriet in memory) he writes:

A flower of the most exquisite form and colouring grows up from a root, comes to perfection in weeks or months, and lasts only a few hours or days. Why should it be otherwise with man? Why indeed? But why, also, should it *not* be otherwise?

Nor is there anything 'so inherently impossible or absolutely incredible' in the Christian revelation as to preclude at least the *hope*—'I go no further'—that it may be true.[25] Conspicuous too in 'Theism' is the role he allows to hope and imagination. Something of this has already appeared in 'Utility'; he had already granted there that 'religion may be morally useful without being intellectually sustainable', and that 'the scepticism of the understanding does not necessarily exclude the Theism of the imagination and feelings'.[26] In 'Theism' he holds still that 'the rational attitude of a thinking mind towards the supernatural . . . is that of scepticism' —a scepticism either way, both for and against; and he is unyielding in his rejection of omnipotence combined with benevolence.[27] However, the limitations of human life stand greatly in need of the elevating inspiration of imaginative ideals—provided they run counter neither to fact nor to reason. Where the latter is allowed due authority, 'the imagination may safely follow its own end, and do its best to make life pleasant and lovely'. Hope too has an elevating influence: it gives strength and solemnity to our feelings for our fellow-creatures; it allays the sense of human insignificance, 'the disastrous feeling of "not worth while"', the pained frustration when the good is destroyed before its fruition; it provides incentive for the improvement of character to the very end of life. Together, hope and imagination offer us the concept of a morally perfect Being as a standard for the regulation of our own lives:

And it cannot be questioned that the undoubting belief of the real existence of a Being who realises our own best ideas of perfection, and of our being in the hands of that Being as the ruler of the universe, gives an increase of force to those feelings beyond what they can receive from reference to a merely ideal conception.[28]

Thus does Mill peer beyond the frontiers of scepticism into a promised land from which he had previously withheld his gaze.

Clearly, he was not the unsympathetic, uncompromising antagonist of religion that he has sometimes been pictured. There is much in his unbelief that is (in his own words) 'more genuinely religious' than the orthodoxy of his time, much that (as *The Spectator* comments) mirrors 'the true language of prophets'.[29] There is even something reminiscent of Christ himself in his denunciation of sophistry, hypocrisy, and Pharisaism in contemporary Christianity. What he stood for was 'a religion of *spirit* not of *dogma*', a religion of high altruism, of uncompromising moral and intellectual integrity, yet touched with sympathy, humility, and a sense of mystery.[30] His was no harsh scepticism but an honest acceptance of the authority of reason and of the limits of knowledge; like Locke he was inclined to be content with 'a quiet ignorance of those things which, upon examination, are found to be beyond the reach of our capacities'.[31] Moreover, twice in his life he underwent a 'conversion experience'; the first, at an intellectual level, was to Bentham's utility principle which gave him 'a creed, a doctrine, a philosophy, in one among the best senses of the word, a religion'.[32] The second, his nervous crisis, shook the depths of his being, released in him forces hitherto suppressed, and was marked by many of the features described by William James in his *Varieties of Religious Experience*. In the month of Mill's death H. R. Fox Bourne wrote of him in *The Examiner*:

If to labour fearlessly and ceaselessly for the good of society, and with the completest self-abnegation that is consistent with healthy individuality, be the true form of religion, Mr. Mill exhibited such genuine and profound religion—so permeating his whole life and so engrossing his every action—as can hardly be looked for in any other man of this generation.[33]

In our own century Edward Alexander has described his life as one of 'secular spirituality'. These are judgements from which, in the opinion of the present writer, it is impossible to dissent.[34]

On the teaching of religion in educational institutions Mill says little directly; what he says is clear and consistent with his opinions on religion itself. He disapproves of doctrinal teaching of Christianity; thus in a letter to T. H. Huxley he declines to associate himself publicly with a proposed international school in London because theology is to be included in the curriculum—'for assuredly I do not think that theology should be taught in any school.'[35] Many years earlier, in a letter to W. J. Fox who at that time was preparing a draft Bill to promote compulsory secular education, he condemns it as useless any way, since such 'stupid *doctrines* . . . generally lie dead in the minds of children'.[36] His objection extended equally to both sectarian and non-sectarian teaching; politically, in view of the part played by the churches in providing schools, it might be necessary to concede undenominational doctrinal teaching in a national system; it was undesirable, however, because it was authoritarian and an affront, therefore, both to children and to truth; it was *indoctrination* in the pejorative sense of the word.[37] Religion cannot be known to be true, and it is wrong to impose it on children as if it were. Dogmatic, authoritarian teaching not only stifles the openness of inquiry which is essential to the discovery of truth; it denies to pupils the right and the dignity of choice. Therefore,

> I do not think it right either oneself to teach, or to allow anyone else to teach, one's children, authoritatively, anything whatever that one does not, from the bottom of one's heart and by the clearest light of one's reason, believe to be true. It seems to me that to act otherwise on any pretext whatever is little if at all short of a crime against one's children, against one's fellow creatures in general, and against abstract truth in whatever form it appears most sacred to one's eyes.[38]

Of course, many Christians, as well as adherents of other religions, would protest that what they proclaim *is* the truth, imparted to mankind by divine revelation and to themselves by inspired insight. It could be so, Mill would reply, but there can be no rational certainty; in any case, if the churches want doctrinal teaching, the place to provide it is within their own precincts, not in schools, and this is a task which they are perfectly competent to perform.

What he wanted was *secular* education. By this he did not mean 'non-sectarian' or 'non-denominational', for such would still include the doctrinal teaching to which he objected. He explains his meaning in a brief address on secular education written in 1849 but not, apparently, delivered.[39] Its occasion was the formation of the Lancashire Public Schools Association, whose purpose had initially been stated as 'the establishment of a general system of secular education in the county of Lancaster'; later, it seems, 'non-sectarian' was substituted for 'secular' and in his address Mill attacks this change. Secular, he explains, is 'whatever has reference to this life. Secular instruction is instruction respecting the concerns of this life. Secular subjects therefore are all subjects except religion'. Secular does not mean *ir*religious but *non*-religious, though the two have been deliberately confused for political ends. He continues: 'Education provided by the public must be education for all, and to be education for all it must be purely secular education.' Clearly, this must exclude doctrinal and denominational teaching; it must also exclude religious tests for teachers—a form of discrimination which was abhorrent to Mill and led him to distrust any sort of state certification of teachers (see above, p.

124).[40] It would also seem, on the face of it, to exclude religion in any form from the curricula of schools, certainly in any national system; this interpretation is supported by the letter to W. J. Fox, referred to above, which was written in the same year and in which Mill asks whether it is 'not better even in policy to make the omission altogether of religion from State schools the avowed object'.[41]

If this is what Mill meant in his address, he changed his mind; for it is clear from what he writes elsewhere that he did not desire such a total exclusion of religious teaching. Previous to this, in *The Monthly Repository* of 1834, he had declared that 'no branch of the general culture of the mental faculties . . . is not a fit subject for a State provision'. He continues: 'When we say that instruction of all kinds, connected with the great interests of man and society, ought to be provided by the State, we by no means . . . except religious instruction.' In the present state of public opinion there are, he admits, formidable difficulties in providing any religious teaching 'as shall not be worse than none'; but these arise from 'the literal and dogmatic character and sectarian spirit of English religion'; they are not inherent in religious teaching. He then presents an argument based on a recognition of the facts of the contemporary situation: moral education is a necessary part of public provision; it must be such as not to clash with the moral convictions of the majority of educated people; in Britain these convictions are 'thoroughly interwoven with, and a great part founded upon, religion'; therefore, he concludes,

to exclude religious instruction is . . . to exclude moral instruction, or to garble it and deprive it of all systematic consistency, or to make it of a kind decidedly objectionable to the majority of the educated classes.[42]

At first sight this argument from expediency seems inconsistent with Mill's position on doctrinal teaching and with his severance of morality from logical and practical dependence on religion—indeed, a wholly uncharacteristic compromise with truth. Against this it can be suggested that he is here recognizing the facts of the contemporary situation; he does not deny the independence of morality, only that it is not in fact independent of religion in Britain then; if moral teaching is for the present unacceptable except in association with religious teaching, so be it; but the situation will change, and meanwhile there are possible safeguards in the manner and content of that teaching. It seems unlikely that Mill would wish to press this argument for religious instruction; he had others more convincing in themselves and more in line with his own thinking.

In the passage at the end of *On Liberty* where Mill discusses the permissible extent of the state's control of education and recommends a state-supervised system of examinations (above, p. 124), he proposes, first, compulsory tests for all children to ensure a minimum educational attainment, second, optional tests to encourage an extended range of knowledge. The latter might include religion, politics, and other controversial topics, but in these the tests would be confined to matters of fact. Obviously this implies that religion may be taught, and Mill says so: 'There would be nothing to hinder [children] from being taught religion, if their parents chose, at the same schools where they were taught other things.'[43] The state's responsibility would be to ensure that they were *instructed* churchmen or dissenters and that they possessed sufficient knowledge to make their opinions worthy of attention. The *Inaugural* allows the teaching of religion in both school and university (its audience did, after all, include theological students— but in any case Mill's attitude to religion was now far less stringent). It would be wrong, he suggests, to exclude from the curriculum a matter which has occupied so important a part of the nation's thought and of its intellectual labours; moreover, the purpose of university education is to provide the information and training which will enable students to form their own beliefs 'in a manner worthy of intelligent beings who seek for truth at all hazards'; the consequences of such belief for conduct are enormous and constitute a further reason for admitting religious teaching which, without dogmatism, offers information, argument, and opportunity for rational choice.[44]

Mill's justification of the teaching of religion may be summarized thus: historically and socially religion has close associations with morality and is a source of moral principles and motivation; it is an important part, however controversial and however dubious its evidential basis, of human experience (or at least of cultural experience in Europe), and a knowledge of it is therefore necessary to a liberal education; unrestricted access to and discussion of all areas of knowledge, including religion, are essential to intellectual freedom and autonomy of belief; they are also essential to the discovery of truth. Possibly he found further justification in that religion was not excluded from his own education; for although he was brought up 'from the first without any religious belief', and although his father impressed on him his own agnosticism as to the nature and origin of the universe, he 'took care that I should be acquainted with what had been thought by mankind on these impenetrable problems', and encouraged him to read ecclesiastical history and to take 'the strongest interest in the Reformation, as the great and decisive contest against priestly tyranny for liberty of thought'.[45]

We must ask now what Mill intended by 'religious teaching' and 'religious instruction'. Much of the answer has already been given or implied in the foregoing paragraphs, but it may be helpful to spell it out more positively. Evidently he had a poor opinion of existing teaching: in his review of the Cousin report on Prussian education he writes of 'the narrowing and perverting tendency of the religious instruction pretended to be given in our schools'; literalism, dogmatism, sectarianism are the charges he levels against it in the passage quoted above from *The Monthly Repository*; in his letter to Fox he doubts the efficacy of any moral instruction given in the same spirit as that of the present religious teaching— '*real* moral instruction', he adds, would be of inestimable value.[46] Mill would have religion taught as fact—not as truth, for in this context they are not the same: fact is open to question, further inquiry, further evidence; truth implies finality. It must be taught as knowledge to be acquired, not as a set of beliefs calling for commitment; it will use the language of statement, not of persuasion. Its content will be principally the history of religion, its institutions, its written records, its prophets and rebels, its great leaders; doctrine, even theology, may be included if taught as fact —what Christians actually believe—and as an occasion for reasoned argument and informed judgement. On teaching the Bible there is a brief letter which is sufficiently interesting to quote in full, for it anticipates remarkably criticisms and recommendations that have been made since 1944 about the Agreed Syllabuses and religious teaching in county schools:

I agree entirely with the general principles and spirit of your letter re-ceived yesterday. I think it highly desirable that the New Testament, and those parts of the Old which are either poetical or properly historical, should be taught *as history* in places of education; and so far my only difference with you would be that nearly all teachers, both churchmen and dissenters, being as yet far short of the enlightened views which you entertain on the subject, would at present be sure to teach and inculcate all that is contained in those books not as matter of history but of positive religious belief. There are, however, other parts of the Old Testament, viz. those which scientific knowledge or historical criticism have shown not to be, in any proper sense of the word, historical, the book of Genesis for example; and I do not think it right to teach these in schools even as history, unless it were avowedly as merely what the Hebrews believed respecting their own origin and the early history of the world.[47]

In short, Mill proposed a neutral teaching of religion as a human phenomenon, a fact of experience evidenced in individual and social life, an open possibility (but no more) for personal commitment; a teaching which made no assumption of supernaturalism, theism, or ecclesiastical authority.

In one respect only does he appear to go beyond this, namely in his plea for the religion of humanity and its educational implementation. He claims in 'Utility of Religion' that it is entitled to be called a religion and a better one than most so-called; in *Utilitarianism* he recommends (or, if this is too strong a word, forcibly envisages) that it be 'taught as a religion', supported by every educational influence and surrounded by the constant profession and practice of it, so that it might 'take hold of human life, and colour all thought, feeling and action'.[48] In this, religion (as Mill here understands it) is clearly linked with persuasion, and his neutral stance abandoned. Is not this inconsistency? Again, on the face of it, yes; but Mill would argue that his religion of humanity is founded on the happiness principle which is in turn founded on a universal human desire and on psychological factors deeply rooted in human nature; it is therefore thoroughly experiential, involves no appeal to the supernatural, and has a firm evidential basis which justifies a persuasive recommendation. It might also be said on his behalf that he is here using 'religion' in a sense peculiar to himself; that he is really talking about *moral* education in which he does accept the need for initiation into basic rules and principles (above, pp. 42–3); and that he would surely wish to apply here the proviso of openness and ultimate autonomy of decision.

Since Mill's time our understanding of religion has been greatly extended by anthropology and psychology and by studies in comparative religion; if he were alive now, there is much that he would wish to add to his proposals. Yet what he says is very much in line with recent changes in the policy and practice of religious instruction in this country. In the upsurge of Christian idealism which accompanied the later stages of the Second World War compulsory religious teaching (and worship) was written into the 1944 Education Act; the Agreed Syllabuses which implemented this were solidly Christian and biblical in content and tended to assume a Christian purpose within the school community. Hindsight has shown that this was naively optimistic: religion in schools is inevitably limited by the beliefs and expectations of heads, staffs, parents, and society at large; our society is increasingly secular in outlook, increasingly sceptical in belief; it follows that religious teaching, if it is to remain in county schools, must be distinguished from Christian evangelism and must justify its place in the curriculum, alongside other humanities like history and literature, on educational grounds, by reason of its intrinsic interest, its importance as an expression of man's response to experience, and (in our own still semi-Christian culture) as a source of moral values.

One further brief point: it could be argued that what Mill proposed (and what is now happening in English schools) is not *religious* teaching at all. W. D. Hudson in an article, 'Is religious education possible?', maintains, first, that religious discourse is logically constituted by the concept of god, a transcendent consciousness and agency; second, that the language of religion has certain inbuilt features which imply, for instance, trust, commitment, belief *in*, recommendation, and which distinguish it *as* religious. It follows that religious education is education into an understanding of the concept of god; and that since religious education must use the language of religion in describing religion, it cannot be held at a purely factual, descriptive level but must include some element or suggestion of persuasion.[49] If one accepts Hudson's view, one must doubt whether the adjective 'religious' is properly applied to Mill's proposals.

In a letter of 1869, quoted above (p. 127), Mill refers to two central principles of the National Education League, compulsory elementary instruction and an undenominational state education; to the former of these, he says, he has been committed for many years, to the latter always. As we have seen, he preferred that education should be secular, by which he intended not a total exclusion of religion but a presentation of it which would be factual and non-persuasive; this implied the exclusion of the churches, since their purpose was clearly missionary as well as educational. However, it was not only consistency with his own views that prompted his opposition to denominational participation in a national, state-supervised or state-provided system of education. The churches had been deeply involved in educational provision from the beginning of the nineteenth century; the two societies, the National Society and the British and Foreign School Society, which pioneered the way towards universal schooling and through which (from 1833) the Government grants were implemented in schools, represented respectively the Church of England and the Free or Dissenting Churches. From the start they had been, and had regarded themselves as, rival institutions committed to promoting not only education but also their own sectarian doctrines. This was an undesirable situation, damaging to the strictly educational objectives which they claimed to serve. W. J. Fox refers to it in introducing his Bill to the Commons in 1850; he complains that the Societies had made popular education subservient to their own (denominational) interests, with the result that 'parties avowedly engaged in the same work of instruction and enlightening the public mind, were continually quarrelling with each other'. Later he quotes from a manifesto issued by working class men in London and rejecting the apportionment of their children among the religious sects, thus fomenting 'those theological distinctions which already so unhappily divide mankind'. It continues:

We have now for several years been spectators of the dispute going on between the denominations on the subject of popular education. We have noticed that they all agree as to its urgent and imperative necessity; each party has vied with the others in eloquent descriptions of the frightful condition of the working classes. . . . We have sat still, expecting that the religious denominations, in holy charity and pity for our sufferings, would for once lay by their peculiarities, which they themselves confess are not essential to salvation, and agree upon some plan by which the resources of the State might be employed to rescue us from our awful condition. But we have waited in vain; the controversy has waxed hotter and more furious; our little ones have been forgotten in the fray, and their golden moments have been allowed to run irrecoverably to waste.[50]

After allowing for exaggeration and rhetoric there remains substantial truth in the charge.

These rivalries were as abhorrent to Mill as they were to Fox and the working men of London. He complains of them in 'The Claims of Labour' (1845): an unhappy consequence of religious liberty, they have so far thwarted attempts to maximize the benefits of schooling; on occasion a Church School has been opened solely to draw off children from an existing Dissenting School and thus ensure its closure; such a spirit of contention was intolerable to 'any person of honest intentions who knew the value of even the commonest knowledge to the poor'. He doubts the Churches' sincerity of purpose: there is no lack of finance for the support of schools, he asserts (dubiously, perhaps); what lacks is a 'sincere desire to attain the end'. He questions the teaching given in denominational schools: too often it is restricted by a fear of 'over-educating' the poor and must be disguised in the garb of religion; thus teachers are driven to ludicrous evasion in order to impart the rudiments of knowledge:

The four rules of arithmetic are often only tolerated through ridiculous questions about Jacob's lambs or the number of the Apostles or of the Patriarchs; and geography can only be taught through maps of Palestine to children who have yet to learn that the earth consists of Europe, Asia, Africa and America.

Anyone who supposes that this contributes to religious teaching or that children can understand the Bible while ignorant of all else is beyond the reach of rational argument.[51] And surely, he suggests in 'Secular Education', it is no compliment to Christianity to insist that mental cultivation must be accompanied by religious indoctrination; Christian truth does not need any such specious protection from the possibility of informed intellectual attack.[52] Another, and not the least, of his objections to denominationalism was its injustice to non-Christian minorities—Jews and agnostics, for instance—who were conscientiously unable to consent to instruction in Christian doctrine or (the latter) to religious teaching of any kind. Even if the Christian denominations could be reconciled, it would be but a compact 'to join in trampling on the weaker'; the result would be 'a national education not for all, but for believers in the New Testament'; this, clearly, was an affront to liberty of conscience and democratic choice.[53]

It was not only in England and Wales that denominationalism was a source of contention and an obstacle (as Mill saw it) to genuine educational advance. He was deeply concerned too about its impact in Ireland: here controversy raged over three issues: denominational schools, the disestablishment of the Irish Church (enacted finally in 1869), and universities.[54] His concern is expressed in a score of letters written between 1865 and 1872, a period which includes the three years when he was a Member of Parliament and therefore more closely and practically involved. A detailed discussion of the various issues would be out of place in the present context (see note 54); it will be sufficient to quote from this correspondence in illustration of Mill's view. 'I shall take my stand', he writes to J. E. Cairnes, 'against the denominational system in any form for Ireland':

No public assistance ought to be given in Ireland to any education involving more or other religious teaching than exists in the mixed or national system. I also think that in Ireland it is so great a point to bring youths of different religions to live together in colleges, as will justify almost any encouragement to the system of the Queen's University, except that of actually refusing degrees to those who have studied elsewhere.

In a later letter he deplores the evident intention of the Tory Government to charter, if not endow, a Catholic university; he agrees with Cairnes on the basic principle that 'no educational institution should be supported or aided by the State but those which are perfectly impartial, as the Queen's Colleges are, in respect to religion'.[55] However, the tide was flowing against him; there was growing pressure for 'freedom of education', which (as Cairnes pointed out in a reply to Mill) meant in practice denominationalism; and although at the university level a greater spirit of liberality and compromise brought a correspondingly greater freedom from sectarian division, the schools were increasingly absorbed into a denominational alignment. It was his hope that eventually a swing in English opinion against denominationalism would produce a similar change in Ireland; but it was not to be.

Despite his hopes and his firm attachment to the principle of non-denominational schools in any national system, Mill came to see that in England at least political reality made his position untenable (and it was impracticable, as he recognized, to have denominationalism here and 'mixed' schools in Ireland). 'The misery is', he writes to Cairnes in 1867, 'that ninety nine hundredths of England wish for only denominational places of education, and will not support any others'. It was a simple fact, unpalatable to Mill but inescapable, that denominationalism was too deeply rooted in English elementary education and English society to be relinquished at a stroke in deference to political or educational principle. To stand by the principle would be to vote against all grants to denominational schools, and 'neither I nor, as far as I know, any other Liberal, would think it right to do this'. Principle must yield, therefore, but only 'as a mere concession to practical difficulties'.[56]

It was one thing to support from public funds denominational schools established by the Churches; to grant to local School Boards the power to establish them was quite another. This latter, in effect, is what the 1870 Bill initially proposed to do: the religious education of the new Board Schools was to be determined by the Boards themselves. The Education League was firmly opposed to the proposal and invited Mill to speak against it at a public meeting in Chelsea on 25 March. Before that date, however, the Prime Minister gave an assurance that the offending clause would be amended; the resolution to which Mill spoke was therefore as follows:

That this meeting condemns the power given to School Boards to found denominational schools at the public expense; and therefore receives with pleasure the assurance by Mr. Gladstone that this portion of the Bill shall be redrawn.

When Mill rose to speak, he was greeted (according to the report in *The Times*) 'with loud and prolonged cheering'[57]—as indeed befitted his reputation as a life-long opponent of sectarian education; and despite Gladstone's assurance he found plenty to say, for there was still, he thought, enough of evil in the Bill to demand a strong protest. For the proposed amendment consisted only in shifting the religious teaching to out-of-school hours; it would still follow the doctrines of the dominant sect in the area of the Board and would still be given at public expense; a minority sect could also teach its doctrines in the Board Schools out of hours but *in addition to* the other religious teaching and *at its own expense*. This introduced 'a new religious inequality' in that teachers were 'to be employed and paid by the entire community to teach the religion of a part', while any minority sect was clearly disadvantaged. So long as the Bill remained infected by such a principle it was unacceptable save to members of the Anglican Church, which was in a majority in most areas. As for the existing denominational schools, their continued existence was no doubt inevitable, but not, he hoped 'as a permanent institution'; in this respect too the Bill was vitiated by the principle of taxing all for 'teaching religions not their own'. At least, in allowing the Boards to subsidize existing schools impartially the Bill abandoned the worst feature of denominationalism, 'the bigoted refusal of aid to secular schools'. If it were objected that the policy of the National Education League violated the majority's conscientious disapproval of schools where there was *no* religious teaching, his answer was that the majority were free to found their own schools and could surely afford to pay for them—'What we demand is that those who make use of religious teaching shall pay for it themselves instead of taxing others to do it.' He concludes:

Let all parties have what religious teaching their conscience approves and they are willing to pay for. But when a man tells me his conscience requires that other people shall have religious teaching, whether they like it or not, and shall have it in schools, though they would prefer having it elsewhere, and shall not be helped like other people with their secular teaching unless they consent to accept religious teaching along with it, I tell him that he is not asserting his own freedom of conscience but trampling on that of other people.

Controversy on the religious issues embittered the progress of the Bill to the end; but the protest of secularists and Dissenters was not unavailing: denominational schools were retained and subsidized from the rates—it was politically impossible to do otherwise; but religious teaching in Board Schools was subjected to the famous Cowper–Temple clause,[58] introduced in the final stages of the Bill and perpetuated almost unmodified in the 1944 Act, that 'no religious catechism or religious formulary which is distinctive of any particular denomination shall be taught' in those schools.

Denominational schools are still with us despite Mill's hope that they would not be a permanent institution. Their total number is smaller, but in some respects their position is even stronger, for their existence has been confirmed by successive Education Acts and fortified by grants extending now to 85 per cent of their capital costs. The majority are Roman Catholic schools, both primary and secondary; other denominations, principally Anglican and Methodist, have increasingly relinquished their hold on schools (but not on education in the broader sense) as a means of evangelism. Of Mill's objections some remain, some are no longer relevant: there are still areas, albeit few, where a denominational primary school (Anglican, Methodist, and a very few shared by these Churches) is the only one available; here there is just cause for complaint in that children, though protected by the Cowper–Temple clause and the right of withdrawal from denominational *instruction*, are still involved in a prevailing religious ethos which may offend the conscience of their parents; and it remains true that some teachers are 'employed and paid by the entire community to teach the religion of a part'. This is a situation which Mill, with his sense of history and of practicality, would no doubt acknowledge (and in some respects deplore) without conceding either its inevitability or its finality.

# 8

# Universities

AT THE beginning of the nineteenth century England had only its
two ancient universities; in Scotland there were four, St. Andrews
(the oldest), Glasgow, Aberdeen, and Edinburgh; Ireland had one
(Trinity College, Dublin) and Wales none. The previous century
had seen Oxford and Cambridge at their lowest ebb: since students
and tutors were generally required to be members (the latter
ordained members) of the Anglican Church, and since both came
predominantly from the aristocratic and wealthy classes, the
universities were a preserve of ecclesiastical and social privilege,
complacent, idle, and understandably resistant to change.[1] Their
statutes were out of date, their curricula dominated by the least
inspiring aspects of classical learning, their examinations often
farcical; in self-contained seclusion they made no response to the
growing commercial and industrial needs of the time. There is
ample witness to this state of affairs, for instance in the diary of
James Woodforde, scholar and fellow of New College, Oxford,
from 1759 to 1776, and in contemporary criticism by Vicesimus
Knox, fellow of St. John's, Oxford, and later headmaster of
Tonbridge School, and by Edward Gibbon, the historian, the last
of whom jibes at 'the monks of Magdalen', 'decent easy men'
supinely enjoying the gifts of the founder.[2] There were, of course,
exceptions among both students and tutors, but the general
picture of eighteenth-century Oxbridge is of inertia, place-seeking
and an absence of scholarly interest or incentive.

At Cambridge there was some improvement from the middle of
the eighteenth century, at Oxford rather later; there was demand
for reform even from within the universities—for the abolition of
religious tests, for the right of fellows to marry, for competitive
election to fellowships, for more rigorous examinations. Change
was slow to come, however—such was the extent of vested interest,
ecclesiastical and otherwise; it could hardly be expected, Gibbon
wrote, 'that any reformation will be a voluntary act'.[3] In fact it was
not until 1850 that a Royal Commission was appointed to inquire

into the state of affairs at Oxford and Cambridge. It reported in 1852, and the ensuing Acts (1854 for Oxford, 1856 for Cambridge) introduced important reforms including competition for fellow-ships and scholarships, the abolition of compulsory ordination for fellows, and the admission of nonconformists to the B.A. (not to the M.A., however, which meant in effect that university govern-ment was still Anglican dominated, and dissenters could still be barred from fellowships); changes in the administration of the universities opened the way for further reform of courses and examinations. It was not until 1871 that religious tests were finally abolished, with the one exception of degrees in Divinity. (It should be noted that in Scotland the situation was very different; here the eighteenth century was a period of vigorous intellectual activity which produced men of academic distinction in various fields of scholarship, especially philosophy, history, and psychology. Among them, to name but a few, were David Hume, Francis Hutcheson, Adam Smith, Thomas Reid, Dugald Steward and William Robertson; perhaps James Mill should be added, for he was after all a Scot and spent eight years at Edinburgh University in the last decade of the century; and John was himself clearly indebted to the intellectual tradition into which his father had been educated.)

John did not go to university, although Sir John Stuart, his father's benefactor and his own godfather, had recently died and left £500 for the express purpose of sending him to Cambridge. To this posthumous persuasion was added the entreaty of a friend of James Mill, Professor Townshend of Trinity College, who urged that John's name be entered 'at that noble college' so that he might make 'an acquaintance at an English University with his Patrician contemporaries'.[4] There were others too who recommended uni-versity life as an antidote to the seclusion of his private education. It was to no avail, however; among the obvious reasons against was the condition of the English universities themselves as outlined above—the religious test was, of course, particularly obnoxious to both father and son. To this, no doubt, was added the advice of Jeremy Bentham, whose experience at Oxford left him with a contempt for that university and a strong preference for home studies, particularly for a boy like John whose resources for academic learning left little to be desired.[5] Finally, it is unlikely that *academically* John had much to learn from going to university:

the bulk of classical literature he had already read by the age of fourteen; in mathematics he had taught his sister Harriet to a level evidently not far short of a final degree (as it then was); in logic he had been thoroughly trained from the age of twelve; at thirteen he was taken through 'a complete course of political economy'; psychology was added after his visit to France in 1820; by the age of seventeen he was deeply read in law (under the guidance of John Austin) and a year or two later was editing the five volumes of Bentham's *Rationale of Judicial Evidence*. What more could a university give? What it *could* give, as James's friend David Ricardo, the economist, saw clearly enough was 'that collision which is obtained only in society and by which a knowledge of the world and its manners is best acquired'.[6]

However, John was not wholly deprived of this benefit. In the summer of 1822 he met John Austin's brother Charles, who was a student of Jesus College, Cambridge, and President of the Cambridge Union (as famous then for its controversial debates as the Oxford Union is today); Charles invited him to a meeting of the Union on 26 March, when the subject for debate was, 'Ought the science of political economy to be encouraged at the present time?'[7] It is not certain that Mill spoke, but on such a subject it seems likely that he would. Michael Packe (without citing evidence) declares positively that he did: 'He went to Cambridge and he spoke. His massive power in disputation, uttered from a flimsy body in the creaking tones of sixteen, stilled the brittle oratory of the adolescent giants. He left a great impression.' This would seem to be a poetic expansion of Bain's description, written almost a century nearer the event: 'The contrast of his boyish figure and thin voice, with his immense conversational power, left a deep impression on the undergraduates of the time; notwithstanding their being familiar with Macaulay and Austin.' Certainly the visit was of great consequence for Mill, for Charles Austin took him under his wing and introduced him to a number of contemporaries, Macaulay included, who were to achieve distinction later. Oddly, the *Autobiography* does not mention the visit but Mill records his respect for and debt to Charles: his was 'the really influential mind among these intellectual gladiators' and 'it was through him that I first felt myself, not a pupil under teachers, but a man among men'.[8] Impressed by his experience of intellectual debate Mill later in the year established a small discussion group which he called the Utilitarian Society and which met fortnightly in London for over three years. A more ambitious project, still an offshoot of his Cambridge visit, was the London Debating Society which he founded in 1825 jointly with Charles Austin, John Roebuck and others; this too continued for several years, meeting fortnightly during the winter and attracting to its membership 'along with several members of Parliament nearly all the most noted speakers of the Cambridge Union and of the Oxford United Debating Society'.[9] It was thus, without residence at university, that Mill experienced that 'collision' of minds and personalities which is perhaps the most valuable element in a university education.

No doubt this lively enthusiasm of intellectual debate, witnessed briefly in the Cambridge Union and for many years in London, sharpened for him the contrast between the inertia of the Oxbridge norm and the adventurous possibilities of university life as he saw it might be. Certainly, in his earlier writings he is an unsparing critic of Oxford and Cambridge; nothing less will suffice than a fundamental reform—'nos Universités ... ont besoin d'une réforme et même d'une réorganisation complète'. So he writes to Victor Cousin in 1834.[10] Oxford, he writes in *The Monthly Repository* of the same year, has lost its former power and prestige; 'it is as effete as the Pope' and having lost its power has lived on to become ridiculous.[11] The two Universities are 'among the last places where any person wishing for education, and knowing what it is, would go to seek it'. The sons of the aristocracy go there because 'it is gentlemanly to have been there'; intending clergymen go there because 'it is very difficult otherwise to get into orders'; barristers go there to save two years of apprenticeship; 'no one else goes at all'.[12] He makes much the same point in a letter to Comte some years later: even when they are not resident in England, 'les riches anglais ... ont l'habitude bien établie d'envoyer leur fils à Oxford ou à Cambridge'; and the qualifications for entry are a mere smattering of the elements of geometry and mathematics.[13] It is not surprising, therefore, so he writes in 'Professor Sedgwick's Discourse', that England has lost the intellectual distinction she once had:

The celebrity of England, in the present day, rests upon her docks, her canals, her railroads. In intellect she is distinguished only for a kind of sober good sense, free from extravagance, but also void of lofty aspirations; and for doing all those things which are best done where man most resembles a machine, with the precision of a machine. Valuable qualities, doubtless; but not precisely those by which mankind raise themselves to the perfection of their nature, or achieve greater and greater conquests over the difficulties which encumber their social arrangements.[14]

Hence the narrowness of vision, the lack of curiosity, of interest in truth and inquiry, that characterizes the English mind in contrast with the French and German.

His strongest condemnation of the Universities is in 'Civilisation':[15] as they have been administered for the past two centuries he regards them 'with sentiments little short of utter abhorrence'; they have acquiesced in imposing on students a nominal assent to the mere articles of religion—'they cared not to make religious men'; they have been content to make Tories instead of patriots, to prevent heresy even at the price of stupidity; it is this last especially which constitutes their 'peculiar baseness'. Meanwhile, though they defend to the last their sectarian character and

the exclusion of all who will not sign away their freedom of thought . . . there is hardly a trace in the system of the Universities that any other object whatever is seriously cared for. Nearly all the professorships have degenerated into sinecures. Few of the professors ever deliver a lecture.

One of their few notable scholars has been dismissed from his tutorship for his honesty in asserting that in his university even theology is not taught. As a means of education such institutions are clearly useless; their ordinary degrees are, at Cambridge, 'utterly contemptible', and little better at Oxford; their honours degrees, while demanding a high level of effort and attainment, promote neither mental excellence nor enthusiasm for research; indeed the latter is discouraged by the system itself, for

when a man is pronounced by them to have excelled in their studies, what do the Universities do? They give him an income, not for continuing to learn, but for having learnt; not for doing anything, but for what he has already done: on condition solely of living like a monk, and putting on the livery of the Church at the end of seven years. They bribe men by high rewards to get their arms ready, but do not require them to fight.

Clearly these are not 'the places of education which are to send forth minds capable of maintaining a victorious struggle with the debilitating influences of the age'.

In addition to these various complaints Mill attacks the Universities for their monopoly in awarding degrees as passports to the professions: degrees should carry only their own intrinsic merit; they should not be necessary for the enjoyment of civil privileges, and the title for exercising a profession should be simply a *good* education (a view which tallies with that expressed years after in the *Inaugural*). He attacks them for their appropriation of endowments to comfortable living instead of the advancement of learning; for their meagre output of scholarly work, as compared with Germany or even France and Italy; for their 'fixity' in the possession of advantage and power, their complacent and self-satisfied acceptance of the *status quo*; for their addiction to conformity as 'the triumph of the system'—which amounts to a total misconception of the purposes of a university education.[16]

He attacks also their impoverished curriculum, which (referring here to Cambridge) 'some few of its pupils actually prosecute'.[17] The traditional core of the university course was the classical languages and literature, whose value Mill, of course, fully acknowledged; but

our two great 'seats of learning', of which no real lover of learning can ever speak but in terms of indignant disgust, bestow attention upon the various branches of classical acquirement in exactly the reverse order to that which would be observed by persons who valued the ancient authors for what is valuable in them; namely, upon the mere niceties of the language *first*; next, upon a few of the poets; next (but at a great distance), some of the historians; next (but at a still greater interval), the orators; last of all, and just above nothing, the philosophers.

Plato, the greatest of the ancient philosophers and 'the most gifted of Greek writers' is scarcely taught at all by 'the impostor universities'.[18] (He admits, however, that at Oxford the *Ethics, Politics,* and *Rhetoric* of Aristotle are reasonably well taught.)[19] Mathematics, though encouraged at Cambridge, is of such a kind and is so taught that it has no tendency to produce superiority of intellect (and in any case 'as an exclusive instrument for fashioning the mental powers [is] greatly overrated'.[20] In philosophy England once stood at the head of Europe, but this has now become 'the mere shell and husk of the syllogistic logic at the one university [i.e. Oxford], the wretchedest smattering of Locke and Paley at the other'.[21] In consequence, while the Universities complacently eulogize their own efforts, philosophy—not any particular school of philosophy, but philosophy altogether—speculation of any comprehensive kind, and upon any deep or extensive subject—has been falling more and more into distasteful-ness and disrepute among the educated classes of England.[22]

The teaching of the physical sciences, such as it is, is over-particu-larized, neglecting the wider issues of the *philosophy* of science, its logic and methodology, and the contribution that a study of the sciences can make to general education, liberating the mind from enslavement to authority and 'its own accidental associations'.[23]

The main obstacle to reform is, of course, the Church, whose obvious interest is to maintain its own dominance and control; 'les établissements d'Oxford et de Cambridge', he writes to Cousin, 'lui appartiennent; et s'ils ne forment pas de chrétiens, ils forment des churchmen'.[24] This is indeed the truth of the matter: Mill ridicules the suggestion that the two Universities encourage in their students a sincere and practical commitment to Christian-ity; to its institutions, yes, for this is a condition of their residence; but to the genuine spirit of religion—*solvuntur risu tabulae*.[25] He deemed the situation little changed in the early 1850s when he wrote his review of Whewell's *Lectures on the History of Moral Philosophy*: the Universities are still 'ecclesiastical institutions' and

it is the essence of all churches to vow adherence to a set of opinions made up and prescribed, it matters little whether three or thirteen centuries ago. Men will some day open their eyes, and perceive how fatal a thing it is that the instruction of those who are intended to be the guides and governors of mankind should be confided to a collection of persons thus pledged.

For it is not simply that they are 'thus pledged', but that they are pledged to doctrines which, unlike the physical sciences, are based not on scrupulous examination of factual evidence but 'on trust and authority'.[26] The remedy is obvious: the Universities must be 'unsectarianised'; to make them genuine places of education, Parliament must 'clean out those sinks of the narrowest and most grovelling Church-of-Englandism, and convert them into reser-voirs of sound learning and genuine spiritual culture'.[27] To allow entry to Dissenters is not enough: 'The principle itself of dog-matic religion, dogmatic morality, dogmatic philosophy is what requires to be rooted out.'[28]

In all this there is no doubt an element of rhetorical exaggeration stemming from his personal abhorrence of sectarianism and from his youthful enthusiasm for reform and for openness of thought, inquiry, and debate. But in general his charges are valid; and they are interestingly substantiated by Alexis de Tocqueville, author of *Democracy in America*, which Mill twice reviewed and by which he was deeply influenced (pp. 86–7). After his return from America in 1832 de Tocqueville visited England and Ireland, recording his impressions with the same acute perceptiveness that he had exercised on the other side of the Atlantic. He came to Oxford in August 1833 and records thus in his notebook:

One's first feeling on visiting Oxford is of unforced admiration for the men of old who founded such immense establishments to aid the development of the human spirit, and for the political institutions of the people who have preserved them intact through the ages. But when one examines these things closely and gets below the surface of this imposing show, admiration almost vanishes and one sees a host of abuses which are not at first sight obvious.

Though richly endowed to attract the best teachers and provide the best education free of charge, the curriculum is still of the fourteenth rather than the nineteenth century; the sciences have been introduced but are undeveloped, and 'the study of living languages is excluded'; fellows share in the college revenues 'without fulfilling any function'; students have several rooms, 'the rich are allowed to enjoy all the pleasures of luxury' and 'all of them have *six* months of vacations'. He confirms, too, writing of both Universities, that a degree is 'necessary, or at least very useful, for the acquisition of great wealth'.[29]

It was noted above that change had begun by 1800; it proceeded slowly against strong resistance until the middle of the century, when progress was accelerated by the Royal Commission of 1850, its Report of 1852 and the subsequent University Acts. The improvements were not unnoticed by Mill, and his views were modified accordingly. In 1845, in a letter to Comte already referred to (p. 165), he admits that the state of mathematics at Cambridge is 'un peu amélioré'; in his review of 1852, while dismissing Whewell's *Elements of Morality* as 'one of the thousand waves on the dead sea of commonplace', he praises the man for assisting the revival of philosophy at Oxford and Cambridge.[30] 'Civilisation' has a footnote written in 1859 affirming that much of what he wrote in the essay has now ceased to be true:

The legislature has at last asserted its right of interference; and even before it did so, those bodies [i.e. the Universities] had already entered into a course of as decided improvement as any other English institutions.

But he leaves it unaltered for the sake of the historical record and 'as an illustration of tendencies'.[31] Some years later again he finds it possible to recommend a correspondent to send her two sons to one or other of the old Universities:

Twenty years ago these were about the last places which I should have recommended . . .; but they are now very much changed, and free inquiry and speculation on the deepest and highest questions, instead of being crushed or deadened, are now more rife there than almost anywhere else in England. And the places not only afford great facilities for study, but a strong stimulus to it, by the competition for honours.

He goes on to recommend in particular Balliol College under Benjamin Jowett, 'not only on account of his liberal tone of thought, but also of his remarkable success in training pupils in the studies of the place'.[32] No less generous are his remarks in the *Inaugural Address*: the old English Universities are doing better work now than within living memory, not only in teaching the ordinary studies of the curriculum, but as 'the great foci of free and manly inquiry'; at last they have recognized that 'to place themselves in hostility to the free use of the understanding is to abdicate their own best privilege, that of guiding it'.[33] Evidently legislation had had its effect and Mill was too honest not to acknowledge the transformation.

It remains now to consider Mill's positive account of what he believed to be the purposes of a university education. Much of his intention can be inferred from the foregoing criticisms; at the other end of his life he describes and argues at length in the *Inaugural Address* his conception of a university course within the notion of a liberal education. In these concluding paragraphs the aim is to make explicit what has already been implied, and to outline the purposes declared in the *Inaugural*.

A university does not exist for the amusement of the idle rich or to provide them with a social *cachet*; this much is obvious and needs no arguing. Less obvious is Mill's contention that it is not a place of professional training; but he insists on this. It is part of his case for endowed institutions of learning that 'there must be places where the teacher can afford to teach other things than those which parents (who in nine cases out of ten think only of qualifying their children to *get on* in life) spontaneously call for'.[34] This was in 'Notes on the Newspapers' in *The Monthly Repository* of 1834; there was no change of view when he wrote the *Inaugural* some thirty years later. Here he states emphatically, and as the generally accepted opinion, that a university 'is not a place of professional education'; its purpose is not 'to teach the knowledge required to fit men for some special mode of gaining their livelihood'. There must of course be schools of law, medicine, engineering, the industrial arts; but these are not an essential part of that culture which each generation has a duty to pass on to the next.[35] A year or two later he complains to a correspondent of the attitude of the middle classes to University College, London: it is not 'good education' they are seeking for their sons, for 'they evidently set no value on any instruction not strictly professional'.[36]

What then should a university aim to provide? In a word, *education*, by which Mill means a 'general' or 'liberal' education as he describes it in the *Inaugural*. Its purpose, for the individual student, is 'the strengthening and enlarging of his own intellect and character', moral elevation by the example of excellence, the broadening of understanding and sympathies into a 'large and catholic toleration', in short the creation of 'capable and cultivated human beings' who can 'bring the light of general culture to illuminate the technicalities of a special pursuit'.[37] Crucial in this is the development of rational skills and an enthusiasm for inquiry:

The very cornerstone of an education intended to form great minds must be the recognition of the principle, that the object is to call forth the greatest possible quantity of intellectual *power*, and to inspire the intensest *love of truth*[38]

—and this even if it should lead the pupil to opinions diametrically opposed to those of his teachers. It is here that Oxford and Cambridge have most conspicuously failed; they are rooted to a wholly false conception of the purpose not simply of academic education but of education itself, namely

that the object is, *not* that the individual should go forth determined and qualified to seek truth ardently, vigorously, and disinterestedly; *not* that he be furnished at setting out with the needful aids and facilities, the needful materials and instruments for that search, and then left to the

unshackled use of them; *not* that, by a free communion with the
thoughts and deeds of the great minds which preceded him, he be
inspired at once with the courage to dare all which truth and conscience
require, and the modesty to weigh well the grounds of what others
think before adopting contrary opinions of his own

—*not* this, but intellectual imprisonment in the prescribed dogma of
a 'favoured set of propositions' irrespective of whether they make
any sense to the student.[39] Elsewhere he proclaims that universities exist 'to keep alive philosophy'; and at St. Andrews he tells his
audience that a university 'ought to be a place of free speculation';
all its teaching should be conducted in a spirit not of dogmatism
but of inquiry, and its aim should be to give the student such
information and training as will enable him to seek truth for himself
and form his own conclusions; 'whatever you do, keep at all risks
your minds open; do not barter away your freedom of thought'.[40]

So much, then, for the individual student and his education; but
universities have obligations also to society, and Mill is not
unaware of these. Partly they are fulfilled through the medium of
the individual student, by the kind and quality of education provided for him and the consequences of this, radiating into society
at large, for his personal and intellectual growth; high attainment
in individuals, whether academic, moral, or any other, presents an
example of excellence which elevates standards generally and at the
same time restrains the depressive cultural impact of democracy.
They are fulfilled too in commitment to intellectual inquiry and
the expansion of knowledge; for truth and enlightenment which
are products of such commitment, are essential to social progress;
(research, it will be remembered, is among the purposes for which
Mill concedes government intervention and support—see p. 121
above). It is thus that universities contribute to what Mill calls
'progression' (pp. 43–4 above); but not only thus, for they provide
(or *should* provide) a leadership which inspires others to 'greater
achievements in virtue, intelligence and social well-being';[41] they
provide, both in themselves as corporate academic bodies and more
widely through the students who pass from them, an élite, a
bastion of cultivated intelligence, which functions continuously to
raise society to higher levels of achievement. They may even, if
endowments are properly used, promote what is now called 'social
mobility' by opening the door of higher education to the able
children of the poor (pp. 138–9 above). They contribute also to

'permanence' by acting, like schools, as instruments of cultural transmission and protection, preserving what is best in a nation's tradition and resisting the countervailing influences of an increasingly commercialized democracy. It is the special duty of universities, he writes,

to counteract the debilitating influence of the circumstances of the age upon individual character, and to send forth into society a succession of minds, not the creatures of their age, but capable of being its improvers and regenerators[42]

—a duty which the English universities have conspicuously neglected. Even politically universities have a function in providing a

counterbalance to the impulses and will of the comparatively uninstructed many [which] lies in a strong and independent organisation of the class whose special business is the cultivation of knowledge; and will better embody itself in Universities than in Senates or Houses of Lords.[43]

In this conception of the purposes of a university education Mill is perpetuating the Greek and Renaissance ideal of the educated gentleman, reinforcing it at the same time with a rigorous intellectual content (including both the traditional Classics and the sciences as essential and complementary constituents) and a firm moral orientation. Thus, while contributing his own emphases, he follows the main stream of English educational thought from Thomas Elyot to the later part of the nineteenth century. (Among the few notable deviants from this stream was John Locke who declared in his *Thoughts concerning Education* that 'most pains should be taken about that which is most necessary, and that principally looked after which will be of most and frequentest use to him in the world'; for this he was criticized, not altogether justly, by Cardinal Newman who wrote that 'the tone of Locke's remarks . . . is condemnatory of any teaching which tends to the general cultivation of the mind'.)[44] Newman, of course, was on Mill's side; so was Matthew Arnold; but other voices were making themselves heard, demanding a greater attention to applied science and technology, without which, they averred, Britain would be unable to compete industrially with her continental neighbours.[45] It was not that Mill was hostile to technology or to the application of science to industrial ends; he admits, as we have seen, the need for colleges of the industrial arts; and it is obvious from his despatches to India that he was aware of the need for technical training in that country. In effect he is anticipating the 'two cultures' debate of our own times, not, however, as an opposition between arts and sciences, but between the liberal (including the sciences) and the vocational; for him the real enemy of culture was not science or technology but the prostitution of learning (as it seemed to him) by confining it to narrow occupational and commercial objectives.

Among contemporary critics of Mill's scheme of university education was Alexander Bain, who considered his Inaugural Address a mistake 'in relation to the time, place and circumstances' and Mill's performance a failure 'for this simple reason that he had no conception of the limits of a University curriculum'.[46] Certainly, the range of content he proposed was far in excess of the capabilities of any but the most talented student; in this he was misled partly by his over-ambitious ideal of the liberally educated man, partly by regarding his own exceptional education and ability as a general norm. Bain also attacks his insistence on retaining the full panoply of classical learning in addition to an extensive course in the sciences; limitations of time alone demand a choice between one or the other as main courses. Moreover, he underestimates the difficulty of Latin and Greek, makes no allowance for the use of translations, exaggerates the literary merit of Greek authors, and erroneously claims that grammar is 'elementary logic'; finally, there are now, Bain urges, other ways of 'correcting the tendency to mistake words for things' than learning foreign languages. Even Mill's claim for freedom of thought in universities Bain dismisses as 'a somewhat impracticable ideal'.[47]

While agreeing with Bain on the Classics a modern critic, from the vantage-point of historical perspective, would insist rather that Mill was either unaware of or refusing to face up to the educational needs of an increasingly industrialized society; the traditional classical and literary disciplines, excellent though they might be as instruments of a liberal education, could not provide the knowledge and skills required for technological and commercial advance; and time and expense prohibited the acquisition of the former merely as an educational basis for the latter. Further, it might be argued that to create a dichotomy between the liberal and the vocational is to impoverish the latter by depriving it of insights and values which can be infused into it by simultaneous rather than successive study. Or again that vocational studies themselves embody liberalizing elements which, combined with the greater motivation implicit in studies whose relevance is perspicuous to the student (and rightly taught, of course), can supply much of the liberal ideal that Mill so insistently pursued.

In mitigation of these criticisms it can be said that Mill was not opposed to vocational studies as such; this has already been made clear. Nor was he averse from including them, presumably as postgraduate studies, within the general confines of universities: 'there is something to be said for having them in the same localities and under the same general superintendence as the establishments devoted to education properly so called'.[48] In this way (though he does not say it) vocational studies might be absorbed into the wider life and purposes of a university and infused with its educational ideals. Where Mill is wrong is in insisting that the educational and vocational objectives are distinct and immiscible; the latter do not, as he assumed, preclude the former. He was wrong too in clinging so firmly, some might say insensitively, to the classical and liberal tradition and to the example of his own highly unusual educational experience, and thus failing to acknowledge the urgent needs of a rapidly changing society. But he was right, not only in pointing to the social contribution that universities can make in promoting truth and knowledge, in providing leadership and standards of excellence, and in serving both 'permanence' and 'progression', but right too, and emphatically so, in demanding areas of higher education where students are unrestrained by immediate vocational pressures and can apply themselves disinterestedly and in a climate of free inquiry to the pursuit of intellectual enlightenment and its concomitant pleasures.

# 9

# Conclusion

IT WAS stated in the Preface that the present book embraces only a part of Mill's educational thought, that it is possible to construct from his writings a theory of education which includes much more than its social and political role. A brief outline of this theory will help to illuminate his concept of educative democracy by placing it within a broader educational perspective. Thence we can proceed to the main purpose of this concluding chapter, namely to summarize the main features of the concept and to assess its strengths and weaknesses.

In his *System of Logic* Mill offers an account of science and its methodology based, as he puts it, on '*experience* only'.[1] Scientific knowledge is derived from observation and experiment; it is expressed in causal laws which enable us to explain, predict, and control. Now Mill was more than an epistemologist; at heart he was a reformer whose earnest desire was to improve human society. For him, therefore, science was not theoretical merely but practical: it aims at the discovery of truth, but it is also an essential instrument of social advance. To be so used its methods must be applicable to human phenomena (individual and social) as well as to the data of the natural sciences. Here Mill found himself in difficulty: there was the problem of accommodating choice and free will within a causally determined universe; and there were problems of method arising from the complexity of behavioural phenomena and the limited scope for experiment. These obstacles he believed he could overcome: his arguments against determinism were briefly reviewed in chapter 5 above; his proposals for a behavioural science based on association psychology and a logically validated sociology are set forth in Book VI of the *Logic*. These proposals included what he calls 'ethology', a practical science of the formation of character which, using education as the means of its implementation, could fashion human character, and with it the character of society, in any desired direction. Thus there was suggested to him the possibility of a programme of social engineering geared to whatever values might be chosen as goals for human improvement: 'We may hereafter succeed not only in looking far forward into the future history of the human race, but in determining what artificial means may be used . . . to accelerate the natural progress in so far as it is beneficial.'[2]

It was his intention to elaborate in his next book this ethological science which he outlines in *Logic* VI. 'With parental fondness', writes Alexander Bain, 'he cherished this subject for a considerable time, regarding it as the foundation and cornerstone of sociology.'[3] In fact it came to nothing and he was soon deeply involved in writing his *Principles of Political Economy*. Thenceforth his interest in the theory of behavioural control gave way before practical preoccupations of matching the realities of contemporary English society with the urgency of his ideals, and it is these last which came to dominate his thinking. Hence he offers no clear logical progression from his behavioural theory to his concept of educative democracy. Yet there is no discontinuity; the influence of the theory is plain in the concept.

It can be seen in his firm commitment to human educability and to the importance of education. All normal human beings are educable; so too, in some sense, are dogs, cats, and other animals. Mill meant more, however, than simple malleability in response to controlled stimuli or techniques of reinforcement. For him educability meant that men, women, and children are susceptible to influences which assist their growth towards goals which are deemed worthwhile, whether happiness, freedom, or any others; that they can be initiated into existing values and thus contribute to society's permanence and cohesion; and that they can be raised to higher levels of experience, to an improved quality of life, thus contributing to social progress and human betterment. This faith is central to his concept of educative democracy. From it there follows inevitably a commitment to education as a prime instrument in the creation and development of a democratic society— education not as the privilege of a few, but as the right and the obligation of all.

The importance of education was, of course, a basic item in his father's creed, impressed on John during his upbringing and reinforced by his reading of Bentham and by his association with other utilitarians; it was also an obvious logical inference from the association psychology in which too he had been drilled from an early age. But it was more than a credal article passively accepted; it became an autonomous belief born of his own investigation into the methodology of the social sciences and their practical applica- tion; and it was as such that it was incorporated into his concept of democracy. Education, he emphatically believed, was a *sine qua non* of a truly democratic society—indeed part of the very concept of democracy and logically implied by it; for only by education (which must in large measure be *self*-education) could there be achieved the release of individual potential, the reservoir of cultivated intelligence, the emergence of truth and exposure of sophistry, the discipline of self-restraint and loyalty to a common interest, the steady growth towards ideals, the administrative expertise, the informed and participant citizenship, all of which he saw as indispensable to its effective functioning.

There follows from his behavioural theory a further consequence whose influence permeates the whole of his educational thought and which, like his commitment to education, is an essential item in his concept of democracy. This is the educative instrumentality of environment. Both experientialism and association psychology, which are the foundations of his ethology, point to the environ- ment as a crucial determinant of mental content and character. For if the primary source of knowledge is the data presented to the mind by the senses; if the bonds which link these data (and thereby predispose our thinking, our attitudes, likes and dislikes) are supplied from the same source; and if the external world and its sensory impact can be manipulated by human agency (as they obviously can) then the environment is inevitably an instrument of undeniable importance in the formation of human character and must be regarded as such by the educator.

Of the total environmental impact much, inevitably, is random and unpredictable; but some is, and more could be, controlled and manipulated with deliberate educational intent. Mill insists that it not only could but *should* be, that the whole human environment is potentially educative (or *mis*educative if ignored and neglected) and must be made instrumental to educational purposes. Education is not, therefore, a matter simply of schools, colleges, and universi- ties—though these are, of course, important as institutions where educative influence is concentrated and focused on clearly formu- lated goals. The home, the local community at work and at leisure, the physical aspect of towns, villages, and countryside, political institutions and forms of government—all these, he contends, are potent educators (indeed the more so, one might add, because their influence is imperceptibly absorbed through suggestion and habit rather than by direct instruction). An educative democracy, therefore, will embody its purposes and ideals not only in educational institutions but in the total life of the people in its total environment; and the extent to which it achieves this will be a principal criterion of its status as a democracy. (Mill was not the first to make such a claim for environmental education; Plato had done so in the *Republic* and others since; but it was of particular significance in nineteenth-century England, where the environment of millions was desperately impoverished and education was commonly equated with the inculcation of fact.)

There is another consequence of Mill's experientialist theory of education, which too is of central importance for his concept of democracy. Knowledge derived from the data of experience (rather than from some *a priori* Platonic pattern of Forms) is a growing and flexible edifice, enlarged and modified as it is supplied with new materials; truth is not final but open, not a finished product but a continuing adventure. Educationally this implies a switch of focus from the teacher and his teaching to the pupil and his learning. Since knowledge is the product of experience, it is in his own experiencing that the pupil comes to know, in his individual response to and interaction with the sensory world (including the books, materials, and fellow human beings who are part of it). This points to an education of involvement, of participation, of experiment, of activity rather than passivity; to an education by discovery whose motivation is from within. Such an education requires freedom—freedom, as far as may be, from external restraint so that the pupil may choose the direction of his interests and energies, put his own questions to experience, establish his own interaction with environment, learn from his own successes and mistakes. There will still be need for restraint, discipline, and respect for authority; but these too will come from within, from the pupil's recognition, borne in upon him by his direct dealings with the world around him, of the need for obedience to natural laws, for rule-governed procedure in order to attain his goals, for deference to the authority (itself vindicated in experience) of superior knowledge and expertise. Such is the picture which emerges from Mill's observations on the educational process.

It is clearly reflected in his educative democracy. Here there is a
similar shift of emphasis, from government to governed. The
individual is encouraged to assume responsibility, to involve himself in the activities of the community, to participate in public
affairs, to identify himself with the common good, to make
decisions instead of accepting them, to act for himself instead of
expecting others to act for him. Such involvement is at the same
time a means of education: the individual learns new skills and
insights; learns the realities of public life—the need for authority,
for restraint, for compromise, for co-operation, for service; learns
to distinguish truth from error, the ingenuous from the humbug;
learns about himself, what he can and cannot do, and what others
can do better. Thereby he becomes a better man, a better citizen;
moreover, by improving himself he improves others, and they likewise him, so that society as a whole is progressively enriched by a
mutual, self-perpetuating educative ferment. Here too freedom is
crucial. Without it individuality is unable to express itself, experiment and innovation are stifled and with them the creative probing
after truth. Without freedom there can be no genuine interaction
with environment, no willing involvement in the life of society;
participation becomes an irksome imposition, the educative ferment ceases.

One prominent feature of Mill's educative democracy derives
partly from his experientialism, partly from other sources; this is
dialogue, the free interchange of ideas within the community. An
epistemology based on experience sees truth as emerging from the
clash of opposing hypotheses and conclusions; no one investigator
sees the whole either of a problem or of its solution; and no solution is final, since new facts may lead to modification of supposedly
established truths. This consequence of his experientialism was
reinforced by his own experience and education and became for
him a firmly held pedagogical principle, the principle, as he calls it,
of 'antagonism'.[4] The discussion groups which he organized among
his contemporaries in the 1820s led him to see argument and debate
as prime means to intellectual clarification; in his review of
Grote's *Aristotle* he recommends their inclusion in all higher
education. The Platonic dialogues confirmed him in this view: here
discussion is refined into a sophisticated technique for the discovery of truth, the Socratic 'dialectic' which is, he believes,
unsurpassed 'as a discipline for correcting the errors and clearing

up the confusions incident to the *intellectus sibi permissus*'.[5] (At this level dialogue has epistemological and metaphysical ramifications, as Mill was well aware; unfortunately there is no space to consider them here.) In his own thinking 'antagonism' appears in various issues—freedom and authority, progression and permanence, nature and discipline, individuality and social restraint; and much of his intellectual endeavour was given to resolving these apparent oppositions into an acceptable pattern of truth.

One can hardly dissent from Mill's conclusions as to the educational value of dialogue at its various levels; in this he anticipates modern practice both in educational institutions and in the media. Discussion contributes not only to clear thinking and the discovery of truth; it has further educational value in encouraging participation and promoting, if not unanimity, at least an agreement to differ which provides a basis for mutual respect and collaboration. For these reasons it is also an essential element in democracy (as Mill understood it), without which it cannot be an *educative* democracy. Dialogue, of course, requires leadership, guidance, and obedience to rule—in other words, technique and discipline. Mill had no illusions about this; nor about the need for fact and access to fact, without which discussion and dialogue become an empty and tedious posturing; hence his insistence on the diffusion of information as one of the prime duties of government.

There are other constituents of Mill's educative democracy which derive from his ideals rather than from his epistemological and educational theories (though the two sources are by no means sharply distinguishable). These include economic sufficiency, equality of opportunity, and universal adult franchise, all of which can be brought under the broad heading of social justice. To these must be added the requirement of a certain quality of life and of personal relationships; for social justice is a means, not an end, and the end to which it points is the good life. All these constituents, Mill would argue, are necessary for a democracy to be educative and not merely a machinery of democratic institutions (and universal franchise necessary for this latter alone). All men *and women*, he believed, have a right to happiness and to a quality of life and relationships beyond mere subsistence and the constraints of daily labour; for this a basic level of material wealth is essential (though not, Mill would again insist, an end in itself)—essential for health, for leisure, for freedom to develop potential and to involve oneself with society. All, therefore, have a claim to a humane standard of living; poverty is an unacceptable evil.

Equality of opportunity depends partly on this, partly on other factors such as the impartial administration of justice, partly on the availability of education for all in both quantity and quality—and by education, as has been made abundantly clear, Mill intended far more than institutional instruction. In society as it was then politically, socially and economically organized, equality of opportunity must have seemed a distant dream; but without it, without the opportunity for all to be and to give their best, there could be no educative ferment and no genuine democracy. (Mill did not, it should be remembered, mistake the meaning and implications of equality: he believed all to be equal in their right of access to the ingredients of the good life, but not equal in their capacity to attain it.) Especially, he believed, there must be opportunity for the emergence of excellence; for it is this, expressing itself diversely but with particular force through 'cultivated intelligence', which elevates society to higher qualities of experience and protects it against that mediocrity to which he believed democracy was dangerously prone. Here there is a crucial role for the universities, appropriately reformed and offering the generous liberal curriculum outlined in the *Inaugural*. Finally, without a universal franchise participation in any meaningful sense is impossible: the disenfranchised are onlookers only, spectators of a political process which they cannot influence and to which they cannot contribute; the effective working of democracy is impaired; there is lacking an essential ingredient of the educative ferment.

Insistence on quality is characteristic of Mill, distinguishing his own utilitarianism from the quantitative version of strict Benthamism and introducing an element of enrichment into his educational thought. Though he is nowhere explicit as to the meaning of 'quality'—his comparison of Socrates dissatisfied with a pig satisfied is vivid but uninformative—his intention is not difficult to infer. There are higher and lower pleasures (some being 'more desirable and more valuable than others')[6] and, correspondingly, there are higher and lower levels of happiness. Instruction is not simply 'that we may live, but that we may live well'; industrial training aims to improve its recipients not 'as workmen merely, but as human beings'.[7] He condemns the 'fopperies of so-called civilisation',[8] commends solitude and contemplation of beauty (in art and nature), insists on moral and aesthetic content for the curriculum, and acknowledges the compelling force in human experience of wonder and mystery. Fitness to live together in mutual respect and reciprocity of give and take is 'the true virtue of human beings'.[9] The higher pleasures are those which employ the higher faculties and employ them *actively*; and the judgement between higher and lower must come from those best qualified by nature, experience, and education to make a proper discrimination. There are obvious problems here, as has already been noted (pp. 4–5); Mill gives them scant attention, assuming uncritically that the milieu of 'cultivated intelligence' in which he himself moved provided the only acceptable criterion of quality. Yet his stance is valuable in its insistence both on qualitative distinctions and, no less, on the crucial role of education in enabling us to make them. Moreover, he was aware that education itself can be qualitatively better or worse, can embody higher or lower values, and that the quality of education depends in no small measure on the creation of 'an improved race of schoolmasters'.[10] The qualitative improvement of education and educators was among his principal justifications for state intervention.

The preceding pages, while tracing the derivation of Mill's educative democracy from theoretical and altruistic sources, has also provided a summary of the concept itself. It remains to attempt some assessment of its worth. Much of this is obvious enough and needs no further elaboration: economic and social justice as a necessary foundation, diversity of self-expression, dialogue, participation, standards of excellence, and qualitative criteria—all of these are now commonly acknowledged to be essential features of the conceptual geography of democracy as well as conditions for its effective practical functioning. So too is education, but on this more needs to be said. Here Mill's importance lies not so much in his insistence on 'certain primary elements and means of knowledge'[11] as necessary for democratic citizenship—by the mid-century this was plain to most of his contemporaries and is even more cogently manifest today. It lies rather in his persistent faith in human educability, in the power of education to release potential, to promote human purposes, to perpetuate and innovate values, and hence to improve both individuals and societies—a faith which led him inexorably to accept state intervention in promoting a universal national system of elementary education.

Without such faith it is impossible for educators whether in administration or the classroom or elsewhere to maintain their own enthusiasm and to secure the backing of popular support; both of these are vital to their task. If education cannot, as Helvetius declared, do *everything*, one must believe that it can do much or else one must revert to other, less desirable, and in the long run less effective means of improvement.

There is more to it than this, however; for Mill, it must always be remembered, consistently thought of education as the total impact of environment (except where, as in the *Inaugural*, he deliberately restricted its meaning). State intervention cannot therefore be a matter simply of supplying money and ensuring the provision of schools and teachers; it must go far beyond this in promoting the creation of a total environment whose influence is educative, supportive of democratic principles and ideals, conducive to improvement. This is not, as has already been noted, an original conception of the educative process; but it is one that needs to be constantly reasserted. The pervasive power of the social environment is now a well established fact; money and effort are wasted, therefore, if the educative ethos of schools, deliberately directed towards improvement, conflicts with and is ultimately overcome by the miseducative impact of society outside them. Though valuable and an immense advance on the restricted view of education as confined to the classroom, this conception of education as the totality of environmental impact is not without its problems; these suggest a weakness in Mill's educational thinking which will be considered below.

There is an element in his account of education which may justifiably be called 'progressive'. Though more obvious in other areas of his educational theory (for instance, in his recommendation of 'discovery' methods), it is apparent also in his conception of the social role of education and its functioning within democracy. His environmentalism is itself suggestive of it; for although others before him had acknowledged the educational importance of environment, it was ignored within the mainstream of traditional educational practice and needed constant reassertion. More distinctively 'progressive' is his switch of emphasis from teacher to child, from government to governed. He recognized clearly—and said so—that the most effective learning comes from within, from the child's own motivation and initiative, from his own personal interaction with the world around him; truth is born of experience; genuine knowledge can never be vicarious; what my teacher tells me 'I must verify . . . by my own observation or by interrogating my own consciousness'.[12] The teacher's task is to furnish his pupil 'with the needful aids and facilities, the needful materials and instruments' and then leave him 'to the unshackled use of them'.[13] Transferred to the political scene this implies, as indicated above, a shift of onus on to the individual citizen; he, through participation and involvement, becomes the initiating force in political decision; he learns from his experience and at the same time contributes to the educative ferment which keeps democracy responsive to new ideas and circumstances.

This individual-centred stance brings Mill very close—sometimes in the actual words he uses—to modern educational thought and practice as seen, for instance, in John Dewey, Sir Percy Nunn, Sir Alec Clegg, even A. S. Neill (much of whose theory and practice Mill would have firmly repudiated) and, more recently, Ivan Illich and John Holt. It also anticipates current pressures for devolution of authority, for a grass-roots democracy where decisions, if not determined, are at least directly influenced by opinion at the shop-floor level of citizenship. (Phone-ins, media participation, works councils, student and pupil representation are all manifestations of this.) It would be foolish to press the parallels too closely or to suggest that Mill has anything very new to say to us, a century later, about education. What he said was advanced for his time. Though it was neither new, even then, nor original (he was indebted, among others, to Rousseau and Pestalozzi and was not ignorant of contemporary educational experiment), it contributed significantly to the growing current of thought which has come to express itself practically in the child-centred, discovery-based, interactional pedagogy which is familiar in the schools of today.

There is one message of special importance which Mill has for us—again not new but worthy of constant re-emphasis as corrective of mistaken interpretations of child-centredness. Although in *On Liberty* he likens human nature to a tree which must 'grow and develop itself on all sides',[14] he avoids the error of supposing that this growth can be uncontrolled. Individuality, it was shown in chapter 5, does not mean for Mill the unrestricted burgeoning of potential, but a growth carefully tended and purposively guided by the educator. His clearest statement of this is in his analysis of 'nature' in the essay of that name in his posthumous *Three Essays on Religion* (there is a brief reference to it on p. 102 above). Here he dismisses the view that 'natural' carries prescriptive force and argues that goodness is not natural, that human potential must be *selectively* developed, that growth must be artificially shaped and directed towards worthwhile goals. It follows that a child-centred education is not one which permits children to grow and to do as they please. Rather, it is a pedagogic technique which facilitates learning by focusing attention on the child and his experience instead of the teacher and his instruction; which allows freedom, but only within a carefully controlled environment (Rousseau's 'well-regulated liberty');[15] and which seeks a *disciplined* development of potential for the child's own good and that of society. There are valuable insights here which illuminate not only the processes of formal education but also, *mutatis mutandis*, the functioning of democracy.

Mill's faith in the improving power of education, coupled with the evident inability of voluntary effort to match the nation's need, convinced him in the end of the necessity for state intervention. However, he was keenly aware of its dangers. Indoctrination was one of them: control of schools was a potent means of controlling opinion and thereby rendering a people pliant in the hands of government. Mediocrity was another, arising from the loss of freedom and the consequent stifling of individual variety and experiment. Bureaucracy too, in education as elsewhere (perhaps especially in education) was prone to pedantocracy and to slow strangulation in the toils of its own immutable maxims. His fears led him to the two distinctions mentioned in chapter 6. The first is between 'authoritative' (or 'authoritarian' as we might now say) and 'non-authoritative', the former relying on precise regulation and central control, the latter on persuasion and example. The second is between 'enforce' and 'direct': since education is an elemental human right and (on the parents' part) obligation, the state must enforce its provision and even, where circumstances require, provide it; but to direct education, in the sense of prescribing aims, content, and methods, would, he believed, be a dangerous intrusion into freedom and a curb on progress. The distinctions are valuable and the issues implied in them as alive today as in Mill's time (though not as clear-cut as he supposed); to achieve a proper balance between the two poles of each is essential, then and now, to the realization of an educative democracy.

Enthusiast though he was for democracy, Mill was not blind to its defects or to the realities of human nature. As already stated, his conception of it was partly shaped by the idealized picture which he drew from Athenian democracy at its best, in the first sixty years of the fifth century B.C. Here, despite the exclusion of women and resident aliens from political rights, there was achieved a high level of free, responsible citizenship which transcended class, allowed virtually unlimited freedom of expression, and was conducive to excellence (as shown, for instance, by Athenian accomplishments in literature and the arts); and within its limitations it was a highly educative democracy. However, it was not immune from 'sinister interest'; and the freedom which enabled became in the second half of that century a licence which destroyed. (Plato's picture of the Athenian demos was far less complimentary than Mill's.) Although the sprawling population of nineteenth-century Britain was scarcely comparable with the compact microcosm of Pericles' Athens, the problems which beset its incipient democracy were not altogether dissimilar; nor were the necessary safeguards. Mill was aware of both. There must, of course, be education—to dispel ignorance, broaden vision, facilitate dialogue; an education which is *total*, environmental as well as institutional. Leadership too is crucial (itself a product of education rightly conceived), a leadership not of rhetoric merely or charisma, but of 'cultivated intelligence' uplifting by its compulsive example of excellence; it was for lack of it that Athens, despite her brilliance, succumbed to Sparta; Mill's world of the nineteenth century and ours of the twentieth provide further illustration. Also necessary is the 'antagonist principle' which balances 'progression' with 'permanence', freedom with authority, individuality with sociality, divergence with coherence, thus protecting democracy from the vicious extremes of its own virtues. Not least there is needed the guidance and inspiration of values—not *any* values but those which are conducive to happiness and have satisfied qualitative criteria in experience. With such safeguards Mill believed a democracy could preserve itself as a focus of self-educative activity spontaneously perpetuated for its own renewing and vitality. That he thus tempered enthusiasm with caution, insisting on his 'antagonist principle' and the authority of values, might suggest ambivalence or even lack of faith (see pp. 26–7 above). A deeper assessment indicates rather a perceptive understanding of the conditions necessary for the success of democracy in his own time and also, one may justly add, in ours.

Mill's educational thought is not without its weaknesses, some of which have already been considered in earlier chapters. He was never *inside* education in the sense of actually teaching children (except within his own family—which can hardly be equated with normal class teaching). He might therefore seem in some of his utterances to be speaking beyond his brief, theorizing where he had no practical experience and to that extent also contradicting his own clearly stated pedagogic principles. It is true that Mill never taught a class of children or of students; but a teacher of a kind he certainly considered himself to be, deeply committed to the task of informing, of broadening intellectual horizons, of transmitting values; his writings and his various public activities all testify to this. He was, he would claim, involved in the educative process and shared its insights with those more overtly engaged in it. Moreover, educational wisdom is not a prerogative of the class teacher. Locke, for instance, though he taught only as a private tutor, wrote an educational classic which combines a sensitive understanding of children with much sound practical pedagogy.

Yet the charge is not without justification. It could be argued, for instance, that his lack of classroom experience contributed to an over-intellectualized conception of education and its content (tradition and his own education were other sources), and thus to an excessive emphasis on the cognitive aspects of learning and on the acquisition of intellectual skills. He does indeed write of the intellect as 'the first of all human possessions, that which in its own nature is fitted to rule';[16] he extols the importance of logic, mathematics, and languages (especially the classical) as intellectual disciplines promoting the capacity for thought; and there is conspicuous in his curricular proposals (in contrast with Locke) an almost total absence of reference to physical education and practical crafts. Yet Mill was not himself a narrow intellectual—one need only recall his lifelong hobby of botanizing, his constant travels abroad, his love of music and art, his sensitivity to beauty, and his revulsion against the emotional anaesthesia induced by excessive analysis; and his educational recommendations include a powerful plea for aesthetic experience and moral training. To the same lack of classroom experience might also be attributed the over-ambitious demands he makes on a university education in the *Inaugural Address*; despite its admirable breadth and balance the course of studies he suggests would be impossible to implement at any worthwhile educational depth, at least within the years available to the ordinary undergraduate. Finally, his defence of payment by results and of the threat of dismissal as necessary incentives to efficiency might similarly be ascribed to a myopic view of the teacher's work arising from lack of contact with the actualities of the classroom.

Mill is open to philosophical as well as educational criticism. His account of self-consciousness in terms of a belief in the permanent possibility of states of consciousness is unconvincing; and he admitted that here he was faced with a 'final inexplicability'.[17] The problem of free will in a causal universe he resolved (to his own satisfaction) only at the cost of ambiguity or, as Packe rather less charitably expresses it, of bending logic.[18] Both these issues were considered in chapter 5; as they are still unresolved, it would be harsh to reproach him for not finding an acceptable answer. Also problematic is the status of happiness in relation to other values (freedom, individuality, and the rest) and the status of these latter in themselves, as ends or means. As suggested in chapter 1, there is here a complex conceptual geography which calls for rigorous analytical exploration. Mill did not undertake it, for his immediate purpose was human improvement and his method prescriptive rather than analytical; but the omission, by a consequent unclarity, weakens the axiological basis of his educative democracy. The criticism can be extended to a more general charge of failing to give due attention to the analysis of important concepts. Happiness is obviously crucial to the exposition of his utilitarianism; but after the bald statement in chapter 2 of *Utilitarianism* that 'by happiness is intended pleasure and the absence of pain' and the admission that 'much more requires to be said' he eschews further examination of the concept as not germane to his purpose. So too, freedom and individuality are central to his thinking, yet they are not exposed to the detailed analysis which, as key concepts, they clearly require; hence the reader of *On Liberty* is faced with obscurities of meaning and logical relationship through which he must force his way as best he can. The same may be said of authority, discipline, democracy, and education (though he does, for this last, make the important distinction between formal and informal). Mill was not incapable of analysis; this is clear from the *Logic* and also, on a much smaller scale, from the analysis of 'nature' referred to earlier. Nor was he unaware of the deceptiveness of language, whose 'pictures', as Wittgenstein reminds us, can so easily hold us captive. 'Language', he writes in 'Nature', 'is as it were the atmosphere of philosophical investigation, which must be made transparent before anything can be seen through it in the true figure and position.'[19] That he did not heed this salutary advice may be due in part to the urgency of his prescriptive intent, the 'improvement of mankind', which assumed precedence over the task of clarification; and in part to the simple fact that analysis was not then the preoccupation which it has become since the so-called twentieth century 'revolution in philosophy'. Whatever the reasons the omission reinforces the impression of ambivalence already noted and makes it easier to see Mill as equivocally committed to inconsistent positions.[20]

Further criticisms might be directed against him on social and political grounds. It could be objected, for instance, that just as he never taught a class of children, so he never saw the 'labouring classes' from inside. He was himself a highly paid civil servant moving in cultural and intellectual circles far removed from the squalor and illiteracy of urban slums. Consequently, despite the strong and sincere idealism that motivated him, he could never fully identify himself in sympathy and understanding with those whom he championed (and so, as Halliday claims, he remained 'by inclination an aristocrat' and distrustful of democracy).[21] As a further consequence he tended to underestimate the infirmity of human nature, its selfishness, its recalcitrance to change even for its own good, and at the same time to overestimate the power of 'cultivated intelligence'; for it is not, as Mill states, 'what men think that determine how they act',[22] but motives more deeply rooted in the grounds of our being. There is some truth in this, but two things can be said in Mill's defence. First, obviously enough, one need not belong to the labouring classes in order to work for their good (any more than one must wear a skirt to champion women's rights); and, at a time when the working classes had too few leaders within their own ranks, inevitably help must come from outside. Nor can there be any doubt of Mill's genuine sympathy, even though from outside and a position of privilege, with the working classes and others whom he felt to be oppressed or unjustly treated

—prostitutes, Irish peasants, American negroes, Jamaicans under Governor Eyre.[23] Second, his faith in 'cultivated intelligence' did not blind him to the realities of human nature: he knew that men are not all equal in either intelligence or virtue, that passion and prejudice can overrule reason, that 'sinister interest' is not confined by class boundaries; it was for this reason, among others, that he advocated participation—to force men out of the narrow circle of 'private partialities' towards a consideration of the public good[24]— and conceded government intervention to secure the good of the people in the face of nonchalance or opposition.

The last of these, intervention for the people's good, suggests a deeper and more intractable criticism. Mill was powerfully motivated by a desire for human improvement; this has been sufficiently emphasized in earlier pages; so too have the values which he thought should give direction to improvement. As a result he found himself in a dilemma which he recognized but never satisfactorily resolved. The dilemma arises partly from a conflict of interests within his own value-goals and partly from the practical implications of his behavioural theory outlined earlier in this chapter; in part it reflects different, and potentially discrepant, aspects of his own nature, the logical and the emotive. Mill was committed to happiness as one, if not the, primary ethical goal—and to happiness of a special quality; he was also committed to individuality and freedom and to democracy as their political expression. But individuality, granted freedom, may through ignorance or preference choose happiness of an inferior quality or other values which conflict with those approved by Mill. Which then has priority, 'the *will* of the people' or 'the *good* of the people'?[25] The dilemma is aggravated by his association psychology and the environmentalism which it implies; these together, if backed by suitable legislation, supply an instrumentality which enables the good (as conceived by those in authority) to be imposed on the people against their will and even, if it is implemented with sufficient subtlety, without their knowledge. Manipulation of environment is a powerful means of influencing behaviour and forming character. The earnest improver is inevitably inclined to use it—and Mill had the example of Plato's *Republic*, familiar to him from boyhood, to reinforce his inclination. No doubt in Mill's time these implications of his behavioural theory were themselves more theoretical than practical —the technology of control has made great advances since his day;

but they point towards the possibility of a totalitarian social engineering which allows only a carefully regulated liberty and subordinates the will of the people to predetermined policies aimed at their good.

How far, then, should intervention go? At what point does a benevolent exercise of authority become unjustifiable intrusion into autonomy? Who decides what *is* good, what values to reject and what to include in the blueprint for the social engineer? Whence comes the authority to make such decisions—is it presupposed in the claim of an élite to possess a more highly cultivated intelligence or is it delegated by the people to an approved leadership? And (a vital question) *quis custodiet ipsos custodes*?[26] Plato's philosopher rulers could rely on the guidance of an objective transcendental Good; no such advantage was available to the imperfect rulers of Mill's imperfect society. Further questions readily suggest themselves. How far, if at all, can human nature (and human society with it) be reshaped to a new pattern of values? May we not be limited, in fact, merely to changing the expression, the outward manifestation, of what is basically the same in all men and all societies? And is it possible to do even this much without exercising a degree of authority which denies that freedom and dignity which (*pace* Skinner)[27] is still for most of us essential to meaningful existence? Yet more questions arise concerning the techniques of control. Environmental planning surely requires the exclusion of undesirable influences by some form of censorship and the inclusion by positive indoctrination of those thought desirable. How else can the will of the people be matched with their good? But here again, who chooses and by what authority and what criteria? And is an aseptic environment, established by a censorship which diminishes choice and an indoctrination which imposes it vicariously, conducive to an *educative* democracy? Finally, the whole concept of social engineering has been attacked by Sir Karl Popper who accuses Mill, together with Plato, Marx and others, of 'psychologism' (the reduction of sociology to psychology) and 'holism' (the notion of society as a complex unity which can be made to respond *as a whole* to blueprint planning).[28]

It is impossible here to consider these criticisms or how Mill himself might have replied to them; nor can we pursue possible answers to the numerous questions in the preceding paragraph. It does seem, however, that Mill leaves us with an extensive and

inadequately explored region of conceptual and practical problems, with controversial issues which are at the heart of his concept
of educative democracy and which, in so far as they are unresolved,
may be thought to diminish its validity. Tentative ventures into
this region he does indeed make. Censorship and indoctrination are
among the issues he discusses in *On Liberty* and elsewhere;
authority he seeks to locate in his élite of cultivated intelligence and
trained expertise (but with insufficient protection, one might
suggest, against human frailty and bureaucratic propensities);
*laissez faire*, the principle of non-interference, is considered in the
final chapter of his *Political Economy* (where the conclusion that
'every departure from it, unless required by some great good, is a
certain evil'[29] leaves the issue as ambiguous as ever). Whether or
not these perplexities are capable of resolution may itself be a
matter for question. Perhaps the only answer lies in there being no
answer but only a sensitive probing which seeks not so much to
solve problems as to keep them poised in the creative tension of
'antagonism'. The central task is to keep democracy *educative*—
through freedom, autonomous decision, dialogue in the pursuit of
truth, participation, and the expression of diverse excellences—
while at the same time contributing to improvement and the sum
of human happiness. Mill's success, it might be argued, lies not in
finding final answers (which he did not) but in correctly siting
interrogation marks on key issues and thus establishing salients for
further exploration. 'Educative democracy' is itself such a salient,
a rich, imaginative, and provocative concept whose full implications
we have yet to unravel.

# Appendix

'A VIOLENT exaggeration of individualism' were the words (quoted on p. 91) of a nineteenth-century critic; but a similar charge has recently been made against Mill in Professor Gertrude Himmelfarb's most interesting and scholarly study, *On Liberty and Liberalism: the case of John Stuart Mill*, to which reference has already been made (chapter 5, note 5). She argues that *On Liberty* contrasts with almost all Mill's other writings by its distinctive view, peculiar to itself, of individuality, freedom, and society; the only works with which it has an affinity are *The Subjection of Women* and the essay 'The Enfranchisement of Women' (the latter of which Mill credits to his wife). The view is not only distinctive (indeed *novel*, she maintains); it is also inconsistent with those expressed elsewhere.

First, Mill proposes in *On Liberty* 'to assert one very simple principle, as entitled to govern absolutely the dealings of society with the individual' (compare his description of the book in his *Autobiography* as 'a kind of philosophic textbook of a single truth'); but such simplistic, single-minded commitment to an absolute principle is precisely what he condemns in Bentham and Comte and even (conceding here the weight of Macaulay's criticism) in his father's theory of government; moreover, it conflicts with the experience of his nervous crisis which drove him to reject the narrow, quantitative utilitarianism of Bentham and James Mill, to sample a variety of thinkers— Wordsworth, Coleridge, Saint-Simon, Carlyle—and to commend the 'many-sidedness' of Goethe.[1]

Second, *On Liberty* expresses a view of the individual in society which is at variance with an early 'Benthamite' article which he wrote for *The Westminster Review* in 1824 and with the much later and mature 1840 essay on Coleridge: in the former he upholds the role of law and government as against the literal interpretation of liberty as total freedom from restraint—'A measure of government, therefore, is not necessarily bad because it is contrary to liberty; and to blame it for that reason leads to confusion of ideas'; in the latter he states three essential conditions for a permanent political society—loyalty to its fundamental principles or values, a 'feeling of common interest', and an education 'continued through life' which includes as its main ingredient a '*restraining discipline*' (Mill's italics). And as if to confirm what he wrote in this passage Mill repeated it in the successive editions of the *Logic* (VI, x). Again, in his second review of *Democracy in America*, while agreeing with de Tocqueville (and with himself in *On Liberty*) in condemning the levelling tendencies of democracy, the dwarfing of individuality and the despotism of public opinion, he nevertheless points to a weakness of democracy in loosening social ties by encouraging each man to 'retire within himself, and concentrate his wishes, interests, and pursuits within his own business and household'; hence comes the 'commercialism' which, though he so much deplored it, was an inevitable outcome of the very individuality he lauded in *On Liberty*.[2]

Third, Mill's view of human nature in *On Liberty* is entirely contrary to that of the essay 'Nature', written at more or less the same time; the latter's doctrine is not the free expression of individuality but its selective and disciplined development; man's duty is to amend and improve nature, whether in himself or outside, to control and suppress instinct, and to strive towards a goodness which, far from being natural, is the outcome of persistent and deliberate endeavour.[3] Fourth, Professor Himmelfarb points to a gradual modification, in the successive editions of *Principles of Political Economy*, of Mill's initial hostility to communist and socialist schemes of social organization and to an increasing sympathy for government control; this is confirmed by the passage in the *Autobiography* where he discusses his own and Harriet's hope for a unison of individual freedom with common ownership and industrial cooperation. It was not only, she writes, the socialist mode of organization that conflicted with *On Liberty*;

it was also the reform of human nature required by the new social organisation. In his other works the 'course of future progress' was seen to lie in the development of the social character of man; in *On Liberty* Mill looked for it in precisely the opposite direction, the development of man's individuality.[4]

These four are not her only illustrations of the distinctiveness of *On Liberty* and its contrast with Mill's other works, but they are sufficient for our purpose. An important conclusion of her argument, and an underlying theme of the book, is that there are two Mills, the Mill of *On Liberty* with its extravagant claims for individuality and non-restraint, and the Mill of rational liberalism which acknowledges a good transcending the individual and his self-expression and which therefore recognizes the need for authority, discipline, and initiation into a culture which both enriches individuality and is enriched by it. In this latter and (in her view) genuine form of liberalism 'Liberty of action is good, but not an absolute or ultimate end, and . . . individuality is good, but again not absolutely, in all forms and under all conditions.' She continues:

Mill had always been concerned with the problem of developing a strong and energetic character. But elsewhere [than in *On Liberty*] he kept clearly in mind the particular kind of character he wanted to see developed

—a character that was not simply strong and energetic in pursuit of its individuality, but was strong and energetic in pursuit of the good. And that good was something other than the individual's desires, impulses, passion and will. There was a virtue that transcended these, an order of goods which might not accord with desire and impulse and which might require the subordination of passion and will. It was the promotion of these goods that was Mill's preoccupation during most of his life.[5]

But *why* does *On Liberty* differ so markedly from the rest of Mill's works (excepting the two named above)? *What* caused him to depart thus from his norm and magnify the claims of individuality?[6] Two possible answers Professor Himmelfarb dismisses briefly as lacking factual support, first that the two Mills represent an earlier and a later stage in his thought, second that Mill was unaware of the contrast. A third answer, initially more plausible, succumbs to a study of the evidence: it is that Mill concentrated his attention on this single limited issue, the threat to individuality from the oppression of social tyranny, because he believed it to be the most momentously urgent problem of his time. If this was so, she argues, then Mill was almost alone in his belief. It was not shared by his reviewers, most of whom were sceptical of his fears; she mentions H. T. Buckle in *Fraser's Magazine*, J. F. Stephen in *The Saturday Review*, and others in *The National Review* and *Bentley's Quarterly*, all insisting that individuality was as vigorous as ever and conformity less of a threat than he supposed; *On Liberty*, one of them suggested, might well be the product of 'the prison-cell of some persecuted thinker'.[7] And there was Macaulay's famous criticism: 'What is meant by the complaint that there is no individuality now? Genius takes its own course, as it always did. . . . He is really crying "Fire!" in Noah's flood.'[8] Furthermore, the Victorian age, contrary to the now popular image of ethical prudery and coercive social conformity, was a time of notable diversity (not to say deviance) in sex, religion, literature, intellect, and leisure; 'most Englishmen in the 1850s,' she writes, 'had a sense of relative ease and freedom, of greater, not fewer, opportunities, options, alternatives'.[9]

What, then, is the correct answer? Professor Himmelfarb finds it in Mill's relationship with Harriet during the years of their marriage, in Harriet's character and influence, and in her contribution to *On Liberty* which, Mill firmly maintained, was 'more directly and literally our joint production' than any other of his books, and which they had constantly revised together, 'reading, weighing and criticising every sentence'. It is impossible in a few paragraphs to do justice to the detailed and well-documented argument which she presents in chapters 9 and 10 of her book. What follows here is a sufficient summary (it is hoped) to indicate its principal grounds and the significance of its implications for *On Liberty*.

She first warns against dismissing as mere eulogy Mill's affirmation of Harriet's influence on him and of her contribution to the essay. That he exaggerated her intellectual ability can hardly be disputed—neither her letters nor her other writings provide evidence of outstanding mental powers, and Carlyle remembered her as 'full of unwise intellect, asking and re-asking stupid questions'. But her intellectual *influence* is a different matter; this, she argues, was powerful and profound. So what kind of a person was she? 'The impression that emerges is of a sharp mind, personal and intuitive, quick to generalise and pronounce judgment, confident in the correctness of her opinions and not at all diffident in advancing them.'[10] Mill himself describes her in the *Autobiography* as 'a woman of deep and strong feeling, of penetrating and intuitive intelligence, and of an eminently meditative and poetic nature', and there is no good reason to disagree with him (intelligence and intellectual ability not being identical). 'Boldness of speculation' he also attributes to her, and with this too one can agree, 'if by boldness is meant a zeal for simple, clear-cut, dramatic solutions, an impatience with the kinds of complexities and difficulties that came more naturally, as he intimated, to himself'.[11] For she was a utopian and a perfectionist, addicted (like Jeremy Bentham) to 'large generalisations and gross simplifications', and her whole mode of thinking was absolutist and simplistic.[12] Mill's attitude to her was one of deferential and self-abasing solicitude, exaggerating her talents at the expense of his own, and assuming the role of interpreter to her inspiring and initiating genius. It is hardly surprising, therefore, that Mill should claim in the *Autobiography* that 'the whole mode of thinking of which [*On Liberty*] was the expression was emphatically hers' and that he 'was so thoroughly imbued with it, that the same thoughts naturally occurred to us both'. There is even less cause for surprise when one considers the circumstances of its composition.

After their marriage in 1851 their life was one of self-contained seclusion: in the seven years of their marriage 'they seldom (if ever) dined out and rarely entertained at home. ... Mill maintained no regular connection with any journal or political group ... attended no meetings except for an occasional session of the Political Economy Club, met few people apart from his colleagues at the India House and some of his more venturesome friends who occasionally visited him there.'[13] Tuberculosis increased their isolation; they both contracted it; they expected to die of it, and even discussed who would be the first to go (it was Harriet, of course—Mill made a remarkable recovery). In this kind of hothouse existence they planned a collection of essays which were to be 'a sort of mental pemican, which thinkers, when there are any after us, may nourish themselves with and then dilute for other people'.[14] *On Liberty* was one of these essays and probably the only one of this period, Professor Himmelfarb asserts, which was both written and revised while they were together; it was the high point of their collaboration (as Mill's own statement suggests). It was thus, more than any other, 'the philosophical expression of their existential situation'.[15] It was a defence and a protest, powered from deep emotional sources—a defence of themselves and the life they had chosen, and a protest, mostly against the conventions which (supposedly) threatened their unique individuality, partly, perhaps, against the mortality which threatened their physical, emotional, and intellectual coexistence. As such it was a very special book, the product of a particular relationship at a particular period of Mill's life. Its simplistic absolutism (the 'one very simple principle') is Harriet's, not Mill's; the extravagant exaltation of individuality and personal freedom derives in part from the same absolutism, in part from their self-assumed stance against the world. (Interestingly, another writer comments: 'Their relationship had been a guilt-ridden one, about which they were hypersensitive.')[16] When Harriet was dead, when his grief was abated, and *On Liberty* had been published as a memorial to their marriage, Mill reverted to his former ways, socially and intellectually—'released from her immediate influence, he entered upon a quite different mode of existence'.[17] (However, his retirement from the India Office a few weeks before Harriet's death may also have contributed to this change of life-style; Professor Himmelfarb does not seem to allow for this possibility.)

Professor Himmelfarb is surely right in pointing to the peculiar circumstances of the composition of *On Liberty*; she is right, too, so the present writer is persuaded, in her estimate of Harriet's character and capabilities and of her influence on Mill during the period of their marriage. It is difficult, therefore, to resist her conclusion that *On Liberty* is a departure from the norm, an exaggerated expression of a view which was not properly Mill's and which, like borrowed clothing, he shed off with Harriet's death. But she is herself guilty of some exaggeration, or at least imbalance, in presenting a partial thesis which, for its particular purpose, isolates *On Liberty* as *contrasted with* rather than *balanced by* Mill's other works. Her two Mills are not strangers to each other but one and the same person seen from different aspects; they represent two currents of thought, each with its own implications and creating a tension of purposes and procedures which at their extremes are irreconcilable but which in rational beings and in democratic societies must be brought together in practicable compromise. Individuality is a part of Mill's thinking at least from the time of his nervous crisis and subconsciously was part of him before that; and although for special reasons it reaches a crescendo of expression in *On Liberty* there are traces of it in all his major and many of his minor writings—*Logic, Political Economy, Sir William Hamilton, Representative Government,*

*Comte*, 'Bentham', even *Utilitarianism* and 'Nature' (which Professor Himmelfarb cites against it). Its sources have already been indicated (in addition to Harriet)—in his own education, in his discovery of the qualitative and affective aspects of experience, in Bentham, de Tocqueville and association psychology; but most of all it was part of the man himself, as is shown for instance by his reverence for the heroic, his passionate response to beauty, his love of music, his moral integrity, and the very boldness with which he defied convention in his love for Harriet. One must remember, too, his botanical interests which would readily suggest to him (without von Humboldt's prompting) the concepts of potentiality and development which are so prominent in *On Liberty*, and also his acquaintance with the educational ideas of Rousseau and Pestalozzi.[18]

If one looks at *On Liberty* from a wider perspective instead of the narrow angle of a single book and a particular relationship, one's impression (as already argued) is not of abnormality or aberration from the true path, but rather of balance, of two modes of thinking, each with its essential value, held in creative tension—the individual and his development, society and its demands upon him. Moreover, the inevitability of the tension can be shown not only from the nature of the human situation—man in and of society, individual potential socially disciplined—but from the implications of Mill's own ethical, psychological and philosophical commitments. Ethically, his utilitarianism sought the greatest happiness of *all*, and this must necessarily conflict at some point with the happiness and self-determination of *each*; the good of society, the improvement of mankind cannot be achieved without limitation of personal freedom (a fact not overlooked in *On Liberty*). Association psychology on the one hand points to an individuality which is unique by reason of the uniqueness of its sensory experience (no two persons have precisely the same mental constituents), on the other it supplies an instrumentality which subordinates the individual to purposes larger than himself (pp. 87 and 176–7 above). Philosophically he was committed to two seeming incompatibles—freedom and a causal universe—and also to a view of human nature as a potential which must be disciplined into conformity with selected values (pp. 81–2). To take this broader view of Mill detracts not at all from the value of Professor Himmelfarb's study in drawing attention to the pecularities of *On Liberty* and to the weaknesses of its doctrine of individuality when isolated from and uncorrected by the counterpoise of 'the other Mill'.

# Note on abbreviations and editions

The following abbreviations are used in the notes to the text and in the bibliography:

| | |
|---|---|
| *Autob.* | *Autobiography*, ed. Laski, H. J., Oxford University Press, World's Classics, 1924 etc. |
| CW | Collected Works, University of Toronto Press and Routledge and Kegan Paul. |
| *D & D* | *Dissertations and Discussions*, vols. I–III (2nd. ed., 1867), vol. IV (1875). |
| EERS | *Essays on Ethics, Religion and Society*, Collected Works X. |
| EES | *Essays on Economics and Society* i and ii, Collected Works IV and V. |
| EL | *Earlier Letters, 1812–1848* i and ii, Collected Works XII and XIII. |
| EPC | *Essays on Philosophy and the Classics*, Collected Works XI. |
| EPS | *Essays on Politics and Society* i and ii, Collected Works XVIII and XIX. |
| *Hamilton* | *An Examination of Sir William Hamilton's Philosophy*, 6th. ed., 1889. |
| *Inaugural* | *Inaugural Address at the University of St. Andrews*, in *John Stuart Mill on Education*, ed. Garforth, F. W., Teachers College Press, New York, 1971. |
| *Lib.* | *On Liberty*, ed. Fawcett, M. G., Oxford University Press, World's Classics, 1912 etc. (in one volume with *Representative Government* and *The Subjection of Women*). |
| LL | *Later Letters, 1849–1873* i–iv, Collected Works XIV–XVII |
| *Logic* | *A System of Logic: Ratiocinative and Inductive* i and ii, Collected Works VII and VIII. |
| PPE | *Principles of Political Economy* i and ii, Collected Works II and III. |
| *Repr. Gov.* | *Considerations on Representative Government*, ed. Fawcett, M. G., Oxford University Press, World's Classics, 1912 etc. (in one volume with *On Liberty* etc.) |
| *S. of W.* | *The Subjection of Women*, ed. Fawcett, M. G., Oxford University Press, World's Classics, 1912 etc. (in one volume with *On Liberty* etc.) |

Schn. *ELS*     *Mill's Essays on Literature and Society*, ed. Schneewind, J. B., Collier Books, New York, 1965.

Schn. *EW*     *Mill's Ethical Writings*, ed. Schneewind, J. B., Collier Books, New York, 1965.

Warnock     *Utilitarianism, On Liberty* etc., ed. Warnock, M., Collins, 1962.

Wherever possible quotations are taken from and references made to the volumes of the Collected Works; some important works have not yet appeared in this series, notably the *Autobiography*, the *Inaugural Address, Sir William Hamilton's Philosophy*, and *The Subjection of Women*; the editions used for these are indicated above. Since the Collected Works may not be easily available to all readers, I have added, for some of Mill's writings, references to more accessible editions.

# Notes

I. AIMS AND VALUES

1. *EERS*, pp. 408–9.
2. 'Nature', *EERS*, p. 397.
3. 'Coleridge', *EERS*, p. 140 (*D & D* I, p. 427; Schn. *ELS*, p. 317); the dictum is attributed to W. E. Hocking by Sir Fred Clarke in his *Freedom in the Educative Society*, p. 16.
4. *LL* i, p. 22; 'Bentham', *EERS*, p. 109 (*D & D* I, p. 381: Schn. *ELS*, p. 279); *Logic* ii, p. 926; *EPS* ii, p. 382. (*Repr. Gov.* p. 156).
5. 'Corporation and Church Property', *EES* i, p. 213 (*D & D* I, p. 28).
6. Quoted in the paper by Hans, N., 'Bentham and the Utilitarians', in Judges, A. V., ed., *Pioneers of English Education*, p. 93.
7. Burston, W. H., ed., *James Mill on Education*, p. 71.
8. On 30 July 1833, Roebuck moved 'that the House would, with the smallest delay possible, consider the means of establishing a system of National Education' (*Hansard*, vol. 20, col. 139); the motion was withdrawn. On 3 June 1834, he moved 'the appointment of a Select Committee to inquire into the means of establishing a system of National Education' (*Hansard*, vol. 24, col. 127); this motion was also withdrawn but another was substituted by Lord Althorp, and accepted, asking for a Select Committee to inquire into the state of education in England and Wales and to investigate the effect of the grant made in 1833 and the need for further grants. An article by Roebuck on 'National Education' appeared in *Tait's Edinburgh Magazine* 2 (Mar. 1833).
9. Burston, W. H., op. cit., p. 41.
10. 'Endowments', *EES* ii, p. 617 (*D & D* IV, p. 5).
11. *EL* i, p. 207; 'Thornton on Labour and its Claims', *EES* ii, pp. 659, 655 (*D & D* IV, pp. 70, 63); *S. of W.*, p. 525; 'Newman's Political Economy', *EES* ii, p. 444; 'Utility of Religion', *EERS*, p. 422.
12. On Ireland see e.g., MacMinn, N., etc., *Bibliography*, October 1846 to April 1847; on slavery and negroes see, e.g., 'The Contest in America', *D & D* III, and 'The Negro Question', *Fraser's Magazine* 41 (1850), pp. 25–31; the letter to his brother-in-law (Arthur Hardy, Harriet's youngest brother, who had founded an institution for working people in Adelaide) is in *LL* ii, pp. 503–4.
13. The quotations in this paragraph are from *Utilitarianism*, ch. 2, *EERS*, pp. 210, 211, 212, 215 (Schn. *EW.*, pp. 281–7; Warnock, pp. 257–64). The identification of happiness with the employment of the 'higher faculties' has a distinctly Aristotelian flavour; see *Nichomachean Ethics* X, 7. John was more explicit than his father felt able to be in describing happiness; for the latter 'Wherein does happiness consist?' was an unanswered question requiring strenuous philosophical inquiry; see Burston, W. H., op. cit., pp. 65–7.

14. *EERS*, p. 234 (Schn. *EW*, p. 309; Warnock, p. 288). For a discussion of Mill's 'proof' see, for example: Warnock, M., *Ethics since 1900*, pp. 28ff., where she examines G. E. Moore's criticism of Mill; also her introduction to the Fontana edition of *Utilitarianism*, pp. 25ff.; MacIntyre, A., *A Short History of Ethics*, pp. 238ff.; Hudson, W. D., *Modern Moral Philosophy*, pp. 74ff.; and Cowan, J. L., *Pleasure and Pain*, pp. 104ff., who strongly opposes the view that Mill is guilty of logical fallacy.
15. *Utilitarianism*, *EERS*, p. 213 (Schn. *EW*, p. 286; Warnock, p. 262).
16. *Logic* ii, p. 952.
17. *Utilitarianism*, *EERS*, pp. 217, 218 (Schn. *EW*, pp. 291–2; Warnock, pp. 267–8). Mill's respect for Jesus appears a number of times in his writings in addition to the passage quoted here; for example, 'Utility of Religion', *EERS*, pp. 416–17, 'Theism', *EERS*, p. 487, *EL* i, pp. 208–9, *LL* i, p. 27.
18. 'Bentham', *EERS*, p. 95 (*D & D* I, p. 359; Schn. *ELS*, p. 262).
19. *Comte and Positivism*, *EERS*, p. 339.
20. *Utilitarianism*, *EERS*, p. 218 (Schn. *EW*, p. 291; Warnock, p. 268).
21. ib., p. 235 (Schn. *EW*, p. 310; Warnock, pp. 289–90).
22. *Logic* ii, p. 949.
23. ib., p. 952.
24. In the introduction to *On Liberty* Mill asserts the principle of non-interference as the norm for society's dealings with the individual, the only exception being the need for society to protect itself; thus freedom means primarily the absence of restraint. He states a more positive view when he writes that 'the only freedom which deserves the name is that of pursuing our own good in our own way' and 'liberty consists in doing what one desires'. In order to have men of genius, he writes in ch. 3, 'it is necessary to preserve the soil in which they grow', and then, changing the metaphor, 'Genius can only breathe freely in an *atmosphere* of freedom' (quotations in *EPS* i, pp. 226, 294, 267 (*Lib.*, pp. 18, 118, 80). (I am not suggesting that there are two kinds of freedom, 'negative' and 'positive'; I believe that freedom means non-restraint and that what one does when one is released from restraint is something quite different. I have tried to elucidate this in 'The "Paradox of Freedom"'; see also below, pp. 102–4 and the article by E. G. West, 'Liberty and Education: John Stuart Mill's Dilemma'. Nor, in this context, am I distinguishing 'freedom' from 'liberty'.)
25. *EPS* i, p. 261 (*Lib.*, p. 70).
26. *S. of W.*, pp. 542, 544, 543.
27. *PPE* i, pp. 208–9.
28. *Utilitarianism*, *EERS*, p. 235 (Schn. *EW*, p. 310; Warnock, p. 290). On freedom as an intrinsic value for Mill see Robson, J. M., *The Improvement of Mankind*, pp. 185–6, McCloskey, H. J., *John Stuart Mill*, p. 127, and Rees, J. C., 'Was Mill for Liberty?'
29. 'Bentham', *EERS*, p. 109 (*D & D* I, p. 381; Schn. *ELS*, p. 279). Mill was well aware of the different aspects of truth—mathematical, scientific, artistic, etc.—but he often used the word in a general sense,

as in the following quotations, ignoring internal distinctions of meaning.

30. 'Utility of Religion', *EERS*, p. 404.
31. 'Civilisation', *EPS* i, p. 144 (*D & D* I, p. 201; Schn. *ELS*, p. 179).
32. *EPS* i, p. 243 (*Lib.*, p. 43).
33. 'Grote's Plato', *EPC*, p. 404 (*D & D* III, p. 319).
34. *Inaugural*, pp. 177, 185, 210.
35. *LL* iii, p. 1346 (cf. p. 1469: 'if there is one thing to which we all ought to give our allegiance irrespective of consequence it is truth').
36. Packe, M. St. J., *The Life of John Stuart Mill*, pp. 450–1.
37. *EPS* i, p. 243 (*Lib.*, p. 44).
38. Burston, W. H., op. cit., p. 66.
39. ib., p. 67.
40. *Inaugural*, p. 226.


2. WHAT KIND OF SOCIETY?

1. *EPS* i, p. 224 (*Lib.*, p. 16); *EPS* ii, p. 418 (*Repr. Gov.*, p. 206). Mill briefly discusses despotic and monarchic government in chs. 3 and 4 of *Repr. Gov.*; he states clearly that 'the ideally best form of government' is not necessarily 'practicable or eligible in all states of civilisation', and that democracy may therefore have to wait on circumstances (*EPS* ii, p. 404 and *Repr. Gov.*, p. 186).
2. *EPS* i, p. 224 (*Lib.*, p. 16).
3. *Spectator*, 16 Mar. 1850, p. 256; *EPS* ii, p. 411 (*Repr. Gov.*, p. 197).
4. *EPS* ii, p. 384 (*Repr. Gov.*, pp. 159, 158).
5. ib., pp. 390–1 (*Repr. Gov.*, pp. 167, 168).
6. ib., p. 392 (*Repr. Gov.*, p. 170).
7. ib., p. 393 (*Repr. Gov.*, p. 171). It is interesting to compare these two criteria with the two principles of good government which he sets forth in his review of Bailey's *Rationale of Political Representation*, published many years earlier in the *London Review*, July 1835; they are, 'identification of interest between the rulers and the ruled' and 'government by a select body, not by the people collectively' (p. 347 and in *EPS* i, p. 23). I have taken the phrase 'educative society' from Sir Fred Clarke's *Freedom in the Educative Society*, but I do not know that he was the first to use it. This educative role of government Mill wished to see extended to Parliamentary debates. In a debate on the Representation of the People Bill (*Hansard*, vol. 182, 13 April 1866, col. 1261) he said: 'I can hardly conceive a nobler course of national education than the debates of this House would become, if the notions, right and wrong, which are fermenting in the minds of the working classes, many of which go down very deep into the foundations of society and government, were fairly stated and genuinely discussed within these walls.'
8. ib., pp. 404, 407 (*Repr. Gov.*, pp. 186, 190, 191).
9. *EPS* i, p. 270 (*Lib.*, p. 84).

10. *EPS* ii, p. 407 (*Repr. Gov.*, p. 190).
11. ib. (*Repr. Gov.*, p. 191). On the power of speculative thought see, for instance, *EPS* ii, p. 382 (*Repr. Gov.*, p. 156) where he asserts that it is 'one of the chief elements of social power', and *Logic* ii, p. 926: 'the evidence of history and that of human nature combine, by a striking instance of consilience, to show that there really is one social element which is thus predominant, and almost paramount, among the agents of the social progression. This is the state of the speculative faculties of mankind'; also *Comte and Positivism, EERS*, pp. 316–17.
12. *EPS* ii, p. 411 (*Repr. Gov.*, pp. 196–7).
13. 'Thoughts on Parliamentary Reform', *EPS* ii, pp. 322–3 (*D & D* III, p. 18).
14. *EPS* ii, p. 412 (*Repr. Gov.*, pp. 197–8); on discipline and the moral effects of participation see also 'Coleridge', *EERS*, pp. 133–4 (*D & D* I, pp. 416–19; Schn. *ELS*, pp. 308–10) and *Comte and Positivism, EERS*, p. 339.
15. On Athens see pp. 16–17 above. Plato's (admittedly prejudiced) estimate of democracy can be found, for example, in *Republic* VI, 488ff. and VII, 555ff. (transl. Lee, H. D. P., 2nd. ed., pp. 282ff. and 372ff.); Thucydides presents contrasting pictures of Athens—her ideal best in Pericles' Funeral Speech (Book II, 35ff.) and the sad days of her degeneracy in the Melian Dialogue (Book V, 84ff.).
16. 'Pledges', *Examiner*, 15 July 1832, p. 450.
17. *PPE* ii, 947ff. (universal education, cf. *EPS* i, pp. 302–4, *Lib.* pp. 129ff.), 941, 970 (and cf. 'Coleridge', *EERS*, p. 156 (*D & D* I, pp. 453–4; Schn. *ELS*, pp. 336–7).
18. *EPS* ii, p. 392 (*Repr. Gov.*, p. 170).
19. 'Pledges', op. cit., p. 449.
20. *EPS* ii, p. 446 (*Repr. Gov.*, p. 245). 'Sinister interest' is a favourite phrase of Mill; he uses it of all social classes to indicate partisan policies contrary to the general good.
21. ib., p. 391 (*Repr. Gov.*, p. 169).
22. 'Appendix', *D & D* I, pp. 470–1; 'Rationale of Political Representation', op. cit., p. 348 and in *EPS* i, p. 23 (see also note 7, above); 'Bentham', *EERS*, p. 109 (*D & D* I, p. 381; Schn. *ELS*, p. 279).
23. 'Pledges', op. cit., p. 449.
24. *PPE* ii, p. 866; *S. of W.*, p. 478; 'Grote's Plato', *EPC*, pp. 435–7 (*D & D* III, pp. 371–2).
25. *Parliamentary Papers 1854–5*, vol. 20, p. 92 (and *EPS* i, p. 207).
26. *EPS* ii, p. 470 (*Repr. Gov.*, pp. 277–8).
27. 'Thoughts on Parliamentary Reform', *EPS* ii, p. 323 (*D & D* III, p. 19).
28. *EPS* ii, p. 473 (*Repr. Gov.*, p. 282) (cf. 'Thoughts on Parliamentary Reform', *EPS* ii, p. 324 (*D & D* III, p. 21)). On plural voting see *Representative Government*, ch. 8, especially *EPS* ii, pp. 472ff. (*Repr. Gov.*, pp. 281ff.), and 'Thoughts on Parliamentary Reform', *EPS* ii, pp. 324ff. (*D & D* III, pp. 18ff.). For his approval and explanation of Hare's system see *EPS* ii, pp. 453ff. (*Repr. Gov.*, pp.

254ff.), a passage added in the second edition, and the footnote, pp. 465–6 (*Repr. Gov.*, pp. 271–3), added in the third edition; also 'Recent Writers on Reform', *EPS* ii, pp. 359ff. (*D & D* III, pp. 74ff.), and *Autob.*, pp. 219–21. Oddly, though at first in favour of a secret ballot, Mill gradually changed his view, arguing that publicity might lead to a greater sense of responsibility, would diminish the pressure of class interest, and would promote mental emancipation; see Robson, J. M., *The Improvement of Mankind*, pp. 233–5.

See also the interesting letter to an unknown correspondent (*LL* ii, pp. 543–4, 11 Dec. 1857): though agreeing that educated people should have a greater weighting in the ballot than that of mere numbers, he has 'not seen any method proposed by which persons of educated minds can be sifted from the rest of the community'; if extra votes were granted to the 'liberal professions', their members would tend to vote as professional rather than as educated men; he suggests two possible measures—excluding the 'uneducated' by appropriate tests, and a plan proposed by a Mr. Marshall for allowing a voter to give all his votes to the same candidate; he adds that he would like to see representation of university graduates, already possessed by Oxford, Cambridge, and Dublin, extended to London (which it was in 1867).

29. 'Centralisation', *Edinburgh Review* 115 (1862), pp. 355–6, and in *EPS* ii, pp. 610–11.
30. 'Thoughts on Parliamentary Reform', *EPS* ii, p. 324 (*D & D* III, p. 21).
31. 'Bentham', *EERS*, p. 107 (*D & D* I, p. 378; Schn. *ELS*, p. 277).
32. *EPS* ii, p. 439 (*Repr. Gov.*, p. 234).
33. 'Centralisation', op. cit., p. 324, and in *EPS* ii, p. 582.
34. *Autob.*, p. 180; *Comte and Positivism*, *EERS*, p. 367.
35. *Comte and Positivism*, *EERS*, p. 306; *PPE* ii, pp. 943–4. Cf. his letter to Bain, *LL* ii, p. 631; 'We *must* be satisfied with keeping alive the sacred fire in a few minds when we are unable to do more—but the notion of an intellectual aristocracy of *lumières* while the rest of the world remains in darkness fulfils none of my aspirations.'
36. *EPS* i, p. 309 (*Lib.*, p. 139): 'Centralisation', op. cit., p. 351, and in *EPS* ii, p. 606).
37. *EPS* ii, pp. 535, 539 (*Repr. Gov.*, pp. 365, 371).
38. *PPE* ii, p. 971.
39. 'Duveyrier's Political Views of French Affairs', *Edinburgh Review* 83 (1846), p. 465; *EPS* ii, p. 446 (*Repr. Gov.*, p. 245).
40. 'Duveyrier's Political Views', op. cit., pp. 465ff.
41. 'de Tocqueville on Democracy', *EPS* i, p. 198 (*D & D* II, p. 73). On the dangers of democracy see, for instance, 'de Tocqueville', *EPS* i, pp. 173ff. (*D & D* II, pp. 36ff.) *Lib.*, ch. 3, and *Repr. Gov.*, ch. 6; note also his statement in *Autob.*, pp. 161–2 on the shifting of his 'political ideal from pure democracy . . . to the modified form of it' set forth in *Repr. Gov.*; and see the essay by J. H. Burns, 'J. S. Mill and Democracy, 1829–61', in Schneewind, J. B., ed., op. cit., where he traces the

evolution of Mill's view through three stages, 1829–40, 1840–49, 1849–61.

42. *EPS* ii, p. 457 (*Repr. Gov.*, p. 259).
43. There will be quacks and rogues in any form of government, he argues in 'Carlyle's French Revolution' (*London and Westminster Review* 5 and 27 (1837), reprinted in Schn. *ELS*), but representative democracy has the advantage that it is government 'by consent ... by mutual compromise and compact', rather than restraint; 'it alone proceeds by quiet muster of opposing strengths', in which the strongest emerge without resort to violence (Schn. *ELS*, pp. 201–2).
44. McCloskey, H. J., *John Stuart Mill*, p. 137; Robson, J. M., *The Improvement of Mankind*, p. 271.
45. 'Chapters on Socialism', *EES* ii, pp. 708, 711.
46. *Autob.*, p. 196.
47. 'Newman's Political Economy', *EES* ii, p. 444.
48. 'Chapters on Socialism', *EES* ii, pp. 712–13; *Utilitarianism, EERS*, p. 216 (Schn. *EW*, p. 289; Warnock, p. 266).
49. 'The Claims of Labour', *EES* i, p. 375 (*D & D* II, p. 197); *PPE* ii, p. 891; *Comte and Positivism, EERS*, p. 341.
50. *EL* i, pp. 31–2.
51. 'de Tocqueville on Democracy', *EPS* i, p. 198 (*D & D* II, p. 73); *PPE* ii, p. 760.
52. *S. of W.*, p. 479; cf. *PPE* ii, p. 768: 'The aim of improvement should be not solely to place human beings in a condition in which they will be able to do without one another, but to enable them to work with or for one another in relations not involving dependence.'
53. *PPE* ii, p. 896. For Mill's views on industrial relations see especially the works named; also 'Thornton on Labour and its Claims', *EES* ii (*D & D* IV); on Parliamentary representation of the working classes see *Autob.*, p. 264, 'Chapters on Socialism', *EES* ii, pp. 707–8, and the passage in Robson, J. M., op. cit., p. 259, quoted from a letter in the Mill–Taylor collection, I (10/11/68). The working class leader, G. J. Holyoake wrote of Mill: 'Of all the public men whom I can recall, there have been none, certainly no philosophers, who personally cared for the people as he did, and aided those in their ranks who showed individuality or capacity of self-help' (*John Stuart Mill, as some of the Working Classes knew him*, London, 1873, p. 5). Note also Mill's apologetic explanation of his use of the term 'labouring classes' in *PPE* ii, p. 758—'in compliance with custom and as descriptive of an existing, but by no means a necessary or permanent, state of social relations'.
54. 'The Claims of Labour', *EES* i, p. 378 (*D & D* II, p. 203).
55. *PPE* ii, p. 763. On the education of the working classes see the chapter in this volume of *Principles*, 'On the Probable Futurity of the Labouring Classes'; also 'The Claims of Labour' and *LL* i, pp. 80–1; their lack of education is his principal argument for plural voting in 'Thoughts on Parliamentary Reform': 'no lover of improvement can desire that the *predominant* power should be turned over to persons in

the mental and moral condition of the English working classes' (*EPS* ii, p. 327, *D & D* III, p. 26).

Mill was particularly concerned to improve the lot of the working classes by encouraging family limitation; he was much impressed by Malthus' work and believed that population control was the principal means of attacking poverty. For this refer to the indices of *PPE* and *EES*, to *Autob.*, pp. 88–9, 93, and to the articles, 'Question of Population', in the *Black Dwarf*, 27 Nov. and 10 Dec. 1823. Packe, op. cit., pp. 56–9, records that Mill was arrested in London in 1823 for distributing leaflets advocating family limitation. Contraceptives were, of course, unknown (at least as we understand them) and Mill underestimated both the difficulty of the task of persuasion and the power of what he tended to disdain as 'mere animal instincts' (*PPE* i, p. 157). See also in Elliot's edition of Mill's letters, vol. 2, p. 382 (26/3/54), the comments from his diary.

56. 'Chapters on Socialism', *EES* ii, p. 736.
57. *PPE* ii, p. 891.
58. ib., i, p. 208.
59. 'Coleridge', *EERS*, p. 157 (*D & D* I, p. 455; Schn. *ELS*, p. 337); cf. 'Leslie on the Land Question', *EES* ii, p. 672 (*D & D* IV, pp. 88–9).
60. *LL* iv, p. 1702; cf. 'Land Tenure Reform', *EES* ii (*D & D* IV). On capitalism see 'Chapters on Socialism' in *EES* ii and the index of that volume. On land tenure and its reform see the various papers in *D & D* IV, and refer to the index of *PPE*; this was another of Mill's major interests; as the chairman of its provisional committee he was involved in the preliminary organization of the Land Tenure Reform Association in 1869–70 and became its chairman when it was established.
61. *PPE* ii, p. 754.
62. 'Newman's Political Economy', *EES* ii, p. 444 (cf. 'Endowments', *EES* ii, pp. 622, 625 (*D & D*, IV pp. 12, 18) on competition in the provision of schools).
63. *PPE* ii, p. 795.
64. 'Endowments', *EES* ii, pp. 622ff. (*D & D* IV, pp. 12ff.).
65. *Autob.*, p. 142.
66. *PPE* i, p. 209. On Mill's increasingly sympathetic attitude to socialism, see his own statement in *Autob.* pp. 195–6, and Robson, J. M., op. cit., pp. 248–9 and 259. There is a lengthy discussion of communism (pre-Marxist) in *PPE* i, pp. 203ff.; he was deeply influenced by the St. Simonians (*Autob.*, pp. 138ff.), whose proposals he considers in *PPE* i, pp. 210ff. (see also 'The Spirit of the Age', in Schn. *ELS*, pp. 27ff., which is much indebted to the St. Simonians, and the correspondence with d'Eichthal in *EL* i); Fourierism he examines in 'Chapters on Socialism' and in *PPE* i, pp. 210ff. For a discussion of Mill and Marx see the article by Harris, A. L., 'John Stuart Mill's Theory of Progress', and Graeme Duncan's *Marx and Mill*.
67. 'Chapters on Socialism', *EES* ii, p. 737.

68. 'The Claims of Labour', *EES* i, p. 376 (*D & D* II. p. 199); 'Chapters on Socialism', ib. ii, p. 737; cf. *PPE* ii, p. 792, on the class struggle.
69. On centralized control see above, pp. 23–6; he strongly advocated a professional civil service (pp. 22–3 above), and was not averse from considering the possibility, at some distant date, of a federation of Europe, though he was keenly aware of the obstacles in the way of the latter (*LL* iv, p. 1800).
70. 'The Negro Question', *Fraser's Magazine* 41 (1850), p. 28; cf. *EL* ii, p. 713.
71. *Comte and Positivism*, *EERS*, p. 339.
72. *PPE* ii, p. 756; cf 'Land Tenure Reform', *EES* ii, p. 693.
73. See 'Coleridge', *EERS*, pp. 133ff. (*D & D* I, pp. 416ff.; Schn. *ELS*, pp. 308ff.), and pp. 41–3 below.
74. McCloskey, H. J., asserts in *John Stuart Mill*, p. 97: 'Mill was seriously exposed to the danger of becoming (what he for a brief time became) a moral totalitarian'; Cowling, M., in *Mill and Liberalism*, argues that Mill is an authoritarian—a view which Rees, J. C., opposes in 'Was Mill for Liberty?'
75. *PPE* i, p. 209.
76. *The Rock* (Faber, 1934), p. 7.
77. *EPS* i, p. 310 (*Lib.*, p. 141).

## 3. THE ROLE OF EDUCATION

1. *Inaugural*, pp. 153–4; cf. James Mill's definition of education in Burston, W. H., *James Mill on Education*, pp. 41–2.
2. Mill was an experientialist, committed to the view that knowledge originates in man's sensory experience of the external world; he was also an associationist, believing that mental content is linked or grouped by the association of one idea with others as a result, e.g., of contiguity or similarity. Now, if the primary source of knowledge is in the data presented to the mind by sensory apprehension of the external world, if the bonds which link these data (and consequently predispose our thinking and our attitudes, likes and dislikes) are supplied from the same source, and if the external world and its impact can be manipulated by human agency (as they obviously can), then clearly the environment assumes enormous importance as an instrument in the formation of human character and the development of human potential. Educationally, therefore, Mill was an environmentalist, a fact which shows itself throughout his writings, including the passage here quoted.
3. This is well stated in the Spens Report (*Secondary Education with Special Reference to Grammar Schools and Technical High Schools*, H.M.S.O., 1939), pp. 147–8: 'the interest of the State is to see that the schools provide the means by which the nation's life may be maintained in its integrity from generation to generation; to make sure that the young are prepared to preserve—and some of them to advance—its standards in all modes of activity which are important to

the common weal. .... Underneath this explicit, overt educational activity of the State, working through laws and regulations, there is the unformulated but very real demand of the community that the young shall grow up in conformity with the national *ethos*.' This was written in the imminence, if not the actuality, of war, when the need for national unity was more obvious than is (mistakenly, I believe) thought to be the case today.

4. 'Coleridge', *EERS*, p. 133 (*D & D* I, pp. 416–17; Schn. *ELS*, pp. 308–9).
5. ib., pp. 133–5 (*D & D* I, pp. 416ff.; Schn. *ELS*, pp. 308ff.).
6. ib., pp. 138, 140 (*D & D* I, pp. 424, 427; Schn. *ELS*, pp. 314, 317).
7. *Comte and Positivism*, *EERS*, pp. 339–40.
8. *EPS* i, p. 282 (*Lib.*, p. 101).
9. *Utilitarianism, EERS*, p. 232 (Schn *EW*, p. 306; Warnock, p. 285).
10. *EPS* ii, pp. 385–6 (*Repr. Gov.*, pp. 160–1).
11. *PPE* ii, p. 763.
12. *Comte and Positivism, EERS*, p. 339.
13. *EPS* i, p. 269 (*Lib.*, p. 82).
14. *S. of W.*, pp. 478, 499, 500.
15. *Logic* ii, p. 833; *PPE* i, p. 139.
16. *LL* ii, p. 631, iv. p. 1662.
17. *Examiner*, 12 June 1831, p. 370.
18. 'Endowments', *EES* ii, pp. 627–9 (*D & D* IV, pp. 20–4). Mill makes the point about the absence of class distinctions in a letter to J. M. Barnard (*LL* iv, pp. 1661–2), where he is referring to America but also, one can assume, making a general observation: 'There are wanted, I do not say a class, but a great number of persons of the highest degree of cultivation which the accumulated acquisitions of the human race make it possible to give them. From such persons, in a community that knows no distinction of ranks, civilisation would rain down its influences upon the remainder of society.'
19. *PPE* i, pp. 43, 42.
20. *Logic* ii, p. 926.
21. *Autob.*, p. 202.
22. 'Coleridge', *EERS*, pp. 147–8 (*D & D* I, pp. 438–42: Schn. *ELS*, pp. 325–8); on Mill's élitism see ch. 4, above.
23. *PPE* i, p. 374.
24. 'The Claims of Labour', *EES* i, p. 376 (*D & D* II, p. 200).
25. *Black Dwarf* 11, pp. 752, 796 (27 Nov., 10 Dec. 1823); cf. *PPE* i, p. 375.
26. *PPE* i, pp. 107, 109, 110.
27. *PPE* ii, p. 948, i, pp. 374–5.
28. 'Speech on Perfectibility', in *Autob.*, p. 298.
29. *LL* i, p. 80.
30. *PPE* ii, p. 763.
31. 'Bentham', *EERS*, p. 99 (*D & D* I, pp. 365–6; Schn. *ELS*, p. 267).
32. *Autob.*, p. 197.

33. 'Chapters on Socialism', *EES* ii, pp. 738–40; cf. 'Newman's Political Economy', *EES* ii, p. 444.
34. *LL* i, pp. 22, 19; *EES* ii, p. 740.
35. *Politics* VIII, i, 1337a, transl. Barker, Sir Ernest (Clarendon Press, 1946), p. 332.
36. 'Grote's Aristotle', *EPC*, p. 505 (*D & D* IV, p. 223.)
37. *EPS* ii, pp. 379–80 (*Repr. Gov.*, p. 153.)
38. ib., p. 417 (*Repr. Gov.*, p. 205).
39. *S. of W.*, p. 501.
40. 'Speech on Perfectibility', in *Autob.*, p. 298.
41. *EPS* i, p. 305 (*Lib.*, p. 134).
42. *Parliamentary Papers 1854–5*, vol. 20, p. 97, and in *EPS* i, p. 210.
43. ib., p. 98 and *EPS* i, p. 211. On Civil Service reform see: Hughes, E., 'Sir Charles Trevelyan and Civil Service Reform, 1853–5' i and ii, and 'Civil Service Reform, 1853–5'.
44. 'Paper Currency and Commercial Distress', *EES* i, pp. 111, 112, 115.
45. *Autob.*, p. 69.
46. For these drafts on education in India see *British Parliamentary Papers 1831–2*, vol. 9 (in the Irish University Press edition, *Colonies: East India*, vol. 6). See also MacMinn, N., etc., *Bibliography*, pp. 27ff. Of interest in this connection is an article by Ballhatchet, K. A., in the *Cambridge Historical Journal* 10 (1950–2), 'The Home Government and Bentinck's Educational Policy' and a note in a later issue, 11 (1953–5), p. 228; these refer to further drafts by Mill on educational policy.
47. op. cit., pp. 393, 489, 385, 497.
48. ib., pp. 392, 529; 488–9; 383–4; 528; 495.
49. This summary of educational advance in India is part of a memorandum submitted to Parliament by the East India Company in 1858 together with an appeal against being deprived of the administration of India; Mill says of it, 'of this I was partly the author and partly the editor' (MacMinn, p. 90). The memorandum was published by the East India Company and appears in *Parliamentary Papers 1857–8*, vol. 43, pp. 1–38, as *Memorandum (prepared at the India House) of the Improvements in the Administration of India during the last Thirty Years*; the educational summary is on pp. 28–31. See also below, the bibliography of Mill's articles etc., 1858.
50. *Parliamentary Papers*, op. cit., p. 495.
51. For this criticism see *The Open Society and its Enemies*, especially vol. 2, and *The Poverty of Historicism*.

## 4. ÉLITISM

1. 'The Spirit of the Age', Schn *ELS*, p. 44 (cf. *EPS* i, p. 232 (*Lib.*, p. 28), *Comte and Positivism*, *EERS*, p. 313).
2. 'Civilisation', *EPS* i, pp. 133–4 (*D & D* I, p. 184; Schn. *ELS*, p. 166).
3. 'Rationale of Political Representation', *EPS* i, p. 23 (*D & D* I, p. 468).
4. *EPS* ii, pp. 459, 460 (*Repr. Gov.*, pp. 263, 264).

5. *EPS* i, p. 267 (*Lib.*, p. 79).
6. *Inaugural*, p. 166.
7. 'Bentham', *EERS*, p.109 (*D & D* I, p. 381: Schn. *ELS*, p. 279);
   *EPS* ii, p. 508 (*Repr. Gov.*, p. 329); 'On the Present State of Literature', *Adelphi* I (1923–4), p. 688; 'Alfred de Vigny', *D & D* I, p. 321;
   *LL* i, p. 68.
8. The word occurs in, e.g., *S. of W.*, p. 478 (quoted above), 'Endowments', *EES* ii, p. 627 (*D & D* IV, p. 22), *EPS* ii, pp. 456, 460
   (*Repr. Gov.*, pp. 258, 263).
9. *Logic* ii, p. 939; *PPE* i, p. 139.
10. On the derivation of 'élite' and its definition in twentieth century
    sociology see Boyd, D., *Elites and their Education*.
11. 'The Spirit of the Age', op. cit., p. 68.
12. *EL* i, p. 48, *LL* iv, p. 1662.
13. *Examiner*, 12 June 1831, p. 370.
14. 'Rationale of Political Representation', *EPS* i, p. 24 (*D & D* I, p.
    469); *EPS* ii, p. 539 (*Repr. Gov.*, p. 370); 'Utility of Religion', *EERS*,
    p. 421; *EPS* i, pp. 242–3 (*Lib.* p. 43). On the beneficent influence of a
    cultured class see also James Mill's article, 'Aristocracy', *London
    Review* 2 (July–Jan. 1835–6); W. H. Burston quotes from it in
    *James Mill on Philosophy and Education*, pp. 215–16; compare with
    this what he writes elsewhere on the influence of the middle classes
    (ib., p. 204).
15. *EPS* i, pp. 267, 261 (*Lib.* pp. 79, 70); 'the uncontented characters' is
    in *EPS* ii, p. 407 (*Repr. Gov.*, p. 190); cf. 'Corporation and Church
    Property', *EES* i, p. 217 (*D & D* I, p. 34): 'All improvements, either
    in opinion or practice, must be in a minority first.'
16. *EPS* ii, pp. 506, 438 (*Repr. Gov.*, pp. 326, 233).
17. 'Rationale of Political Representation', *EPS* i, p., 24 (*D & D* I, p.
    469); on self-interest see 'Coleridge', *EERS*, p. 124 (*D & D* I, pp.
    401–2; Schn. *ELS*, p. 297), *EPS* ii, pp. 444–5 (*Repr. Gov.*, pp. 241–2).
18. *EL* ii, p. 713; on a cultural élite see, e.g., 'Coleridge', *EERS*, pp. 123–
    4 (*D & D* I, pp. 401–2; Schn. *ELS*, pp. 296–7), and 'Civilisation',
    *EPS* i, pp. 136–7 (*D & D* I, pp. 189–90; Schn. *ELS* 170–1); and on
    reform of society, e.g., 'The Spirit of the Age', Schn. *ELS*, p. 45.
19. Also 'Corporation and Church Property', *EES* i, pp. 220–1 (*D & D* I,
    pp. 37–9): 'training and rearing them by systematic culture continued
    throughout life, to the highest perfection of their mental and spiritual
    nature.'
20. *EPS* i, p. 306 (*Lib.*, p. 135).
21. *PPE* ii, p. 943 (cf. *Comte and Positivism*, *EERS*, p. 352).
22. *Comte and Positivism*, *EERS*, pp. 326, 313, 314.
23. 'Coleridge', *EERS*, pp. 147, 150 (*D & D* I, pp. 439, 444–5; Schn.
    *ELS*, pp. 326, 329–30).
24. *Autob.*, p. 26.
25. Mill coined the word 'pédantocratie' in a letter to Comte, Feb. 1842
    (*EL* ii, p. 502), and Comte, attracted by it, asked Mill's permission to
    use it (ib., p. 524); see also *EPS* i, p. 308 (*Lib.*, p. 138).

26. *Hansard*, vol. 20, 30 July 1833, col. 151. Mill's comments on English residents and fellow tourists whom he met in Sicily and Greece in 1855 have now and then a hint of self-conscious educational and cultural superiority, e.g., *LL* i, pp. 342, 424, 437 (but cf. 448). His draft despatches to India have an élitist flavour in their recommendations for the education of the higher classes.

27. See *EPS* i, pp. 232, 267–8, 269 (*Lib.*, pp. 27–9, 79–80, 82).

28. See *Utilitarianism, EERS*, pp. 211–12 (Schn. *EW*, pp. 283–4; Warnock, pp. 259–60), *S. of W.*, pp. 499–500, *EPS* ii, pp. 473–4 (*Repr. Gov.*, p. 282).

29. 'The Spirit of the Age', Schn. *ELS*, p. 40.

30. ib., p. 41.

31. 'de Tocqueville on Democracy in America', *London Review* 1, Oct. 1835, pp. 110–11; and in *EPS* i, pp. 71–2; for the effect on Mill of his reading of de Tocqueville see *Autob.*, pp. 162–4.

32. *Autob.*, p. 121.

33. For the development of Mill's view of education as an improving force see the article by Roellinger, F. X., 'Mill on Education'.

34. *Autob.*, pp. 194, 196.

35. *PPE* ii, p. 760.

36. 'Civilisation', *EPS* i, p. 147 (*D & D* I, p. 205; Schn. *ELS*, p. 182).

37. For the movement of the working classes towards autonomy see *PPE* ii, pp. 763ff.

38. On educating the 'élite' of the poor see 'Endowments', *EES* ii, pp. 627–8 (*D & D* IV, pp. 20–23); on dialogue and its conditions, above, p. 64; on social justice, above, pp. 27–9; the phrase 'a renovated social fabric' occurs in 'Chapters on Socialism', *EES* ii, p. 708.

39. Parry, G., *Political Elites*, p. 18; also of interest for political and educational élitism are:

| | |
|---|---|
| Boyd, D. | *Elites and their Education* |
| Guttsmann, W. L. | *The British Political Elite* |
| Wakeford, J. | *The Cloistered Elite* |
| Weinberg, I. | *The English Public Schools* |
| Wilkinson, R. H., ed. | *Governing Elites* |

40. On middle class tutelage see above p. 68; 'leading strings'. *PPE* ii, p. 763; for unanimity, see Stillinger, J., ed., *The Early Draft of John Stuart Mill's Autobiography*, pp. 188–9 ('the authority of the instructed', 'of one mind on these subjects' [n. 42], 'united authority').

A further criticism which deserves mention is made by Harris, A. L., in 'John Stuart Mill's Theory of Progress', pp. 172–3: 'He greatly underestimated the role power plays in connection with the exercise of social leadership by intellectual elites' (p. 172); for instance, objectivity of judgement may be impaired by competition for status and power; to win popular recognition the élite may be tempted to descend to the public's level of thinking; the free market of ideas may degenerate into competitive salesmanship. There is truth in this criticism; on the other hand, Mill was not unaware of the corruptive effect of power, as can be seen, for instance, in the passage from

'Centralisation' quoted above (p. 24) and in the following passage from 'Writings of Junius Redivivus', *Monthly Repository* 7 (Apr. 1833), p. 268:

> Our author is a radical, because he is convinced both from principle and from history, that is both from the experience of men and of nations, that power, without accountability to those over whom, and for whose benefit it is to be exercised, is for the most part a source of oppression to them, and of moral corruption to those in whom the power resides. On the same principle *we* are radicals also: not that we consider the above proposition to be true without exception: nor do we in any case look upon it as embracing the *whole* of what ought to be taken into consideration in forming our practical conclusions: but we hold it to contain as much of the truth, as is amply sufficient to prove all institutions worthless, which like most of those which now exist, are constructed in utter defiance, or entire negligence of it.

And Mill was fully alive to the danger of class interests (pp. 21–2 above).

41. ed. Stillinger, J., op. cit., p. 188.
42. 'The Spirit of the Age', Schn. *ELS*, p. 44 (cf. *EL* i, p. 48); on the apparent inconsistency between Mill's view of authority in 'The Spirit of the Age' and his defence of liberty and individuality in *On Liberty*, see Friedman, R. B., 'An Introduction to Mill's Theory of Authority', in Schneewind, J. B., ed., *Mill: a Collection of Critical Essays*.
43. Mill's élitism has some resemblance to the 'pluralism' described by Parry, op. cit., ch. 3.
44. *Education and Leadership*, p. 12.
45. 'Bentham', *EERS*, p. 109 (*D & D* I, p. 381; Schn. *ELS*, p. 279); *EPS* i, p. 268 (*Lib.*, p. 81); *S. of W.*, pp. 500, 499; *EPS* ii, p. 460 (*Repr. Gov.*, p. 263); *S. of W.*, p. 500; *EPS* ii, p. 460 (*Repr. Gov.*, p. 264.
46. op. cit., p. 27.
47. Hughes, A. G., *Education and the Democratic Ideal*, pp. 38–9.
48. Reeves, M., *Growing up in a Modern Society*, p. 46. In an article, 'Lord Durham's Return', *London and Westminster Review* 32 (December 1838), p. 243, Mill describes the qualities he looks for in a leader of the Radical Party:

> But the man we want is the one who can recommend himself not solely by the ability to talk, nor even merely to think, but by ability to *do*. We want a man who can wrestle with actual difficulties and subdue them; who can read 'the aim of selfish natures hard to be spelled,' can bend men's stubborn minds to things against which their passions rise in arms; who needs not sacrifice justice to policy, or policy to justice, but knows how to do justice and attain the ends of policy by it. We want a man who can sustain himself where the consequences of every error he commits, instead of being left to accumulate for posterity, come back to him the next week or the next month, and throw themselves in his path; where no voting of bystanders can make that success, which is, in truth, failure; where there is a real thing to be done, a positive result to be brought about, to have accomplished which is success – not to have accomplished it defeat.

49. On participation see above, pp. 19–20; just laws, *PPE* ii, p. 886; equitable taxation, *EPS* ii, pp. 386–7 (*Repr. Gov.*, pp. 162–3); cooperation, *PPE* ii, pp. 768–9; the press, ib., p. 861; home life, *Inaugural*, pp. 211, 214; initiation and conservation, pp. 40ff. above. Note also the following passage from his article, 'The Monthly Repository for December', in *Examiner*, 15 Dec. 1833, p. 789:

> In every word of this we concur; but with the qualification, that not *only* the more vigorous minds in the poorer class, but persons also with the superior opportunities of instruction afforded by a higher station, *may* be, (and of this the writer himself is an example) most efficient instructors of the poorer classes, provided they have sufficient freedom from the littleness of mind which caste-distinctions engender, and a sufficiently just appreciation of the intelligence of the reading part of the working-classes, to prevent them from being condescending instructors. No gentleman is fit to write for the poor who cannot help betraying in every line that he habitually deems himself a being of a different order from them, and vastly their superior, that he cannot for one half hour lose the consciousness of his artificial and conventional rank, but is perpetually showing it in the most offensive of all ways, that of taking credit for not showing it. He must learn to speak to the working-people as an equal to his equals, as he would speak to persons less informed than himself on the particular subject, but with minds quite as capable of understanding it. When, moreover, the assumption of superiority over their intellect, and the ostentation of descending to make himself intelligible to their ignorant minds is accompanied with an attempt to pass off upon them, even though in a good cause, palpable sophisms which the least discerning of them has intellect enough to see through, he but excites the contempt, mingled with aversion, which a large portion of the reading mechanics feel for the instructions in political economy which have been put forth to the 'working man' by the Society for the Diffusion of Useful Knowledge.

It was clear to Mill that effective dialogue is possible only when, despite differences of education and expertise, there is a relationship of equality between the participants and an absence of condescension on the part of the few.

## 5. INDIVIDUALITY

1. *EPS* ii, pp. 389ff. (*Repr. Gov.*, pp. 166ff.); *PPE* ii, pp. 939–42 (quotation on p. 940).
2. Mill's ethology assumes that the formation of human character is subject to causality, yet within this causal determination he feels bound to find a place for freedom and genuine choice; he argues the case for free will in *Logic* VI, ch. 2, and also in *Hamilton*, ch. 26.
3. For example in *Logic* ii, pp. 936–9.
4. *EPS* i, pp. 269, 266 (*Lib.*, pp. 82, 78).
5. For our present purpose I follow tradition in referring to the ideas expressed in the essay as Mill's; he did, of course, insist in the *Autobiography* that the work was a 'joint production' with his wife and that 'the whole mode of thinking of which the book was the expression

was emphatically hers' (op. cit., pp. 213–14). For discussion of this issue see Pappé, H. O., *John Stuart Mill and the Harriet Taylor Myth*, Ree, J. C., 'H. O. Pappé on Mill', and Himmelfarb, G., *On Liberty and Liberalism* (and for this last see also the appendix to the present book, pp. 195ff. below).

6. *EPS* i, pp. 266, 280, 274, 268 (*Lib.*, pp. 78, 99, 89, 81).
7. ib., pp. 266, 267 (*Lib.*, pp. 77, 80).
8. ib., p. 276 (*Lib.*, p. 92).
9. ib., p. 263 (*Lib.*, p. 73); on von Humboldt see Himmelfarb, G., op. cit., pp. 60–62.
10. ib., p. 265 (*Lib.*, p. 77).
11. ib., pp. 263, 264, 268 (*Lib.*, pp. 74, 75, 80.)
12. *Autob.*, p. 216.
13. *EPS* i, p. 267 (*Lib.*, p. 79).
14. ib., pp. 266, 262, 270 (*Lib.*, pp. 78, 72, 84).
15. ib., pp. 267, 269 (*Lib.*, pp. 79, 82).
16. 'Endowments', *EES* ii, p. 618 (*D & D* IV, p. 6); cf. *Logic* ii, pp. 936–9.
17. *EPS* i, p. 262 (*Lib.*, p. 72).
18. op. cit., pp. 59–60.
19. E.g., Sir Percy Nunn, *Education: its data and first principles*, p. 13: Education must aim at securing for everyone 'the conditions under which individuality is most completely developed'; the Spens Report on secondary education (1939), p. 152: a school fulfils its purpose when it helps 'every boy and girl to achieve the highest degree of individual development of which he or she is capable'.
20. *EPS* i, pp. 261, 268, 261, 269 (eccentricity), 215 (*Lib.*, pp. 70, 80, 70, 83, 2).
21. ib., pp. 266, 264 (*Lib.*, pp. 77, 75); *Logic* ii, App. H, p. 1155; cf. 'Nature', *EERS*, pp. 396–7.
22. *EPS* i, p. 281 (*Lib.*, p. 99).
23. 'Nature', *EERS*, p. 402.
24. *EPS* i, pp. 266, 261, 269, 267 (*Lib.*, pp. 78, 70, 82, 79).
25. *EPS* ii, p. 439 (*Repr. Gov.*, pp. 234–5).
26. *PPE* ii, pp. 794–6 (but cf. pp. 753–4: 'I confess I am not charmed with the ideal of life held out by those who think that the normal state of human beings is that of struggling to get on; that the trampling, crushing, elbowing, and treading on each others' heels, which form the existing type of social life, are the most desirable lot of human kind, or anything but the disagreeable symptoms of one of the stages of industrial progress').
27. *EPS* i, pp. 261, 263, 270 (*Lib.*, pp. 70, 73, 83).
28. *PPE* ii, p. 938.
29. 'Utility of Religion', *EERS*, pp. 420ff.; see also 'Bentham', *EERS*, p. 95 (*D & D* I, p. 359; Schn. *ELS*, p. 262): 'Man is never recognised by him as a being capable of pursuing spiritual perfection as an end; of desiring for its own sake the conformity of his own character to his standard of excellence, without hope of good or fear of evil from other source than his own inward consciousness.'

30. *Utilitarianism, EERS*, p. 210 (Schn. *EW*, p. 281, Warnock, p. 257).
31. 'Thoughts on Parliamentary Reform', *EPS* ii, p. 323 (*D & D* III, p. 19).
32. There is some evidence that Mill shifted his stance in regard to the equality or otherwise of human potential. In his earlier years, when he was still strongly influenced by Bentham and orthodox utilitarianism, he was inclined to regard human nature as basically equal and subject to unlimited improvement by a kind of environmental conditioning. He is criticized for this, one of 'his greatest theoretical errors', by his biographer Alexander Bain: 'He inherited the mistake from his father, and could neither learn nor unlearn in regard to it' (*John Stuart Mill: a criticism* etc., p. 146). But while he never abandoned his belief in the educative power of environment, he did apparently come to acknowledge differences in human educability—though he was against over-stressing their innateness and underestimating the impact of circumstances (*Autob.*, pp. 232–3); this is clear in his comments on his own ability in the *Autobiography* ('if I had been by nature . . .'; 'in all these natural gifts', p. 26); and it is implied in all he writes about the exceptionally great, as in *Logic* VI, xi, 3. See the article by Roellinger, F. X., 'Mill on Education'.
33. See the interesting comparison of Mill with Marx in Ward, J. W., 'Mill, Marx and Modern Individualism': for Mill individuality was a 'primary commitment'; for Marx it was a historical goal.
34. *Autob.*, pp. 26–7; see also pp. 18, 39 on the Socratic *elenchus* and on Socrates himself.
35. *EPS* i, p. 266 (*Lib.*, p. 77); 'Early Grecian History and Legend', *EPC*, pp. 299–303 (*D & D* II, pp. 326–32); 'Grote's History', *EPC*, pp. 333–4 (*D & D* II, pp. 549–50); *EPC*, pp. 315ff. (*D & D* II, pp. 520ff.).
36. *Autob.*, p. 121.
37. On sex and sexual relations see Mill's diary entry for 26 Mar. 1854, in Elliot, H. S. R., *The Letters of John Stuart Mill*, vol. 2, Appendix A, p. 382. He asserts that no 'great improvement in human life is . . . to be looked for so long as the animal instinct of sex occupies the absurdly disproportionate place it does therein'; but 'what any persons may freely do with respect to sexual relations should be deemed to be an unimportant and purely private matter, which concerns no one but themselves'—except, he adds, where children result.
38. But see also *Autob.*, p. 217, where he mentions the enthusiastic assertion of individuality by a Mr. William Maccall in a series of writings, especially *The Elements of Individualism*, and the foundation in America by a Mr. Warren of a community pledged to 'equal freedom of development for all individualities'. Maccall's *Elements* was published in 1847, and a lecture, *The Outlines of Individualism*, in 1853.
39. 'de Tocqueville on Democracy in America', *EPS* i, p. 194 (*D & D* II, pp. 67–8).
40. *Hamilton*, p. 138.

41. ib., pp. 233, 241, 247, 248; the paragraph on p. 248 is worth quoting in full:

> The truth is that we are here face to face with that final inexplicability, at which, as Sir W. Hamilton observes, we inevitably arrive when we reach ultimate facts; and in general, one mode of stating it only appears more incomprehensible than another, because the whole of human language is accommodated to the one, and is so incongruous with the other, that it cannot be expressed in any terms which do not deny its truth. The real stumbling block is perhaps, not in any theory of the fact, but in the fact itself. The true incomprehensibility perhaps is, that something which has ceased, or is not yet in existence, can still be, in a manner, present: that a series of feelings, the infinitely greater part of which is past or future, can be gathered up, as it were, into a single present conception, accompanied by a belief of reality. I think, by far the wisest thing we can do, is to accept the inexplicable fact, without any theory of how it takes place: and when we are obliged to speak of it in terms which assume a theory, to use them with a reservation as to their meaning.

42. *Analysis of the Phenomena of the Human Mind*, vol. 2, ch. 14, p. 175 (see also vol. 1, pp. 229–30; 339–40).
43. Packe, M. St. J., op. cit., p. 267 (see p. 90 below).
44. *Logic* i, p. 379.
45. ib., ii, pp. 836, 837.
46. ib., ii, pp. 839, 838, 839.
47. *Hamilton*, p. 576; see also *Autob.*, pp. 143–4.
48. *Logic* ii, pp. 839, 840, 841.
49. Packe, M. St. J., op. cit., p. 267.
50. *EPS* ii, pp. 385–6 (*Repr. Gov.*, pp. 160–1).
51. *Logic* ii, pp. 937–8.
52. Harrison, F., 'John Stuart Mill', pp. 493, 504, 493; in fact the quotatation on p. 504 is directed against *The Subjection of Women*, but the writer claims that both works are vitiated by the same 'root error' of regarding the individual as a primary social unit and by the same pervading exaggeration. The critic's own position is that individuals, in any absolute sense, are non-existent; a social philosophy based on such 'is founded not on real facts and living beings as we find them and know them, but upon mental abstractions . . . upon postulates, not on realities' (p. 495).
53. *Logic* ii, p. 879.
54. *Comte and Positivism, EERS*, p. 337; cf. *EPS* ii, p. 389 (*Repr. Gov.*, p. 166): the principal source of good government is 'the qualities of the human beings composing the society over which the government is exercised'.
55. *EPS* i, pp. 223, 272 (*Lib.*, pp. 15, 87); *S. of W.*, p. 479. For Harriet's influence on Mill see p. 86 above and the Appendix.
56. *Autob.*, pp. 46–7, 48.
57. ib., p. 121; *Inaugural*, p. 154.
58. 'The Claims of Labour', *EES* i, p. 376 (*D & D* II, p. 200).
59. *PPE* ii, pp. 938, 947, 948.
60. *EPS* i, p. 301 (*Lib.*, p. 129).

61. 'Civilisation', *EPS* i, p. 122 (*D & D* I, p. 165; Schn. *ELS*, p. 152).
62. *EPS* i, pp. 276–7 (*Lib.*, pp. 92, 93).
63. *Utilitarianism, EERS*, p. 231 (Schn. *EW*, p. 305; Warnock, p. 284.)
64. For these see Packe, M. St. J., op.cit., pp. 56–9, 467ff. On the balance between individuality and the demands of society see also: Schneewind, J. B., ed., *Mill: a Collection of Critical Essays*, the articles by Burns, J. H., Cowling, M., Halliday, R. J., and Friedman, R. B.; the very interesting article by West, E. G., 'Liberty and Education: John Stuart Mill's Dilemma'; and Rees, J. C., 'Was Mill for Liberty?'
65. *EPS* i, p. 224 (*Lib.*, pp. 15–16).
66. ib., p. 226 (*Lib.*, p. 18).
67. *Autob.*, pp. 196, 197.
68. Rees, J. C., 'Was Mill for Liberty?', p. 73 (quoting Cowling).
69. 'Civilisation', *EPS* i, pp. 136, 135 (*D & D* I, pp. 188, 187; (Schn. *ELS*, p. 169).
70. 'de Tocqueville on Democracy in America', *EPS* i, p. 194 (*D & D* II, p. 67).
71. 'Bentham', *EERS*, pp. 106–7 (*D & D* I, pp. 378–9; Schn. *ELS*, pp. 277–8).
72. *EPS* i, p. 310 (*Lib.*, p. 141).
73. Robert Waley Cohen Memorial Lecture, p. 34.
74. On the theme of human improvement see his early 'Speech on Perfectibility', in *Autob.*, pp. 288ff.
75. 'Utility of Religion', *EERS*, p. 418 (cf. *Hamilton*, pp. 630–1: 'I do wonder at the barrenness of imagination of a man who can see nothing wonderful in the material universe').
76. 'Bentham', *EERS*, pp. 95–6, 112 (*D & D* I, pp. 359–61, 386–8; Schn. *ELS*, pp. 262–4, 283–4).
77. See note 52, above.
78. Notice of Grant's *Arithmetic*, the *Globe*, 23 Oct. 1835.
79. *Inaugural*, p. 163.
80. On religious and moral indoctrination see, for example, his speech at the public meeting of the National Education League (*The Times*, 26 Mar. 1870), and his letters to W. J. Fox (*LL* i, pp. 39–40), the Rev. T. W. Fowle (*LL* iii, pp. 1235–6) and Charles Friend (ib., pp. 1468–70.)
81. *LL* iii, pp. 1304–5.
82. ib., p. 1304.
83. 'On Genius', Schn. *ELS*, p. 101.
84. Hollis, M., 'The Pen and the Purse', p. 153.
85. *Inaugural*, p. 205; *Comte and Positivism, EERS*, p. 339.
86. *Emile* (Dent, Everyman ed.), pp. 14, 5.
87. 'Nature', *EERS*, pp. 396–7; for his analysis see pp. 373ff. He expresses a view more favourable to innate goodness in human nature in *Inaugural*, p. 211.
88. See p. 9, note 24, above.
89. *EPS* i, pp. 226, 294 (*Lib.*, pp. 18, 118).
90. ib., p. 224 (*Lib.*, p. 15).
91. *Inaugural*, p. 154; cf. *PPE* ii, pp. 948ff., where he argues for com-

pulsory education on the grounds that, 'There are certain primary elements and means of knowledge . . . that all human beings born into the community should acquire during childhood'.

92. 'Nature', *EERS*, p. 393.
93. 'Coleridge', *EERS*, p. 133 (*D & D* I, p. 416; Schn. *ELS*, p. 308).
94. *Comte and Positivism, EERS*, p. 339.
95. *Autob.*, p. 44.
96. 'Bentham', *EERS*, p. 106 (*D & D* I, pp. 376–7; Schn. *ELS*, p. 276).
97. ib., pp. 108, 109 (*D & D* I, pp. 380, 381; Schn. *ELS*, pp. 278, 279); cf. *PPE* ii, pp. 936ff.
98. 'Sedgwick's Discourse', *EERS*, p. 33 (*D & D* I, pp. 95–6).
99. *EPS* i, p. 246 (Lib., p. 48).
100. *Logic* ii, p. 951.
101. On secondary principles see 'Bentham', *EERS*, pp. 110–12 (Schn. *ELS*, pp. 281–3).
102. *Inaugural*, p. 223; 'Utility of Religion', *EERS*, p. 422; *Utilitarianism*, *EERS*, pp. 228–9 (Schn. *EW*, pp. 302–3; Warnock, p. 281), and cf. 'Bentham', *EERS*, pp. 95–6 (*D & D* I, pp. 359–61; Schn. *ELS*, pp. 262–4).
103. *Inaugural*, p. 226.

6. THE STATE AND EDUCATION

1. For a survey of the period 1780 to 1869 see Lawson, J., and Silver, H., *A Social History of Education in England,* chs. 7 and 8, and Adamson, J. W., *English Education 1789–1902*; and for a more detailed examination of various persons and aspects of educational advance in Britain and on the continent see Pollard, H. M., *Pioneers of Popular Education.*
2. Parliament showed a tentative and limited interest in education in passing the Health and Morals of Apprentices Act of 1802.
3. The DNB comments thus on Joseph Hume: 'He spoke longer and oftener and probably worse than any other private member, but he saw most of the causes which he advocated succeed in the end' (J. A. Hamilton, Lord Sumner of Ibstone).
4. For Roebuck's resolution of 1833 see Hansard, vol. 20, 30 July 1833, cols. 139ff.; and for his motion in the following year proposing a Select Committee 'to inquire into the means of establishing a system of National Education , see vol. 24, 3 June 1834, cols. 127ff.; see also his article, 'National Education , in *Tait's Edinburgh Magazine* 2 (Mar. 1833).
5. On the termination of this friendship see Packe, M. St. J., op. cit., pp. 152–3; it came in 1834 after Roebuck, with the best of intentions, warned Mill of the possible effects of his relationship with Harriet; but it was not Roebuck's wish that they should part: 'His part of our friendship was rooted out, nay destroyed, but mine was left untouched.'
6. *PPE* ii, p. 938; *EPS* i, p. 223 (*Lib.*, p. 15).

7. *EPS* i, p. 224 (*Lib.*, p. 16); 'Pledges', *Examiner*, 15 July 1832, p. 450; *PPE* ii, p. 970 (general interest).
8. *PPE* ii, p. 938; cf. *EPS* i, pp. 280–1 (*Lib.*, pp. 98–9).
9. *EPS* i, p. 225 (*Lib.*, pp. 16–17) (inaction); *PPE* ii, pp. 936–7 (interference); *PPE* ii, pp. 937ff., and *EPS* i, pp. 305ff. (*Lib.*, pp. 133ff.) (objections to intervention); *PPE* ii, pp. 947ff., and *EPS* i, pp. 301ff. (*Lib.*, pp. 128–32) (exceptions to non-interference).
10. *The Improvement of Mankind*, pp. 208–9.
11. *PPE* ii, pp. 947ff.; quotations in this paragraph are on pp. 947 (consumer judgement), 952 (animals), 964 (colonization), 962 (the destitute); assistance to voluntary enterprise in navigation, research etc., pp. 968ff.
12. Quotations in this paragraph, pp. 970–1; cf. pp. 803–4 and 'Centralisation', *Edinburgh Review* 115 (1862), pp. 323, 355, and in *EPS* ii, pp. 581, 609–10.
13. *EPS* i, p. 305 (*Lib.*, p. 134).
14. ib., p. 306 (*Lib.*, p. 135); cf. 'Centralisation', op. cit., p. 350., and in *EPS* ii, p. 605.
15. *PPE* ii, p. 940.
16. ib., (cf. pp. 943–4).
17. ib., p. 939.
18. For instance, the articles 'National Education' (17 Apr. pp. 356ff.), 'Lord Brougham's Defence of the Church Establishment' (13 May pp. 441ff.), 'Debate on the Universities Admission Bill' (21 June pp. 591ff.).
19. *EL* i, pp. 233, 198–9 (and on Roebuck see also Mill's letter to Carlyle, p. 171). Further evidence of his interest in education at this time can be found in, e.g., 'Corporation and Church Property' (*EES* i, pp. 213ff., *D & D* I, pp. 28ff.), 'Professor Sedgwick's Discourse' (*EERS*, pp. 33ff., *D & D* I, pp. 95ff.), and in his review of the Cousin report on Prussian education, mentioned in the next but one paragraph.
20. Burston, W. H., *James Mill on Philosophy and Education*, p. 243, quoted from the *Edinburgh Review*, Feb. 1813.
21. *Monthly Repository* 8 (1834), p. 356.
22. 'Mrs. Austin's Translation of M. Cousin's Report', ib., p. 504 (and on this see Pollard, H. M., *Pioneers of Popular Education*, chs. 8, 16).
23. op. cit., pp. 356–7 (cf. *LL* iv, p. 1659: 'unfortunately it is much easier to improve education in quantity than in quality'; and see his criticism of elementary schools in 'The Claims of Labour' (*EES* i, pp. 376ff., *D & D* II, pp. 200ff.)).
24. ib., p. 358. 'Normal Schools' were so called after the French 'Écoles Normales', the first of which was established in Paris in 1794 specifically for the training of teachers; the term was commonly used on the continent for teacher-training institutions and came into use in Britain in the 1830s.
25. ib., p. 443.
26. ib., p. 358.

27. ib., p. 442.
28. ib., p. 503.
29. *Monthly Repository* 8 (May 1834), p. 383.
30. op. cit., p. 503.
31. *PPE* ii, p. 948; *EPS* i, p. 301 (*Lib.*, p. 129).
32. *EL* i, pp. 199, 233.
33. 'Sedgwick's Discourse', *EERS*, p. 33 (*D & D* I, p. 95).
34. *EL* i, p. 233. The extent of misapplication of educational endowments was made clear by the reports of Brougham's charity commissioners, 1818–37.
35. 'Civilisation', *EPS* i, pp. 140–1 (*D & D* I, pp. 195–6; Schn. *ELS.*, p. 175).
36. For the views stated here see *PPE* i and ii, pp. 108–9, 374–5, 763ff., 948–50.
37. ib., pp. 949–50; the longer quotation (p. 950) shows an interesting variation in this, the 7th. ed. text, from earlier versions (1848, 1849, 1852) which have 'supply the defect by providing elementary schools'. On working class education see also 'The Claims of Labour', *EES* i, pp. 376–8.
38. *PPE* ii, pp. 763–5.
39. 'Thoughts on Parliamentary Reform', *EPS* ii, pp. 327–8 (*D & D* III, p. 26).
40. *EPS* ii, p. 470 (*Repr. Gov.*, pp. 277–8).
41. 'Thoughts on Parliamentary Reform', *EPS* ii, p. 328 (*D & D* III, p. 27).
42. 'The Rationale of Political Representation', *London Review* 1 (July 1835), p. 357, and in *EPS* i, p. 32.
43. On education and the franchise see *EPS* ii, pp. 470–1, 474ff. (*Repr. Gov.*, pp. 278, 284ff.).
44. 'de Tocqueville on Democracy in America', *EPS* i, pp. 197–8 (*D & D* II, pp. 72–3).
45. *PPE* ii, p. 968.
46. 'Centralisation', *Edinburgh Review* 115 (1862), p. 334, and in *EPS* ii, p. 591.
47. *PPE* ii, p. 950.
48. 'Endowments', *EES* ii, p. 621 (*D & D* IV, p. 10).
49. 'Centralisation', *op. cit.*, p. 349, and *EPS* ii, p. 605.
50. *PPE* ii, p. 950; *EPS* i, p. 302 (*Lib.*, p. 130); cf. 'Bentham', *EERS*, pp. 106–7 (*D & D* I, pp. 376–9; Schn. *ELS*, pp. 276–7), and *Comte and Positivism, EERS*, pp. 314–15.
51. *PPE* ii, p. 950.
52. *EPS* i, p. 302 (*Lib.*, p. 129).
53. *LL* iii, p. 1348.
54. *EPS* i, p. 303 (*Lib.*, p. 130); *PPE* ii, p. 950.
55. *EPS* i, p. 302 (*Lib.*, p. 130).
56. On authorization of private establishments see *PPE* ii, p. 950; and on certification of teachers, *LL* iii, p. 1348 and *EPS* i, p. 304 (*Lib.*, p. 132); the last of these passages, 'The examinations . . . in the higher

branches of knowledge . . . deficiency of qualifications', I interpret to suggest non-interference with teacher-qualification; but earlier in the paragraph Mill allows that the state 'may very properly offer to ascertain and certify that a person possesses the knowledge requisite to make his conclusions on any given subject worth attending to'. Perhaps the point is merely that the state may *offer* certification of teachers but not require it or assume sole responsibility for it; but clearly he is uneasy about government control over qualification for the teaching profession.

57. *LL* iii, p. 1348 (cf. 'Centralisation', op. cit., p. 346 (*EPS* ii, pp. 601–2) on the function of the inspectorate).
58. *EPS* i, pp. 303–4 (*Lib.*, pp. 130–2); cf. *EPS* ii, pp. 529ff. (*Repr. Gov.*, pp. 357ff.) on impartiality in examinations for the public service.
59. *EPS* i, pp. 303–4 (*Lib.*, pp. 131–2).
60. *PPE* ii, p. 949; *EPS* i, p. 303 (*Lib.*, p. 131); *LL* iv, p. 1658.
61. *LL* ii, p. 733 (see also iii, p. 1237, referring to Mill's comments on Classics in the Inaugural Address).
62. *LL* iii, pp. 1087, 1093.
63. ib., p. 1246 (cf. *Inaugural*, p. 163).
64. ib., iv, p. 1550.
65. ib., pp. 1661–2 (see *Autob.*, pp. 46–7).
66. *LL* ii, p. 815.
67. ib., iii, p. 1116.
68. ib., pp. 1304–5 (ref. to *Inaugural*, p. 211).
69. ib., iv, p. 1666. The National Education League, founded in Birmingham in October 1869, aimed at coordinating the work of the many local societies which were campaigning for a universal national system of education.
70. ib., pp. 1820–1.
71. ib., p. 1807.
72. ib., ii, p. 720; iii, p. 1224. For Chadwick's report see *Parliamentary Papers 1861–2*, vol. 21, part 6, in the Irish University Press edition, *Education: General*, vol. 8, pp. 775ff.
73. *The Times*, 19 March 1862.
74. *LL* ii, p. 829.
75. 'Endowments', *EES* ii, p. 624 (*D & D* IV, pp. 15–16). See also Mill's submission to the Schools Inquiry Commission, *Parliamentary Papers 1867–8*, vol. 28, part 2, vol. ii, p. 61: 'The true principle for the remuneration of schoolmasters of all classes and grades, wherever it is possible to apply it, is that of payment for results.'
76. *LL* i, pp. 169, 206; iv, p. 1613.
77. This Bill, introduced by W. E. Forster on 17 February, allowed School Boards to decide what kind of religious instruction should be given in their schools and thus enabled the financing of denominational teaching from the rates. For Mill's comments see *LL* iv, pp. 1699, 1724, 1799.
78. *Hansard*, vol. 182, 13 Apr. 1866, col. 1263.
79. ib., vol. 187, 20 May 1867, cols. 826–7.

80. ib., vol. 189, 29 July 1867, col. 374.
81. For Mill's contributions to the Committee debates on the Public Schools Bill see *Hansard*, vol. 192, 16 June 1868, cols. 1650, 1655; ib., 23 June cols. 1928–9, 1931–2 (endowments); vol. 193, 7 July 1868, col. 823. The Clarendon Commission had investigated nine schools — Eton, Winchester, Westminster, Charterhouse, Harrow, Rugby, Shrewsbury, St. Paul's and Merchant Taylors'; the Bill excluded the two last, the only day schools among the nine.
82. *LL* ii, p. 732.
83. ib., iv, p. 1674. The Birmingham etc. Institute was founded in 1853 for the education of working men, Mill's interest in which was well known.
84. ib., pp. 1768, 1770.
85. ib., pp. 1658; 1702–3.
86. ib., iii, pp. 1377–9; iv, p. 1624 (see also p. 1695).
87. *S. of W.*, p. 494; on the aptitudes and education of women see especially pp. 493ff.
88. 'Enfranchisement of Women', *D & D* II, p. 438. Mill assigns the authorship of 'Enfranchisement of Women' to Harriet, his own share 'being little more than that of an editor and amanuensis' (p. 411); whether this is true or not, the article certainly represents his own views. On his marriage to Harriet, Mill signed a statement protesting at the existing law of marriage and renouncing all rights over her person and property; it is included in Elliot's edition of his letters, vol. i, pp. 158–9.
89. 'Endowments', *EES* ii, p. 629 (*D & D* IV, p. 24).
90. *LL* ii, p. 890 (cf. 864–5); ib., p. 787; iv, p. 1755. See also the memorandum of improvements in India (*Parliamentary Papers*, vol. 43, 1857–8) of which Mill claims he was 'partly the author and partly the editor'; see ch. 3, note 49, above. In this the progress in girls' education is welcomed and the hope expressed that it will continue. Mill was over-optimistic about degrees for women; they were admitted to London University degrees in 1878, but to Oxford degrees not until 1920, and to Cambridge degrees in 1948.
91. *LL* iv, pp. 1635; 1684: 'Je crois que l'on finira par n'avoir que des écoles communes aux deux sexes.'
92. *Parliamentary Papers 1854–5*, vol. 20, pp. 92–8 (*EPS* i, pp. 207–11); quotations in this and the following paragraph are on pp. 97, 98, 92, 94, 95, 93. (The *Report on the Organisation of the Permanent Civil Service*, signed in 1853 by Stafford H. Northcote and C. E. Trevelyan, was published in 1854; the various submitted papers, including Mill's, were published in the following year.) *The Times* also strongly supported selective examinations for the Civil Service, e.g., its leader of 3 Apr. 1962: despite the reactionary protests of 'the Bourbonists of the Parliamentary lobbies', the proposal 'has conquered . . . is conquering, but slowly and by the great and unceasing efforts of a few clear-headed men, who knew the scandals of the old system, and seized the opportunity to unite the reform of the public administration with the indirect encouragement of education among all ranks of the people'.

93. *LL* iii, pp. 1168, 1172; for Mill's reply to the request see *Parliamentary Papers 1867–8*, vol. 28, part 2, vol. ii, pp. 61ff.
94. *EES* i (*D & D* I); quotations in this paragraph are on pp. 213, 214, 215 (pp. 28–31).
95. ib., p. 216 (*D & D* I, p. 32).
96. 'Debate on the Universities Admission Bill', op. cit., p. 592.
97. 'Sedgwick's Discourse', *EERS*, p. 33 (*D & D* I, pp. 95–6); 'Coleridge', ib., p. 150 (*D & D* I, pp. 444–5; Schn. *ELS*, pp. 329–30).
98. *Examiner*, 12 June 1831, p. 370.
99. 'Endowments', *EES* ii (*D & D* IV); quotations in this paragraph are on pp. 621, 623, 626, 628 (*D & D* IV, pp. 10, 14, 19, 22). See also Robert Lowe's *Middle Class Education: Endowment or Free Trade* (1868), in which he attacks the Commission's proposals and strongly supports free enterprise in education: 'I prefer the simple and natural proceeding of instruction by private enterprise, as against ... decentralised bureaucracy' (p. 25).
100. op. cit. (note 93, above); quotations in this paragraph are on pp. 65, 66.

## 7. RELIGION AND EDUCATION

1. *LL* iii, pp. 1068–9; the notes on these pages give the references to the various journals; and for the offending passage in *Hamilton* see *LL* iii, p. 1079 (in *Hamilton*, pp. 128–9).
2. *Autob.*, pp. 34 (cf. 41), 121.
3. 'Theism', the last in his *Three Essays on Religion*, was written in 1868–70, ten years after the first two; for his noticeably more conciliatory attitude to religion in this essay see pp. 147–8 below; also the valuable article by Robert Carr, 'The Religious Thought of John Stuart Mill: a Study in Reluctant Scepticism'.
4. 'Coleridge', *EERS*, pp. 144–5 (*D & D* I, pp. 433–6; Schn. *ELS* pp. 321–3); cf. *Inaugural*, p. 218, and 'A Prophecy', *D & D* I, pp. 284ff.
5. *Logic* ii, p. 681.
6. 'Civilisation', *EPS* i, p. 128 (*D & D* I, pp. 175–6; Schn. *ELS*, p. 160); 'Corporation and Church Property', *EES* i, p. 202 (*D & D* I, p. 12).
7. *LL* i, p. 53; ib., iii, p. 1274.
8. *Autob.*, p. 38.
9. 'Utility of Religion', *EERS*, p. 423.
10. *Autob.*, pp. 32–3.
11. 'Nature', *EERS*, p. 388.
12. 'Theism', *EERS*; p. 456.
13. *Hamilton*, p. 129.
14. Packe, M. St. J., op. cit., p. 451.
15. 'Theism', *EERS*, pp. 446ff. (quotations on pp. 446, 450, 457–8, 459 (cf. *LL* ii, pp. 754–6). Mill refers to the watch analogy on p. 447; William Paley, well known at the time as a Christian apologist, used it in his *Natural Theology* (1802) to support his argument from design.
16. On Manichaeism see 'Nature', op. cit., pp. 389–90, 'Utility of Religion', op. cit., pp. 425–6, *Autob.*, p. 33, and *LL* ii, p. 709).

17. *LL* ii, p. 754.
18. *EPS* i, p. 257 (*Lib.*, p. 63).
19. 'Utility of Religion', *EERS*, p. 417.
20. 'Theism', *EERS*, pp. 487–8.
21. *Utilitarianism, EERS*, pp. 231–2 (Schn. *EW*, pp. 305–7; Warnock, pp. 284–6); for the non-dependence of morality on religion see 'Utility of Religion', *EERS*, pp. 407ff., 415ff., and *Utilitarianism*, op. cit., pp. 230ff. (Schn. *EW*, pp. 304ff.; Warnock, pp. 283ff.).
22. 'Utility of Religion', *EERS*, p. 422; on his 'Religion of Humanity' see 'Utility of Religion', op. cit., pp. 422ff., and *Comte and Positivism*, ib., pp. 333ff.
23. *Autob.*, pp. 58–9.
24. 'Utility of Religion', *EERS*, pp. 418ff. (quotations on pp. 418, 419, 426).
25. 'Theism', *EERS*, pp. 461–2, 481.
26. 'Utility of Religion', *EERS*, pp. 405, 426.
27. 'Theism', *EERS*, p. 482.
28. ib., pp. 485, 486. Mill's more conciliatory attitude to religion can be seen earlier in a letter of 1861 already referred to (*LL* ii, pp. 754–5): theism is 'a legitimate subject of imagination, and hope, and even belief (not amounting to faith) but not of knowledge'.
29. pp. 142 and 143 above.
30. *EL* i, p. 210 (cf. *LL* iii, p. 1469: 'the immense value attached to worldly prosperity by the bulk of so-called Christians is to me the best proof that their doctrine is hollow and effete').
31. *Essay concerning Human Understanding* I, i, 4.
32. *Autob.*, p. 56.
33. *Examiner*, 17 May 1873, and in the collected notices published on 29 May, p. 16.
34. *Matthew Arnold and John Stuart Mill*, p. 128.
35. *LL* iii, p. 1092 (and see the note, p. 1087).
36. ib., i, p. 39.
37. ib., iii, pp. 1313–14 (and cf. i, pp. 38–40).
38. ib., pp. 1468–9 (and cf. *Inaugural*, pp. 214–15).
39. Included in *Autob.*, pp. 326ff. (quotations on pp. 327–8). On the Lancashire Public School Association see Janes, D. K., 'The Educational Legacy of the Anti-Corn Law League', and Maltby, S. E., *Manchester and the Movement for National Elementary Education 1800–1870*. Mill explains what he means by 'secular' on p. 327 of his speech; it is interesting to compare Roebuck on this, speaking for Fox's Education Bill, in *Hansard*, vol. 110, col. 451 (17 Apr. 1850).
40. On tests for teachers see *LL* i, p. 40, *EPS* i, pp. 303–4 (*Lib.*, p. 132) and 'Coleridge', *EERS*, pp. 149–50 (*D & D* I, pp. 442–4; Schn. *ELS*, pp. 328–9).
41. *LL* i, pp. 39–40.
42. 'Lord Brougham's Defence of the Church Establishment', *Monthly Repository*, vol. 8 (1834), pp. 442–3.

43. *EPS* i, p. 303 (*Lib.*, p. 131).
44. *Inaugural*, pp. 214ff. (quotation on p. 215).
45. *Autob.*, pp. 32, 36.
46. 'Mrs. Austin's Translation of M. Cousin's Report etc.', *Monthly Repository*, vol. 8 (1834), p. 506, and cf. 'The Claims of Labour', *EES* i, pp. 376–7 (*D & D* II, pp. 200–1); *LL* i, p. 39.
47. *LL* iii, pp. 1235–6.
48. 'Utility of Religion', *EERS*, pp. 422ff.; *Utilitarianism, EERS*, p. 232 (Schn. *EW*, p. 307; Warnock, p. 286).
49. Langford, G. and O'Connor, D. J., eds., *New Essays in the Philosophy of Education*, ch. 10.
50. *Hansard*, vol. 109, cols. 28, 41–2 (26 Feb. 1850).
51. 'The Claims of Labour', *EES* i, pp. 377, 376, 377 (*D & D* II, pp. 200–1).
52. 'Secular Education', in *Autob.*, p. 329.
53. ib., p. 328.
54. A non-denominational system of elementary education for Ireland was proposed in 1828 by a Select Committee of the House of Commons; it was to be supported by Parliamentary grant administered by a Board of Commissioners; instruction was to be given to Catholics and Protestants alike in the same schools and classes, but with separate provision for denominational religious teaching. The proposals were implemented and the first grant paid in 1831. However, there was strong opposition from Anglicans and Presbyterians, who regarded education as a means of proselytizing for their faiths; Catholics, at first approving, moved towards the other sects in favouring denominational schools.

    The Queen's College (from 1908 the Queen's University), Belfast, was specifically non-denominational; so too were the original Queen's Colleges at Cork and Galway (from 1908 constituent colleges of the National University of Ireland), which were founded with it in 1845. Pressure for a specifically Catholic higher education led to the opening in 1854 of the Catholic University (later, University College), Dublin, with J. H. Newman as its first Rector. However, it had no charter and could not award degrees—a situation which was not remedied until the University Education (Ireland) Act of 1879, which established the Royal University as an examining and degree-awarding body for all the university institutions in Ireland. This body was dissolved in 1908 when there were established two universities for Ireland, the National University with colleges at Dublin, Cork, and Galway, and the Queen's University at Belfast; Magee University College, Londonderry, was at first affiliated to the National University, but from 1951 to 1965 was a college within Queen's University and from 1965 was absorbed into the New University of Ulster.
55. *LL* iii, pp. 1133–4; 1313; see also p. 1507n. From 1859 J. E. Cairnes was one of Mill's most frequent and valued correspondents; he was Professor of Political Economy at Trinity College, Dublin, Queen's College, Galway, and University College, London.

56. *LL* iii, pp. 1313, 1133.
57. *The Times*, 26 March 1870.
58. So called after the M.P. who introduced it as an amendment to the Bill.

## 8. UNIVERSITIES

1. The situation was not quite as simple as this summary statement may suggest. At Oxford in order to *matriculate*, i.e. enrol as a student, it was necessary to be a full member of the Anglican Church, subscribing to the Thirty-Nine Articles and the doctrines of the Prayer Book. At Cambridge this condition was enforced only for *graduation*; it was possible for a student to enter a Cambridge college and pursue his studies but not to graduate unless he was an Anglican; however, the college regulations in regard to chapel attendance etc. were such that nonconformists (and more especially secularists like Mill) would have found themselves in a very uncomfortable position to say the least.
2. Hargreaves-Mawdesley, W. N., ed., *Woodforde at Oxford 1759–1776*; Knox, V., 'On some parts of the discipline in our English Universities', *Essays Moral and Literary* (1778–9); Gibbon, E., *Autobiography* (Dent), p. 44.
3. op. cit., p. 41.
4. Bain, A., *John Stuart Mill*, p. 29.
5. See Packe, M. St. J., op. cit., p. 19, and Mill's 'Bentham', *EERS*, p. 81 (*D & D* I, pp. 336–7; Schn. *ELS*, pp. 245–6); his signing of a declaration accepting the Thirty-Nine Articles left him with a permanent impression of having done 'an immoral act'.
6. On Mill's educational attainments see Burston, W. H., op. cit., pp. 87–8, and Packe, M. St. J., op. cit., pp. 47–8; Ricardo's comment is quoted in Burston, p. 88. See also, of course, the *Autobiography*; the quotation here is on p. 23.
7. On Mill's visit to Cambridge see Professor Karl Britton's article, 'J. S. Mill and the Cambridge Union Society', Packe, M. St. J., op. cit., p. 52, and Bain, A., op. cit., p. 28.
8. *Autob.*, p. 65.
9. For the Utilitarian Society see *Autob.*, pp. 67ff., Packe, op. cit., pp. 52–3, and Bain, op. cit., pp. 30–1; for the London Debating Society see *Autob.*, pp. 104ff. (quotation on p. 107), and Packe, op. cit., pp. 69ff., also Britton's article (above, note 7) and another, 'J. S. Mill: a Debating Speech on Wordsworth'.
10. *EL* i, p. 233.
11. 'The Tom-foolery at Oxford', *Monthly Repository*, vol. 8 (1834), p. 525.
12. 'Debate on the Universities Admission Bill', ib., p. 592.
13. *EL* ii, p. 663.
14. 'Sedgwick's Discourse', *EERS*, pp. 33–4 (*D & D* I, pp. 96–7).
15. *EPS* i, pp. 138ff (*D & D* I, pp. 193ff.; Schn. *ELS*, pp. 172ff.) The 'notable scholar' who suffered dismissal was the Rev. Connop

Thirlwall, historian and theologian; while assistant tutor at Trinity College, Cambridge, he published a pamphlet in May 1834, in which he stated that 'we have no theological colleges, no theological tutors, no theological students' and that Cambridge colleges were not 'schools of religious instruction'; further, he complained of compulsory attendance at college chapel, with its 'constant repetition of a heartless, mechanical service' (DNB). This was in answer to arguments against the admission of Dissenters to degrees. Dr. Christopher Wordsworth, Master of Trinity, asked for his resignation five days later and Thirlwall obeyed at once. Mill refers to the incident also in the *Monthly Repository*, vol. 8 (1834). p. 592.

16. For these criticisms of the universities see *Monthly Repository*, vol. 8 (1834), pp. 592–3, 'Corporation and Church Property', *EES* i, pp. 202ff. (*D & D* I, pp. 11ff.), 'Civilisation' *EPS* i, pp. 140ff. (*D & D* I, pp. 195ff.; Schn. *ELS*, pp. 174ff.), and 'Sedgwick's Discourse', *EERS*, pp. 33–5, 38–9, (*D & D* I, pp. 95–9, 102–5).
17. 'Sedgwick's Discourse', *EERS*, p. 36 (*D & D* I, p. 99).
18. *EPC*, p. 39 (Borchard, R., ed., *Four Dialogues of Plato*, p. 41).
19. 'Civilisation', *EPS* i, p. 143 (*D & D* I, p. 199; Schn. *ELS*, p. 178).
20. ib., p. 142 (*D & D* I, pp. 198–9; Schn. *ELS*, p. 177).
21. ib., pp. 142–3 (*D & D* I, pp. 199; Schn. *ELS*, p. 177).
22. 'Sedgwick's Discourse', *EERS*, p. 35 (*D & D* I, pp. 98–9).
23. ib., p. 39 (*D & D* I, p. 104).
24. *EL* i, p. 233.
25. 'Debate on the Universities Admission Bill', *Monthly Repository*, vol. 8 (1834), p. 593.
26. 'Dr. Whewell on Moral Philosophy', *EERS*, p. 168.
27. 'Civilisation', *EPS* i, p. 144 (*D & D* I, p. 201; Schn *ELS*, p. 179), 'unsectarianise'; 'Debate on the Universities Admission Bill', op. cit., p. 592.
28. 'Civilisation', *EPS* i, p. 144 (*D & D* I, p. 201; Schn. *ELS*, p. 179).
29. de Tocqueville, Alexis, *Journeys to England and Ireland*, ed. Mayer, J.P., pp. 48, 49, 50, 92.
30. *EL* ii, p. 663; 'Dr. Whewell on Moral Philosophy', *EERS*, p. 169.
31. 'Civilisation', *EPS* i, p. 143 (*D & D* I, p. 200; Schn. *ELS*, p. 178).
32. *LL* ii, p. 819.
33. *Inaugural*, pp. 216, 217.
34. 'Debate on the Universities Admission Bill', op. cit., p. 592.
35. *Inaugural*, p. 155.
36. *LL* iv, p. 1663.
37. 'Civilisation', *EPS* i, pp. 139, 145 (*D & D* I, pp. 193, 202; Schn. *ELS*, pp. 173, 180); *Inaugural*, pp. 155, 156.
38. 'Civilisation', *EPS* i, p. 144 (*D & D* I, p. 201; Schn. *ELS*, p. 179).
39. ib., p. 141 (*D & D* I, pp. 196–7; Schn. *ELS*, pp. 175–6).
40. 'Sedgwick's Discourse', *EERS*, p. 33 (*D & D* I, p. 95); *Inaugural*, pp. 216, 215, 217.
41. 'Sedgwick's Discourse', *EERS*, p. 33 (*D & D* I, pp. 95–6).

42. 'Civilisation', *EPS* i, p. 128 (*D & D* I, p. 175; Schn. *ELS*, p. 159).
43. 'Vindication of the French Revolution of 1848', *D & D* II, p. 402.
44. *Some Thoughts concerning Education,* ed. Garforth, F. W., p. 117 (para. 94); Newman is quoted on p. 13 of the same edition.
45. On the growing demand for technical education see Lawson, J. and Silver, H., op. cit., pp. 303, 346ff.
46. *John Stuart Mill*, pp. 126, 127.
47. ib., pp. 127, 128; the reference to grammar and logic is in *Inaugural,* p. 174 (and see note).
48. *Inaugural*, p. 155.

9. CONCLUSION

1. *EL* ii. p. 412.
2. *Logic* ii, p. 929.
3. *John Stuart Mill*, p. 78.
4. 'Sedgwick's Discourse', *EERS*, p. 39 (*D & D* I, p. 104), 'Coleridge', ib., p. 122 (*D & D* I, p. 399; Schn. *ELS*, p. 295).
5. *EPC*, pp. 509–10 (*D & D* IV, pp. 227–8); *Autob.*, p. 18.
6. *Utilitarianism, EERS*, p. 211 (Schn. *EW*, pp. 282–3, Warnock, p. 258).
7. 'Lord Brougham's Defence of the Church Establishment', *Monthly Repository* 8 (May 1834), p. 443; 'The Claims of Labour' *EES* i, p. 378 (*D & D* II, p. 203).
8. 'The Negro Question', *Fraser's Magazine* 41 (Jan. 1850), p. 28.
9. *S. of W.*, p. 479.
10. 'National Education', *Monthly Repository* 8 (Apr. 1834), p. 358.
11. *PPE* ii, p. 948.
12. 'On Genius', Schn. *ELS*, p. 90.
13. 'Civilisation', *EPS* i, p. 141 (*D & D* I, p. 196, Schn. *ELS*, p. 175).
14. *EPS* i, p. 263 (*Lib.*, p. 73).
15. *Emile* (Dent, Everyman ed., 1911, repr. 1948), p. 56.
16. 'Honours to Science', *Monthly Repository* 8 (May 1834), p. 455.
17. *Hamilton*, p. 248.
18. op. cit., p. 267.
19. *Three Essays on Religion, EERS*, p. 378.
20. See above, p. 35 and note 74, p. 95 and note 68; also Halliday, R. J., *John Stuart Mill*, pp. 138–9.
21. op. cit., p. 138.
22. *EPS* ii, p. 382 (*Repr. Gov.*, p. 156).
23. For these see Packe, op. cit., pp. 501–3 (prostitutes) and 467ff. (Governor Eyre); and for the others see above, p. 4 note 12.
24. *EPS* ii p. 412 (*Repr. Gov.*, p. 197).
25. *Examiner*, 15 July 1832, p. 450; 'the test of what is right in politics is not the *will* of the people, but the *good* of the people'; and see above, pp. 20–1.
26. Juvenal, *Satires* II vi, 347–8.
27. Skinner, B. F., *Beyond Freedom and Dignity* (Cape, 1972).

28. See above, p. 56 and note 51.
29. *PPE* ii, p. 945.

APPENDIX

1. Himmelfarb, G., op. cit., ch. 1.
2. ib., ch. 3, pp. 73ff.
3. ib., pp. 85ff.
4. ib., pp. 126ff.
5. ib., pp. 72–3 (cf. pp. 337–8).
6. ib., ch. 6.
7. ib., pp. 163–5.
8. ib., pp. 162–3.
9. ib., p. 161.
10. ib., pp. 225–6.
11. ib., p. 232.
12. ib., p. 238.
13. ib., pp. 212–13.
14. ib., p. 243, quoted from *LL* i, pp. 141–2.
15. ib., p. 254.
16. McCloskey, H. J., *John Stuart Mill*, p. 13. Professor Himmelfarb draws attention to their letters of this period, which, she says, give the 'impression of two beleaguered souls, the only remnants of virtue and wisdom in a corrupt and Philistine world' (p. 253).
17. Himmelfarb, G., op. cit., p. 214.
18. For individuality in writings other than in *On Liberty*, see ch. 5 above; also:
    a) *Hamilton*, ch. 12, on consciousness, self and self-awareness, where he admits to the 'final inexplicability' of the ego's awareness of itself as a series of feelings or possibilities of feelings (6th. ed., p. 248, and see above, ch. 5, note 41, where the full paragraph is quoted).
    b) *Comte and Positivism*: in his criticisms of Comte's demand for unity and systematization: 'May it not be the fact that mankind, who after all are made up of single human beings, obtain a greater sum of happiness when each person pursues his own?' (*EERS*, p. 337.)
    c) *Utilitarianism*, ch. 2, in his plea for higher qualities of pleasure, 'Socrates dissatisfied' etc. (*EERS*, p. 212).
    d) 'Nature' (*EERS*, p. 393): 'there is hardly anything in the natural man except capacities—a whole world of possibilities' but, he goes on, dependent on artificial discipline for their realization.
    Love of music is not *in itself*, of course, a mark of individuality, but *in Mill* it has some claim to be; see, for instance, *Autob.*, pp. 122–3; and there is the picture of him in one of his mother's letters playing 'upon the piano without music some of his own compositions' (Hayek, F. A., *John Stuart Mill and Harriet Taylor*, p. 133). Nor is moral integrity, but *in Mill* it reached at times levels almost of eccentricity; e.g., his repudiation at the time of his marriage of all legal rights over his wife and her property (in Elliot, H. S. R. *The Letters of John Stuart Mill*, vol. 1, pp. 158–9).

# Bibliography

THE FOLLOWING lists of Mill's writings include only works used or referred to in the text and notes. Mill compiled his own full list of his published writings; this has been edited by MacMinn, N., Hainds, J. R., and McCrimmon, J. M., *Bibliography of the Published Writings of John Stuart Mill* (Evanston: Northwestern University Press, 1945); it excludes the few works published posthumously.

Since the present book is confined to a limited area of Mill's thought, no attempt has been made to provide a full bibliography of secondary sources. The list includes those drawn on in the text and notes, others which have helped the writer in understanding Mill and his educational thought, and others again which supply useful biographical, historical, or critical material. More extensive bibliographies can be found in van Holthoon's *The Road to Utopia*, Robson's *The Improvement of Mankind*, and Ryan's *J. S. Mill* and *The Philosophy of John Stuart Mill*; a complete, cumulative list is provided in *The Mill News Letter*, nos. 1 ff. (1965–   ).

For the life of Mill one should, of course, read the *Autobiography* (including Stillinger's *Early Draft*); there is also much biographical material in the six volumes of letters in the Collected Works. Bain's *John Stuart Mill* is a valuable contemporary source; also useful is another nineteenth-century book, Courtney's *The Life of John Stuart Mill*, and there are many fascinating personal glimpses of Mill in Caroline Fox's *Memories of Old Friends*. Of modern biographies the fullest is Packe's; there are also Borchard's and Cranston's (the latter a brief critical essay.) Hayek's *John Stuart Mill and Harriet Taylor* and Pappé's *John Stuart Mill and the Harriet Taylor Myth* deal with a specific (and crucial) personal relationship; so too does Josephine Kamm's *John Stuart Mill in Love*. Mazlish's *James and John Stuart Mill* combines biography with psychology in what is claimed to be 'a contribution to psychohistory'.

1. MILL'S WRITINGS (in chronological order of publication)

(i) *Books*

1843   *A System of Logic: Ratiocinative and Inductive* i and ii; CW VII and VIII, textual editor Robson, J. M., introduction by McRae, R. F., 1973.

1844   *Essays on Some Unsettled Questions of Political Economy;* in *EES* i, CW IV.

1848    *Principles of Political Economy* i and ii; CW II and III, textual editor Robson, J. M., introduction by Bladen, V. W., 1965.

1859    *Dissertations and Discussions*, an anthology of Mill's periodical writings, of which two volumes were published in 1859, a third in 1867, and a fourth in 1875.

1859    *On Liberty;* in *EPS* i, CW XVIII; ed Fawcett, M. G., Oxford University Press, World's Classics, 1912 etc. (with *Representative Government* and *The Subjection of Women*); and ed. Himmelfarb, G., Penguin Books, 1974.

1861    *Considerations on Representative Government;* in *EPS* ii, CW XIX; ed. Fawcett, M. G., Oxford University Press, World's Classics, 1912 etc. (with *On Liberty* and *The Subjection of Women*).

1863    *Utilitarianism* (reprinted from *Fraser's Magazine* 64 (1861); in *EERS*, CW X; ed. Warnock, M., Collins Fontana, 1962; and in *Mill's Ethical Writings*, ed. Schneewind, J. B., Collier Books, New York, 1965.

1865    *Auguste Comte and Positivism* (reprinted from *The Westminster Review* of the same year, vols 83, 84, N. S. 27, 28); in *EERS*, CW X.

1865    *An Examination of Sir William Hamilton's Philosophy.*

1867    *Inaugural Address at the University of St. Andrews;* in Garforth, F. W., ed., *John Stuart Mill on Education,* Teachers College Press, New York, 1971; and in Schneewind, J. B., ed., *Mill's Essays on Literature and Society*, Collier Books, New York, 1965.

1869    *The Subjection of Women;* ed. Fawcett, M. G., Oxford University Press, World's Classics, 1912 etc. (with *On Liberty* and *Representative Government*).

1873    *Autobiography* (published posthumously); Laski's edition (Oxford University Press, World's Classics, 1924 etc.) is the text as published by Mill's step-daughter, Helen Taylor, with certain passages excised; the full text is in the Columbia University Press editions of 1924 and 1944 (ed. Howson, R., preface by Coss, J. J.); the original draft, written probably between 1853 and 1856, has been published as *The Early Draft of John Stuart Mill's Autobiography*, ed. Stillinger, J., University of Illinois Press, Urbana, 1961.

1874    *Three Essays on Religion* (published posthumously); in *EERS*, CW X. The three essays are 'Nature', 'Utility of Religion', and 'Theism'.

Collected writings have been published in the following volumes of the Collected Works:

*Earlier Letters, 1812–1848* i and ii, CW XII and XIII, ed. Mineka, F. E., 1963.
*Later Letters, 1849–1873* i–iv, CW XIV–XVII, ed. Mineka, F. E. and Lindley, D. W., 1972.
*Essays on Economics and Society* i and ii, CW IV and V, textual editor Robson, J. M., introduction by Lord Robbins, 1967.
*Essays on Ethics, Religion and Society,* CW X, textual introduction by Robson, J. M., introduction by Priestly, F. E. L. and Dryer, D. P., 1969.
*Essays on Philosophy and the Classics*, CW XI, textual editor Robson, J. M., introduction by Sparshott, F. E., 1978.
*Essays on Politics and Society* i and ii, CW XVIII and XIX, textual editor Robson, J. M., introduction by Brady, A., 1977.
Selected writings include:
*Essays on Politics and Culture by John Stuart Mill*, ed. Himmelfarb, G., Doubleday, New York, 1962.
*John Stuart Mill: a Selection of his Works*, ed. Robson, J. M., Macmillan, Toronto, 1966 (this includes *On Liberty* and *Utilitarianism* in full).
*Mill's Essays on Literature and Society*, ed. Schneewind, J. B., Collier Books, New York, 1965.
*Mill's Ethical Writings*, ed. Schneewind, J. B., Collier Books, New York, 1965.
*John Stuart Mill on Politics and Society,* ed. Williams, G. L., Fontana/Collins, Glasgow, 1976.

(ii) *Articles, essays etc.*

1823  'Question of Population', *Black Dwarf* 11 (27 Nov., 10 Dec. 1823).
1824  'Edinburgh Review', *Westminster Review* 1 (1824).
1826  'Paper Currency and Commercial Distress'; published, unsigned, in *Parliamentary Review: Session of 1826* (London: Longman, Rees etc., 1826); *EES* i, CW IV.
1827/8 'On the Present State of Literature'; an unpublished speech; *Adelphi* 1, no. 2 (1923–4).
1828  'Speech on Perfectibility'; an unpublished speech; included in Laski, H. J., ed., *Autobiography*.
1831  'The Spirit of the Age', *Examiner*, Jan.–May 1831; Schneewind, J. B., ed., *Mill's Essays on Literature and Society*.
1831  'Attack on Literature', *Examiner*, 12 June 1831.
1831/2 Despatches to India, *British Parliamentary Papers 1831–2*, vol. 9; Irish University Press edition, *Colonies: East India*, vol. 6, pp. 377ff.
1832  'Pledges', *Examiner*, 1, 15 July 1832.

1832 'On Genius', *Monthly Repository* 6 (Oct. 1832); Schneewind, J. B., ed., *Mill's Essays on Literature and Society*; Borchard, R., ed., *Four Dialogues of Plato*.

1833 'Corporation and Church Property', *Jurist* 4 (Feb. 1833); *EES* i, CW IV; *D & D* I, 'The Right and Wrong of State Interference with Corporation and Church Property'.

1833 'Writings of Junius Redivivus' [W. B. Adams], *Monthly Repository* 7 (Apr. 1833); another review of one work only, in *Tait's Edinburgh Magazine* in June of the same year.

1833 'The Monthly Repository for December', *Examiner*, 15 Dec. 1833.

1834 'National Education', in 'Notes on the Newspapers', *Monthly Repository* 8 (17 Apr. 1834).

1834 'Lord Brougham's Defence of the Church Establishment', in 'Notes on the Newspapers', *Monthly Repository* 8 (13 May 1834).

1834 'The Tom-foolery at Oxford', in 'Notes on the Newspapers', *Monthly Repository* 8 (14 June 1834).

1834 'Debate on the Universities Admission Bill', in 'Notes on the Newspapers', *Monthly Repository* 8 (21 June 1834).

1834 'Mrs. Austin's Translation of M. Cousin's Report on the State of Public Instruction in Prussia', *Monthly Repository* 8 (July 1834); MacMinn etc. have 'Miss' in their *Bibliography* (p. 40), but the article has 'Mrs.'

1834/5 'Notes on Some of the More Popular Dialogues of Plato', *Monthly Repository* 8, 9 (Feb. 1834–Mar. 1835); *EPC*, CW XI. These 'Notes' are a combination of comment, paraphrase, and translation; a selection from them (*Protagoras, Phaedrus, Gorgias, Apology*) is published in Borchard, R., ed., *Four Dialogues of Plato*.

1835 'Professor Sedgwick's Discourse—State of Philosophy in England', *London Review* 1 (Apr. 1835); *EERS*, CW X; *D & D* I, 'Professor Sedgwick's Discourse on the Studies of the University of Cambridge'.

1835 'The Rationale of Political Representation', *London Review* 1 (July 1835); reprinted in part in *D & D* I, pp. 467ff., as 'Appendix'.

1835 'De Tocqueville on Democracy in America', *London Review* 1 (Oct. 1835), a review of the first volume (a later review, on the publication of the second volume, appeared in the *Edinburgh Review* in 1840); *EPS* i, CW XVIII.

1835 Notice of Grant's *Arithmetic for Young Children* and *Exercises for the Improvement of the Senses*, the *Globe*, Oct. 1835.

1836 'Civilisation', *London and Westminster Review* 3 and 25 (Apr.

1836); *EPS* i, CW XVIII; *D & D* I; Schneewind, J. B., ed., *Mill's Essays on Literature and Society*.

1837    'Carlyle's French Revolution', *London and Westminster Review* 5 and 27 (July 1837); Schneewind, J. B., ed., *Mill's Essays on Literature and Society* (omits excerpts from Carlyle).

1838    'Letters from Palmyra', *London and Westminster Review* 6 and 28 (Jan. 1838); a review of William Hare's *Letters of Lucius Manlius Piso, from Palmyra, to his Friend, Marcus Curtius, at Rome*, a historical novel; reprinted in part in *D & D* I, pp. 284–6, 'A Prophecy'.

1838    'Writings of Alfred de Vigny', *London and Westminster Review* 7 and 29 (N. S. 31) (Apr. 1838); *D & D* I; Schneewind, J. B., ed., *Mill's Essays on Literature and Society*.

1838    'Bentham', *London and Westminster Review* 7 and 29 (N. S. 31) (Aug. 1838); *EERS*, CW X; *D & D* I; Schneewind, J. B., ed., *Mill's Essays on Literature and Society*.

1838    'Lord Durham's Return', *London and Westminster Review* 32 (Dec. 1838).

1840    'Coleridge', *London and Westminster Review* 33 (Mar. 1840); *EERS*, CW X; *D & D* I; Schneewind, J. B., ed., *Mill's Essays on Literature and Society*.

1840    'M. de Tocqueville on Democracy in America', *Edinburgh Review* 72 (Oct. 1840); *EPS* i, CW XVIII; *D & D* II; Schneewind, J. B., ed., *Mill's Ethical Writings*; an earlier review, of the first volume, appeared in the *London Review* 1 (Oct. 1835).

1845    'The Claims of Labour', *Edinburgh Review* 81 (Apr. 1845); *EES* i, CW IV; *D & D* II.

1846    'Duveyrier's Political Views of French Affairs', *Edinburgh Review* 83 (Apr. 1846).

1846    'Grote's History of Greece', *Edinburgh Review* 84 (Oct. 1846), a review of the first two volumes of Grote's *History of Greece*; *EPC*, CW XI; reprinted in *D & D* II as 'Early Grecian History and Legend'. A brief review of these two volumes appeared in the *Spectator*, 4 Apr. 1846; for his reviews of later volumes, including his major review of vols. 9, 10, 11, see below, 1853, 'Grote's History of Greece'.

1849    'The French Revolution of 1848 and its Assailants', *Westminster Review* 51 (Apr. 1849); reprinted in *D & D* II as 'Vindication of the French Revolution of 1848'. This was a review of a pamphlet of Lord Brougham attacking the revolution, *Letter to the Marquess of Lansdowne, K. G., Lord President of the Council, on the late Revolution in France* (London: Ridgway, 1848).

1849    'Speech on Secular Education', included in Laski, H. J., ed.,
        *Autobiography*.

1850    'The Negro Question', *Fraser's Magazine* 41 (Jan. 1850); a
        vehement reply to an article by Carlyle in the previous issue.

1851    'Enfranchisement of Women', *Westminster Review* 55 (July
        1851); in the preface to the reprint in *D & D* II Mill claims
        that this was Harriet's work, his own part in it being 'little more
        than [as] an editor and amanuensis'; it is not included in
        MacMinn's *Bibliography*. See the note in Robson, J. M., *The
        Improvement of Mankind*, pp. 55-6.

1851    'Newman's Political Economy', *Westminster Review* 56 (Oct.
        1851); *EES* ii, CW V.

1852    'Dr. Whewell on Moral Philosophy', *Westminster Review* 58
        (Oct. 1852); *EERS*, CW X; *D & D* II; Schneewind, J. B., ed.,
        *Mill's Ethical Writings*.

1853    'Grote's History of Greece', *Edinburgh Review* 98 (Oct. 1853),
        review of vols. 9, 10, 11; *EPC*, CW XI; *D & D* II. Reviews of
        vols. 1 and 2 were published in the *Edinburgh Review*, Oct.
        1846, and in the *Spectator*, Apr. 1846; notices of other volumes
        appeared in the *Spectator*, 5 June 1847 (vols. 3 and 4), 3 and 10
        March 1849 (vols. 5 and 6), and 16 March 1850 (vols. 7 and 8).

1854    Diary, 8 Jan. to 13 Apr. 1854; in Elliot, H. S. R., *The Letters of
        John Stuart Mill*, vol. 2, pp. 357-86; excerpts in Schneewind,
        J. B., ed., *Mill's Essays on Literature and Society*.

1854/5  Paper relating to the Re-organisation of the Civil Service
        (competitive examinations), *Parliamentary Papers 1854-5*, vol.
        20, pp. 92-8; *EPS* i, CW XVIII.

1858    *Memorandum of the Improvements in the Administration of India
        during the last Thirty Years, and the Petition of the East-India
        Company to Parliament* (London: Cox and Wyman, 1858), pp.
        75-85; Education. Mill says of this summary of educational
        advance, included in the Memorandum, 'of this I was partly the
        author and partly the editor' (MacMinn, p. 90); it appears
        under Mill's name in the British Museum Catalogue and in the
        special East India Index of the Irish University Press edition of
        *Parliamentary Papers*. The Memorandum was published in
        *Parliamentary Papers 1857-8*, vol. 43 (Education, pp. 28-31),
        and republished in its original form in 1968 by Gregg Inter-
        national, Farnborough, Hants.

1859    *Thoughts on Parliamentary Reform* (London: Parker and Son,
        1859); *EPS* ii, CW XIX; *D & D* III.

1859    'Recent Writers on Reform', *Fraser's Magazine* 59 (Apr.
        1859); *EPS* ii, CW XIX; *D & D* III.

1862    'The Contest in America', *Fraser's Magazine* 65 (Feb. 1862).

1862   'Centralisation', *Edinburgh Review* 115 (Apr. 1862); *EPS* ii, CW XIX.

1866   Speech in Parliament, *Hansard*, vol. 182, 13 Apr. 1866, Representation of the People Bill, cols. 1253–63.

1866   'Grote's Plato', *Edinburgh Review* 123 (Apr. 1866); *EPC*, CW XI; *D & D* III.

1866   Paper on Endowed Schools (submitted in reply to questions addressed to him by the Schools Inquiry Commission), *Parliamentary Papers 1867–8*, vol. 28, part 2, vol. ii, pp. 61ff. (the paper is dated 9 Aug. 1866); IUP, *Educ.: Gen.* vol. 18.

1868   Speeches in Parliament, *Hansard*, vol. 192, 16 June 1868, cols. 1650, 1655; 23 June, cols. 1928–9, 1931–2; vol. 193, 7 July, col. 823; these are brief contributions to the Committee debates on the Public Schools Bill.

1869   'Endowments', *Fortnightly Review* 11 (N.S.5) (1 Apr. 1869); *EES* ii, CW V; *D & D* IV (1875).

1869   'Thornton on Labour and its Claims', *Fortnightly Review* 11 (N.S.5) (May 1869); *EES* ii, CW V; *D & D* IV (1875).

1869   Notes to James Mill's *Analysis of the Phenomena of the Human Mind* (new ed., 1869), edited by Bain, A., Findlater, A., and Grote, G., with additional notes by J. S. Mill.

1870   Speech at a Public Meeting of the National Education League (25 Mar. 1870), reported in *The Times*, 26 Mar.; for the resolution put to the meeting and carried unanimously, see the issue of 24 Mar.

1870   'Leslie on the Land Question', *Fortnightly Review* 7 (N.S.) (1 June 1870); *EES* ii, CW V; *D & D* IV (1875).

1871   *Programme of the Land Tenure Reform Association, with an Explanatory Statement by John Stuart Mill* (London: Longmans, Green, Reader and Dyer, 1871); *EES* ii, CW V; republished in *D & D* IV (1875) as 'Explanatory Statement of the Programme of the Land Tenure Reform Association'.

1871   *Speech on Land Tenure Reform*, spoken at a public meeting called by the Land Tenure Reform Association, by whom it was published on 15 May 1871; *D & D* IV (1875).

1873   'Grote's Aristotle', *Fortnightly Review* 19 (N.S.) (1 Jan. 1873); *EPC*, CW XI; *D & D* IV (1875).

1874   'Nature' (written 1850–58); in *Three Essays on Religion; EERS*, CW X.

1874   'Utility of Religion' (written 1850–8); in *Three Essays on Religion; EERS*, CW X.

1874   'Theism' (written 1868–70), in *Three Essays on Religion; EERS* CW X.

1879 'Chapters on Socialism', *Fortnightly Review* 25 (N.S.) (Feb., Mar., Apr. 1879); *EES* ii, CW V (see note, p. 704).

## 2. SECONDARY SOURCES

ADAMSON, J. W., *English Education 1789–1902* (London: Cambridge University Press, 1930).

ALEXANDER, E., *Matthew Arnold and John Stuart Mill* (London: Routledge and Kegan Paul, 1965).

—— 'Mill's Theory of Culture: the Wedding of Literature and Democracy', *University of Toronto Quarterly* 35 (1965–6).

—— 'The Principles of Permanence and Progression in the Thought of J. S. Mill', in Robson, J. M., and Laine, M., *James and John Stuart Mill*.

ANON., 'Mr. Mill on Education', a review of the *Inaugural Address, Saturday Review* 23 (9 Feb. 1867).

ANON., Review of the *Autobiography, Edinburgh Review* 139 (Jan.–Apr. 1874).

ANON., Review of the *Autobiography, Quarterly Review* 136 (Jan.–Apr. 1874).

ANSCHUTZ, R. P., *The Philosophy of J. S. Mill* (Oxford: Clarendon Press, 1953; repr. with appendix, 1963).

ARISTOTLE, *The Ethics of Aristotle*, transl. Thomson, J. A. K. (Harmondsworth: Penguin Books, 1955).

—— *The Politics of Aristotle*, transl. Barker, Sir Ernest (Oxford: Clarendon Press, 1946).

ARNOLD, M., *A French Eton: or Middle Class Education and the State* (London: Macmillan, 1892).

AUGUST, E., *John Stuart Mill: a Mind at Large* (London: Vision Press, 1976).

BAIN, A., *John Stuart Mill: a Criticism with Personal Recollections* (London: Longmans, Green, 1882; repr. New York: Kelley, 1969).

—— *James Mill* (London: Longmans, Green, 1882).

BAKER, W. J., 'Gradgrindery and the Education of J. S. Mill: a Clarification', *Western Humanities Review* 24 (Winter, 1970).

BALLHATCHET, K. A., 'The Home Government and Bentinck's Educational Policy', *Cambridge Historical Journal* 10 (1950–2); there is also a brief note, 'John Stuart Mill and Indian Education', in vol. 11 (1953–5), p. 228.

BAMFORD, T. W., ed., *Thomas Arnold on Education* (London: Cambridge University Press, 1970).

BARROW, R., *Plato, Utilitarianism and Education* (London: Routledge and Kegan Paul, 1975).

BENTHAM, J., *Chrestomathia*, in *Works*, vol. 8, ed. Bowring, J. (Edinburgh: William Tait, 1843–59).

BERLIN, SIR ISAIAH, *John Stuart Mill and the Ends of Life,* Robert Waley Cohen Memorial Lecture (London: Council of Christians and Jews, 1959).

BOARD OF EDUCATION, *Secondary Education with Special Reference to Grammar Schools and Technical High Schools* (Spens Report) (London: H.M.S.O., 1939).

BORCHARD, R., *John Stuart Mill: the Man* (London: Watts, 1957).

—— ed., *Four Dialogues of Plato* (London: Watts, 1946); see under Mill's articles, 1834/5, 'Notes on some of the More Popular Dialogues of Plato'.

BOURNE, H. R. FOX, 'John Stuart Mill: a Sketch of his Life', *Examiner,* 17 May 1873; included among the articles collected and separately printed (see next item).

—— ed. *John Stuart Mill: Notices of his Life and Works together with two Papers written by him on the Land Question* (London: E. Dallas, 1873, repr. from the *Examiner,* 17 May 1873).

BOYD, D., *Elites and their Education* (Windsor: National Foundation for Educational Research, 1973).

BRITTON, K. *John Stuart Mill* (Harmondsworth: Penguin Books, 1953).

—— 'John Stuart Mill: the Ordeal of an Intellectual', *Cambridge Journal* 2, no. 2 (1948).

—— 'J. S. Mill and the Cambridge Union Society', *Cambridge Review* 76 (29 Oct. 1955).

—— 'J. S. Mill: a Debating Speech on Wordsworth, 1829', *Cambridge Review* 79 (8 Mar. 1958).

—— 'John Stuart Mill on Christianity', in Robson, J. M., and Laine, M., eds., *James and John Stuart Mill.*

BRITTON, K., and ROBSON, J. M., 'Mill's Debating Speeches', *Mill News Letter* 1, no. 1 (Fall, 1965).

BROGAN, H., *Tocqueville* (London: Collins/Fontana, 1973).

BURNS, J. H., 'J. S. Mill and Democracy, 1829–61', in Schneewind, J. B., ed., *Mill: a Collection of Critical Essays.*

BURSTON, W. H., *James Mill on Philosophy and Education* (London: Athlone Press, 1973).

—— ed., *James Mill on Education* (London: Cambridge University Press, 1969).

—— 'The Utilitarians and the Monitorial System of Teaching', *The Year Book of Education 1957* (London: Evans, 1957).

CAPES, J. M., 'The Autobiography of John Stuart Mill', *Contemporary Review* 23 (Dec. 1873–May 1874).

CARR, R., 'The Religious Thought of John Stuart Mill: a Study in Reluctant Scepticism', *Journal of the History of Ideas* 23 (1962).

CHADWICK, E., 'Communications on Half-Time Teaching and on Military Drills', with a letter explanatory of the former, in Papers submitted to the Education Commission, 1 July 1861, *Parliament-ary Papers 1861-2*, vol. 21, part 6, Irish University Press edition, *Education: General*, vol. 8.

CLARKE, SIR FRED, *Freedom in the Educative Society* (London: Univers-ity of London Press, 1948).

COMMISSION ON RELIGIOUS EDUCATION IN SCHOOLS, *The Fourth R: the Durham Report on Religious Education* (London: National Society and SPCK, 1970).

COURTNEY, W. L., *Life of John Stuart Mill* (London: Walter Scott, 1889).

COWAN, J. L., *Pleasure and Pain* (London: Macmillan, 1968).

COWLING, M., *Mill and Liberalism* (London: Cambridge University Press, 1963).

CRANSTON, M., *John Stuart Mill* (London: Longmans, Writers and their Work, no. 99, 1958).

CUMMING, I., *A Manufactured Man* (Auckland: University of Auckland, Bulletin no. 55, Educational Series no. 2, 1960).

DEWEY, J., *Democracy and Education* (New York: Macmillan, 1916).

DUNCAN, G., *Marx and Mill* (London: Cambridge University Press, 1973).

ELIOT, T. S., *The Rock* (London: Faber, 1934).

ELLIOT, H. S. R., ed., *The Letters of John Stuart Mill*, 2 vols. (London: Longmans, Green, 1910).

FEUER, L. S., 'John Stuart Mill as a Sociologist: The Unwritten Ethology', in Robson, J. M. and Laine, M., eds., *James and John Stuart Mill*.

FOX, W. J., Speech on Education Bill, *Hansard*, vol. 109, 26 Feb. 1850, cols. 28, 41-2.

FRIEDMAN, R. B., 'An Introduction to Mill's Theory of Authority', in Schneewind, J. B., ed., *Mill: a Collection of Critical Essays*.

GARFORTH, F. W., 'The "Paradox of Freedom"', *Studies in Education* (University of Hull Institute of Education, July 1962).

GIBBON, E., *Autobiography*, ed. Smeaton, O. (London: Dent, Everyman Library, 1911, repr, 1923).

GROTE, G. (pseudonym, PHILIP BEAUCHAMP) ed., *Analysis of the Influence of Natural Religion on the Temporal Happiness of Mankind*, edited from the MSS of Jeremy Bentham (London: Carlile, 1822).

GUTTSMANN, W. L., *The British Political Elite* (London: MacGibbon and Kee, 1963).

HAINDS, J. R., 'J. S. Mill's *Examiner* Articles on Art', *Journal of the History of Ideas* 11 (1950).

HALLIDAY, R. J., *John Stuart Mill* (London: Allen and Unwin, 1976).

—— 'Some Recent Interpretations of John Stuart Mill', *Philosophy* 43 (Jan. 1968).

HAMBURGER, J., *Intellectuals in Politics* (New Haven: Yale University Press, 1965).
—— 'Mill and Tocqueville on Liberty', in Robson, J. M., and Laine, M., eds., *James and John Stuart Mill.*
HANS, N., 'Bentham and the Utilitarians', in Judges, A. V., ed., *Pioneers of English Education.*
HARGREAVES-MAWDESLEY, W. N., ed., *Woodforde at Oxford, 1759–1776* (Oxford: Oxford Historical Society, 1969).
HARRIS, A. L., 'John Stuart Mill's Theory of Progress', *Ethics* 66 (Apr. 1956).
—— 'John Stuart Mill: Servant of the East India Company', *Canadian Journal of Economics and Political Science* 30 (1964).
HARRISON, F., 'John Stuart Mill', *Nineteenth Century* 40 (July–Dec. 1896).
HAWTREY, S., *A Letter containing an account of St. Mark's School, Windsor, and Embodying some suggestions on the Subject of Education* (London: 1859).
—— *Reminiscences of a French Eton* (London: 1867). It consists mostly of a letter to Matthew Arnold on the latter's *A French Eton*; he quotes from Mill's *Inaugural*: 'It is beyond the power of schools and universities to educate morally or religiously.'
HAYEK, F. A., *John Stuart Mill and Harriet Taylor* (London: Routledge and Kegan Paul, 1951).
HIMMELFARB, G., *Victorian Minds* (London: Weidenfeld and Nicolson, 1968), ch. 4, 'The Other John Stuart Mill'.
—— *On Liberty and Liberalism: the Case of John Stuart Mill* (New York: Knopf, 1974).
—— 'The Two Mills', *New Leader*, 10 May 1965.
—— 'Mill on Liberty', *Inquiry* 10 (1967).
HOLLIS, M., 'The Pen and the Purse', *Proceedings of the Philosophy of Education Society of Great Britain*, vol. V, no. 2 (July 1971).
VAN HOLTHOON, F. L., *The Road to Utopia: a Study of John Stuart Mill's Social Thought* (Assen: van Gorcum, 1971).
HOLYOAKE, G. J., *John Stuart Mill as Some of the Working Classes knew him* (London: Trubner, 1873).
HUDSON, W. D., *Modern Moral Philosophy* (London: Macmillan, 1970).
—— 'Is religious education possible?', in Langford, G., and O'Connor, D. J., *New Essays in the Philosophy of Education.*
HUGHES, A. G., *Education and the Democratic Ideal* (London: Longmans, 1951).
HUGHES, E., 'Sir Charles Trevelyan, and Civil Service Reform, 1853–5' i and ii, *English Historical Review* 64 (1949).
—— 'Civil Service Reform, 1853–5', *Public Administration* 32 (1954).

ILLICH, I. D., *Deschooling Society* (New York: Harper and Row, 1971; Harmondsworth: Penguin Books, 1973).

JACK, D. R. L., *John Stuart Mill: Philosophy and Education*, M.Ed. Thesis, University of Birmingham, 1972/3.

JAMES, ERIC, LORD, *Education and Leadership* (London: Harrap, 1951).

JAMES, WILLIAM, *The Varieties of Religious Experience* (London: Longmans, Green, 1902).

JANES, D. K., 'The Educational Legacy of the Anti-Corn Law League', *History of Education* 3 (Jan. 1974).

JANES, G. M., 'J. S. Mill's Education', *Quarterly Journal of the University of North Dakota* 21 (1931).

JEFFREYS, M. V. C., *Personal Values in the Modern World* (Harmondsworth: Penguin Books, 1962).

JUDGES, A. V., ed., *Pioneers of English Education* (London: Faber, 1952).

KAMM, J., *John Stuart Mill in Love* (London: Gordon and Cremonesi, 1977).

KNOX, V., 'On some parts of the discipline in our English Universities', in *Essays Moral and Literary* (London: 1778).

LANGFORD, G., and O'CONNOR, D. J., eds., *New Essays in the Philosophy of Education* (London: Routledge and Kegan Paul, 1973).

LAWSON, J. and SILVER, H., *A Social History of Education in England* (London: Methuen, 1973).

LEE, H. D. P., trans. and ed., *Plato: the Republic* (Harmondsworth: Penguin Books, 2nd. ed., 1974).

LEVI, A. W., 'The "Mental Crisis" of John Stuart Mill', *Psychoanalytic Review* 32 (1945).

—— 'The Idea of Socrates: the Philosophic Hero in the Nineteenth Century', *Journal of the History of Ideas* 17 (1956).

LOCKE, J., *Some Thoughts concerning Education*, ed. Garforth, F. W. (London: Heinemann, 1964).

—— *An Essay concerning Human Understanding*, abridged and ed. Pringle-Pattison, A. S. (Oxford: Clarendon Press, 1924 etc.).

LOWE, R., *Middle Class Education: Endowment or Free Trade* (London: 1868).

MACAULAY, T. B., 'Mr. Mill's Essay on Government', *Edinburgh Review* 49 (Mar. 1829).

MACCALL, W., *The Elements of Individualism* (London: 1847).

—— *The Outlines of Individualism* (London: 1853).

McCLOSKEY, H. J., *John Stuart Mill: a Critical Study* (London: Macmillan, 1971).

MACINTYRE, A., *A Short History of Ethics* (London: Routledge and Kegan Paul, 1967).

McREADY, H. W., 'The Defence of Individualism', *Queen's Quarterly* 52 (1945).

MAGID, H. M., 'Mill and the Problem of Freedom of Thought', *Social Research* 21 (1954).

MALTBY, S. E., *Manchester and the Movement for National Elementary Education, 1800–1870* (Manchester: Manchester University Press, 1918).

MAZLISH, B., *James and John Stuart Mill: Father and Son in the Nineteenth Century* (London: Hutchinson, 1975).

MILL, ANNA, J., *John Mill's Boyhood Visit to France* (Toronto: University of Toronto Press, 1960).

—— 'John Stuart Mill's Visit to Wordsworth, 1831', *Modern Languages Review* 44 (1949),

MILL, J., *Analysis of the Phenomena of the Human Mind*, 2 vols., notes by Bain, A., Findlater, A., Grote, G., edited with additional notes by John Stuart Mill (London: Longmans, Green, Reader and Dyer, new edition, 1869).

—— 'Education of the Poor', *Edinburgh Review* 21 (Feb. 1813).

—— 'Education', article contributed to the 5th. edition of the *Encyclopaedia Britannica* (written in 1818 according to Bain, A., *James Mill*, p. 247).

—— 'Aristocracy', *London Review* 2 (July–Jan. 1935–6).

*Mill News Letter*, Toronto: University of Toronto Press, in association with Victoria College, 1965– .

MORLEY, J., 'The Death of Mr. Mill', *Fortnightly Review* 78 (N.S.) (1 June 1873).

NEFF, E., *Carlyle and Mill: an Introduction to Victorian Thought* (New York: Columbia University Press, 1926, Octagon Books, 1964, repr. 1974).

NUNN, SIR PERCY, *Education: its Data and First Principles* (London: Arnold, 3rd. ed., 1945).

PACKE, M., ST. J., *The Life of John Stuart Mill* (London: Secker and Warburg, 1954).

PALEY, W., *Natural Theology* (London: 1802).

PAPPÉ, H. O., *John Stuart Mill and the Harriet Taylor Myth* (London: Cambridge University Press, 1960).

—— 'Mill and Tocqueville', *Journal of the History of Ideas* 25 (1964).

PARRY, G., *Political Elites* (London: Allen and Unwin, 1969).

PETERS, R. S., *Ethics and Education* (Allen and Unwin, 1966).

—— *Education as Initiation* (London: University of London Institute of Education, 1964).

PILLON, F., 'La Raison Profonde de la Crise Mentale de Stuart Mill', *La Critique Philosophique* 2 (1873).

PLAMENATZ, J., *The English Utilitarians* (Oxford: Blackwell, 2nd. ed., 1958).

PLATO, *Republic*, trans. and ed., Lee, H. D. P. (Harmondsworth: Penguin Books, 1955, 2nd. ed., 1974).

POLLARD, H. M., *Pioneers of Popular Education 1760–1850* (London: Murray, 1956).

POPPER, Sir Karl, *The Open Society and its Enemies*, vols. i and ii (London: Routledge and Kegan Paul, 4th ed., 1962).

—— *The Poverty of Historicism* (London: Routledge and Kegan Paul, paperb. ed., 1961).

PRICE, A., 'J. S. Mill and the Combination of Logic and Poetry in Education', *Researches and Studies* 24 (Oct. 1962).

PRINGLE, G. O. S., 'Mill's Humanity', *Westminster Review* 150 (July–Dec. 1898).

REES, J. C., *Mill and his Early Critics* (Leicester: University College, Leicester, 1956).

—— 'A Phase in the Development of Mill's Ideas on Liberty', *Political Studies* 6 (1958).

—— 'A Re-reading of Mill on Liberty', *Political Studies* 8 (1960).

—— 'H. O. Pappé on Mill', *Political Studies* 10 (1962); a review of Pappé, op. cit.

—— 'Was Mill for Liberty?', *Political Studies* 14 (1966); a review of Cowling, M., op. cit.

REEVES, M., *Growing up in a Modern Society* (London: University of London Press, 1946).

ROBSON, J. M., *The Improvement of Mankind* (Toronto: University of Toronto Press, and London: Routledge and Kegan Paul, 1968).

—— 'J. S. Mill's Theory of Poetry', *University of Toronto Quarterly* 29 (1960).

—— 'Harriet Taylor and John Stuart Mill: Artist and Scientist', *Queen's Quarterly* 73 (1966).

—— 'Rational Animals and Others', in Robson, J. M., and Laine, M., eds., *James and John Stuart Mill*.

ROBSON, J. M., and LAINE, M., *James and John Stuart Mill: Papers of the Centenary Conference* (Toronto and Buffalo: University of Toronto Press, 1976).

ROEBUCK, J., Speeches in Parliament, *Hansard*, vol. 20, 30 July 1833, cols. 139ff.; vol. 24, 3 June 1834, cols. 127ff.; vol. 110, 17 Apr. 1850, col. 451.

—— 'National Education', *Tait's Edinburgh Magazine* 2 (Mar. 1833).

ROELLINGER, F. X., 'Mill on Education', *Journal of General Education* 6 (Apr. 1952).

ROUSSEAU, J.-J., *Emile*, trans., Foxley, B. (London: Dent, Everyman Library, 1911, repr. 1948).

RUSSELL, BERTRAND, LORD, 'John Stuart Mill', *Proceedings of the British Academy* 41 (1955).

RYAN, A., *The Philosophy of John Stuart Mill* (London: Macmillan, 1970).

—— *J. S. Mill* (London: Routledge and Kegan Paul, 1974).

RYLE, G., *The Concept of Mind* (London: Hutchinson, 1949; Harmondsworth, Penguin Books, 1963).

SCHAPIRO, J. S., 'Utilitarianism and the Foundation of English Liberalism', *Journal of Social Psychology* 4 (1939).

—— 'John Stuart Mill, Pioneer of Democratic Liberalism in England', *Journal of the History of Ideas* 4 (Apr. 1943).

SCHNEEWIND, J. B., ed., *Mill's Essays on Literature and Society* (New York: Collier Books, 1965).

—— ed., *Mill's Ethical Writings* (New York: Collier Books, 1965).

—— ed., *Mill: a Collection of Critical Essays* (London: Macmillan, 1969).

—— 'Concerning some Criticisms of Mill's *Utilitarianism* 1861–76', in Robson, J. M., and Laine, M., eds., *James and John Stuart Mill.*

SPENCER, H., *Education* (London: 1861; Watts, Thinker's Library, 1929).

STEPHEN, L., *The English Utilitarians*, 3 vols. (London: Duckworth, 1900).

—— 'Social Macadamisation', *Fraser's Magazine* 6 (N.S.) (July–Dec. 1872).

STEWART, W. A. C., *Progressives and Radicals in English Education, 1750–1970* (London: Macmillan, 1972).

STOKES, E., *The English Utilitarians and India* (London: Oxford University Press, 1959).

SUMNER, L. W., 'More Light on the Later Mill', *Philosophical Review* 83 (Oct. 1974).

TAYLOR, A. (son of HARRIET TAYLOR), *Memories of a Student* (London: Simkin, Marshall, etc., 1895); contains some interesting glimpses of Mill.

THILLY, F., 'The Individualism of John Stuart Mill', *Philosophical Review* 32 (Jan. 1923).

THOMAS, W., 'John Stuart Mill and the Uses of Autobiography', *History* 56 (Oct. 1971).

THORNTON, W. T., 'John Stuart Mill at the India House', *Examiner*, 17 May 1873 (see above, Bourne, H. R. Fox, ed.)

THWING, C. F., 'Education according to John Stuart Mill', *School and Society* 3 (Jan. 1916).

*The Times*, Leading article, 3 Apr. 1862, on selective examinations for the Civil Service.

THUCYDIDES, *History of the Peloponnesian War*, edited in translation by Livingstone, Sir Richard (London: Oxford University Press, World's Classics, 1943).

248 *Bibliography*

Tocqueville, Alexis de, *Democracy in America*, a new translation by Lawrence, G., ed. Mayer, J. P., and Lerner, M. (New York: Harper and Row, 1966).
—— *Journeys to England and Ireland*, transl. Lawrence, G., and Mayer K. P., ed. Mayer, J. P. (London: Faber, 1958).
Wakeford, J., *The Cloistered Elite* (London: Macmillan, 1969).
Ward, J., 'J. S. Mill's Science of Ethology', *International Journal of Ethics* (later *Ethics*) 1 (July 1891).
Ward, J. W., 'Mill, Marx and Modern Individualism', *Virginia Quarterly Review* 35 (1959).
Warnock, M., *Ethics since 1900* (London: Oxford University Press, 1960).
—— ed., *Utilitarianism, On Liberty, Essay on Bentham*, etc. (London: Collins/Fontana, 1962).
Weinberg, A., *Theodor Gomperz and John Stuart Mill* (Geneva: Librairie Droz, 1963).
Weinberg, I., *The English Public Schools* (New York: Atherton Press, 1967).
West, E. G., 'The Role of Education in Nineteenth Century Doctrines of Political Economy', *British Journal of Educational Studies* 12 (1963-4).
—— 'Liberty and Education: John Stuart Mill's Dilemma', *Philosophy* 40 (1965).
Whewell, M., *The Elements of Morality*, 2 vols. (London: 1845).
Wilkinson, R. H., ed., *Governing Elites: Studies in Training and Selection* (New York: Oxford University Press, 1969).
Woods, T., *Poetry and Philosophy: a Study in the Thought of John Stuart Mill* (London: Hutchinson, 1961).

# Index